CONFLICT AND CONSENSUS

CONFLICT AND CONSENSUS

A General Theory
of Collective Decisions

Serge Moscovici and Willem Doise

translated by

W.D. Halls

SAGE Publications

London · Thousand Oaks · New Delhi

SAGE Publications Ltd
6 Bonhill Street
London EC2A 4PU

SAGE Publications Inc
2455 Teller Road
Thousand Oaks, California 91320

SAGE Publications India Pvt Ltd
32, M-Block Market
Greater Kailash - I
New Delhi 110 048

British Library Cataloguing in Publication data

Moscovici, Serge
 Conflict and Consensus:General Theory of Collective
 Decisions
 I. Title II. Doise, Willem III. Halls, W. D.
 302.34

 ISBN 0–8039–8456–1
 ISBN 0–8039–8457–X (pbk)

Library of Congress catalog card number 94–066466

Typeset by Type Study, Scarborough
Printed in Great Britain by The Cromwell Press Ltd,
Broughton Gifford, Wiltshire

Contents

Introduction: The Problem

The subject of this book is one simple, basic fact of community life: consensus, necessary when people seek to associate together, act in concert and make decisions. However, the very banality, like the banality of the procedures – discussion and voting – through which they arrive at consensus, makes it difficult to understand. It is true that one often hears criticism of the volatility of opinions, the tyranny of the majority and the manipulation of the mass media that precedes consensus. On all sides there is a revolt against the lack of information, the poverty of the debate and the public apathy that accompany consensus. One comes to believe that up to a certain point communication manufactures consensus by tricks of rhetoric, giving too much weight to the arguments of certain groups and to distorting choices. In short, communication is accused, assisted by images and slogans, of reconciling the prejudices of individuals instead of reconciling their interests and ideas. Harmonized before reaching harmonious agreement, individuals tend unwittingly towards an agreed solution. Consequently they conform, rather than forming a consensus.

None the less, however justified such criticisms may be, modern societies increasingly seek consensus. The reason is plain. It may be claimed that there are only three authorities that can cut through disagreements and put an end to our dissensions by a choice that each of us accepts. The first is tradition, which encapsulates and accumulates past experience, a legacy of rules and examples that in every set of circumstances point the path to be followed. The next is science, whose judgement, based on observation and computation, can discern the solution that best corresponds to the objective facts. Finally, there is consensus, which explores various conflicting viewpoints and possibilities, focuses them, and directs them towards an entente that all acknowledge. But tradition has lost its age-old ascendancy over people, their beliefs and lifestyles. As for science, it has recently seen its authority undermined; its absolute principles of progress and truth no longer command respect, and no longer mark the path along which to proceed.

Thus, of these three authorities, the ultimate one to hold good and answer the need for individuals and groups to make decisions, to resolve their arguments, to demarcate what is permitted and what is forbidden, remains consensus. Its role, increasing at the expense of the other two, is performed by leading conflicting prejudices and competing desires to discover a unifying bond. In the end it not only relies on reason but emerges from an exchange of views and discussion. It represents much more than the use of discussion as serving to resolve conflicts; it is a type of institution, the handiwork of everyone, and accepted by everyone. Individuals are conscious of having given their consent to a decision if they have had some part in it, and have consciously made the sacrifices required. In short, what effects consensus and makes it convincing is not the agreement itself, but participation by those who have arrived at it. Thus it imposes no constraints upon them and possesses legitimacy only insofar as each individual has participated in it. It might be said that the fewer the parties involved, the easier it is to bring them to agreement. On the other hand, in that case its value is diminished through the number of abstentions on the part of those who remain hostile or apathetic. Upon deeper reflection, we can see that it is an institution that excludes our remaining indifferent to public affairs or withdrawing from them.

It is understandable that consensus is needed all the more when society is changing. By raising new problems, by holding up instances of novel modes of behaviour, by creating unexpected differences, change naturally provokes dissent and the breaking of ties. There is nothing more physiological in social life than this sporadic eruption of contrasts between terms that must be made compatible in order to avoid such disruptions, choose a course of action and pursue a task correctly. Indeed, although the conflict may be waged remorselessly, any committee has to come up with a proposal, a panel of experts has to opt for an exact diagnosis, a scientific community set up a research programme, or an electoral body has to vote. We note that nowadays the process rules out reliance on custom, or even faith in the methods of science – on which there is rarely unanimity – substituting for these a public debate in which those participating state their views.

The task, therefore, remains of stimulating the desire for consensus, to function as a framework for assimilating new ideas and controversies focusing on ever-changing dilemmas. This is so when a decision has to be made as to whether we should accept the risks of nuclear energy, sanction euthanasia, encourage the systematic diagnosis of AIDS or resolve the other problems that crop up daily and set us at odds with one another. One may object that the institution of consensus has existed throughout history. This is certainly true. What is novel is that from now on it prevails over other means whereby individual attitudes and decisions are transformed into social ones. This leads us to speculate on how consensus arises. What are its various sources? How are relationships between individuals expressed in their judgements and discussions? And in what common direction, if there is one, do they converge? It is these questions that make consensus an interesting topic. They permit consideration of it as a helpful approach to a better understanding of the nature of groups.

Yet it is not enough to define consensus: its meaning must be made clear. The following three ideas seem essential to us.

In every social situation where consensus develops, its characteristic source is choice. The widely held conviction is that the genuineness and strength of a choice depend upon the existence of a consensus that eliminates the danger of error. One resorts to consensus in order to overcome the doubt that emerges from the comparison of opinions, and from the exchange of arguments for and against, as the sole possible chance not only of forestalling an error of judgement, but also of ending divisions and misunderstandings between the defenders of different positions. Indeed we believe that mutual criticism and the examination together of various viewpoints lead to a decision free from prejudices and subjective distortions. Sound reasons militate in favour of such a procedure, the best one perhaps being that there is no alternative. How otherwise can one proceed when none of the alternatives presented is entirely satisfactory, and on which neither science nor tradition cast any sure light?

For example, hospital authorities may have available only one organ for transplant. They are faced with a dilemma: to carry out the transplant on one of their patients, a great artist, whose life they might be able to save, or to perform it on a child suffering from the same illness. How should the choice between the two be made? In what scales should human beings be weighed in order to decree that one or the other has the greater need, when either can equally expect a cure from the transplant? No criterion exists for allowing us to evaluate the various possibilities or establish that one is more objective than the other. There is only an incompatible situation – to save the great artist or the child – that is, either the one or the other must be sacrificed.

One is faced with a similar situation, although a less dramatic one, when it is a question of deciding between several scientific projects originating from several disciplines which require expenditure as considerable as that for a super-particle accelerator, a project for the charting of a genome, extended explorations by satellite as a response to the global modification of the environment, etc. Even supposing that criteria exist for establishing which has the greatest scientific value and what are the expected benefits, the fact remains that a choice has to be made. To assess the various proposals coming from different sciences, and to establish priorities, one submits to a debate that ends in agreement among the interested parties. Not surprisingly, since these kinds of dilemma abound, committees of 'wise men', or ethical committees, are set up to review the various options in order to decide, and even propose rules for choosing between them. In that case we accept their choice, on the base of the *consensus omnium*, which opts for a single one as being the sole real one, in conformity with what we know and believe. Bergson wrote: 'So long as experimental science is not soundly constituted, there will be no more certain guarantee of truth than universal consent. Truth will more often than not be that very consent' (1976: 209). Even when consent has crystallized, it remains, as it were, a kind of guiding light, as fragile as it is indisputable, an arbitrary but constraining convention.

The act of consent can be understood as the will of the individual to associate with others and, what is more, to approve their value system and be ready to share their fate, whatever that may be. Mostly all that is required is to place a voting paper into a ballot box, to append one's signature to a document, or to speak out at some meeting. On all such occasions, consent publicly given puts the seal on our commitment, attests to others that we are people of the same kind as themselves, that we share an attitude in common and that they can expect that we will behave accordingly. This is what entitles them to rely upon our embarking on a particular action, to include us in their plans and to treat us as members of the same group, country or undertaking, and so on. It goes without saying that all this makes for unity, because, as Durkheim remarks,

> What makes for the unity of organized societies, as of any organism, is that spontaneous *consensus* between parties, an internal solidarity that is not only as indispensable as the regulatory action of the higher centres, but which is even the necessary condition for it, because they only translate it into another language and, in a manner of speaking, consecrate it. (1978: 351)

Thus consensus goes well beyond mere acceptance and agreement. We must state at the outset that the convergence of individuals, which binds them mutually as regards interests and ideas, fosters their confidence in one another. It signifies that everything can be discussed and questioned, in actions or in words; everything save the obligation in the last resort to conclude by an agreement and rely on it being kept. From this it follows that one need have no fear of violence, that suspicion is eliminated and a gamble is taken on the good faith of each individual. However fragile that confidence may be, individuals must nevertheless preserve it, on pain of causing disarray and disorder in their relationships. This course is voluntary, and therefore not imposed upon them by any external constraint or emotional conformity. For, as everyone knows, what *manifestly* arises from external pressure cannot be considered *as agreement*. Agreement rests constantly on common convictions (Habermas, 1990).

This is why each individual, reflecting in solitude, should not ask himself whether he falls in with the attitudes and choices of the majority. Nor should the members of a group decide on a solution in silence before validating it by a vote. A meeting and debate are necessary, even a public statement, to prevent any hardening of consciences, affording an opportunity to renew the credence those consciences can give one another. Those individuals who take part in this process can in this way consider their situation objectively and have some conception of what they can expect of others in matters that remain unresolved. Who would take the risks inevitable in politics, or dare to express a personal opinion, or associate himself with others, if he had not received publicly some sign of credence or promise of agreement? Whatever the form in which it is envisaged – an alliance, a contract or act of solidarity – the propensity to consensus is inherent in any voluntary grouping and has to be constantly renewed. What contributes to that renewal is the shared conviction that, once established, the climate of confidence can endure indefinitely, unless there are good reasons to assume the contrary. Nothing, of course, lasts for ever. But, by increasing the degree of liberty to individuals without diminishing the degree of constraint upon the group, this conviction brings a measure of stability into our lives.

Finally, it is undeniably the fact that there is a link between consensus and the use and cultivation of the reason. From Hobbes to Spinoza, and, later Rousseau, everything rests on the conception that a principle of intelligence exists whereby people associate together and attribute to themselves a form of power. Convinced that human nature is the same in every clime and age, they believe in a harmony between ideas or goals once these are known. This sweeps away prejudices, rejects obedience not based on reason as well as blind imitation, and leads individuals into the paths of science and harmony. The only way in which to approach difficult choices in social life in accordance with the reason is to be well informed and recognize the reality of clashes of opinion and interests, so that all concerned may be induced to seek an enlightened solution despite their holding opposing positions. Expressed differently, this entails discovering what, beneath their apparent divergences, can bring them to a consensus. The assumption is that in a democracy, where all men and women are equal and free to express their viewpoint without fear of punishment, there is no other way of reaching an agreement and winning adherence to it. At least, this is the means that has gradually been enshrined in state constitutions, in social representations, and in the usages of collective psychology. Consensus and compromise have thus become the true categorical imperatives of our morality.

The three concepts of choice, trust and reason are subsumed under the idea of consensus. Together they are the sign of a bond between people, of a commitment born of convictions held in common, and above all in usages inherent in a modern democracy, and consequently anonymous; even without the dual prestige of tradition and science, they are totally effective.

2

In the end every consensus is useful in dealing with a margin of disagreement, by allowing a common relationship or action to be pursued. The unknowns in this equation are to know the basis for establishing consensus and the conditions for it to be realized. The classic theories on decision-making relating to consensus have tried to resolve this from a general viewpoint, if not a particular one. The theories all depend on two postulates that are assumed to be taken for granted, namely:

1 Consensus is better arrived at if one can benefit from very precise information regarding its purpose and if very many individuals are involved in discussing it. In other words, the choices of a group will have more chance of being rational if it has assembled an optimum amount of knowledge which it has carefully examined. One may hypothesize that, in the absence of experimental and scientific criteria, the truth will be arrived at more precisely if a great number of ideas and facts volunteered by the individuals concerned have been brought together. Of course it would be wrong to say that this is sufficient. But such a procedure seems so simple, and very plainly

reduces the degree of uncertainty among those who are the actors in it. Thus the verdict of an electoral body, like that of a meeting or a jury, is held to be correct provided that its members have learnt the facts, listened to the various viewpoints, and compared opposing arguments. This is why so much importance is attached to them. There are many who assert that committees are ineffectual, and meetings and associations valueless, being mere occasions for verbiage and time-wasting. They suggest we abandon them and delegate their tasks to well-qualified persons. This seems a reasonable arrangement to those who have so much else to occupy them. At the same time, however, public or private persons would lose all the benefits accruing from inquiry or discussion, which renders understanding easier and ensures the objectivity of conclusions. 'Social intercourse', Heider, the American psychologist, reminds us, 'talking to other people and being involved in their point of view, is considered of great importance for the establishment of cognitive objectivity' (1958: 228).

This does not mean that participants all subscribe to the same conception of what ought to be the intended objective emerging from their deliberations. It does mean they accept collectively the right of each individual to voice his disagreement, and the duty of everybody to weigh up the arguments of both majority and minority in order to discover what unifying link exists between them. Whatever impedes the transmission and discussion of information, on the other hand, hinders arriving at a rational decision and weakens the objective authority of the group over individuals. This is, moreover, a moral authority in a democracy that espouses freedom of expression and the discussion of opinions as 'the most suitable techniques' (Arrow, 1963: 85) to transform an opinion into a rule of behaviour and a rule for living implicitly approved by everyone.

2   The normal tendency in a consensus is to arrive at a compromise. The two words are so often used in conjunction that they have become synonymous. Very often to envision a consensus or a compromise comes to the same thing, so great is the power that this counsel of moderation has acquired among us. In other words, differences between individuals are assumed to be settled by concessions that draw them nearer to the mean point between their positions and distance them from extremes. The quest for the golden mean, the middle of the road or the reconciliation of conflicting opinions is aimed at diminishing conflict in social life. To employ a metaphor, it is notable that one can usually predict, even before negotiations have begun, that the pear will be cut in half, or in quarters, or even in eight pieces. There is talk of a 50–50 division, or of mutual concessions, indicating from the outset what will be clearly the point of convergence. This is why in social psychology it is expected that the choices made by groups will be more moderate than those made by individuals. They represent an averaging, the lowest common denominator of the choices made by individuals. Many experimental observations can be adduced to support this prevailing viewpoint (Clark, 1971).

Such convergences occasionally emerge from a process of careful reflection, or from the prudent expression of an opinion or judgement in the presence of others. Most often they serve to avoid confrontations that would run the risk of causing the group to disrupt if each participant took the expression of his ideas to the limit. It is even the duty of certain persons – for example, the foreman of a jury or the secretary of a party – to be watchful so that the protagonists and groups tip some of the 'ballast' overboard in order to preserve the common interest. Thus, as a journalist remarked concerning the secretary of the French Socialist Party, 'squeezed in this collective vice, M. Jospin was constrained always to speak in the language of compromise and express a kind of mean in his thinking'.[1]

In the event, each person sacrifices fragments of his conviction, facets of his own reality; he gives up a degree of individuality in order to seek an understanding and vision in which all can share. Compromise is therefore the solution whereby each actor in a possible conflict gives up what he cherishes, but what is not vital to him, in order to enlist the support of others, a support which is truly indispensable. This avoids extremism, which in contrast appears an abnormal solution, and even runs counter to common sense. This is what two economists suggested when they adopted as a principle that the 'consensual probability will tend, being an average, to swarm the more extreme points of view. They will be pressed towards the centre, and therefore iconoclasm will be repressed' (Lehrer and Wagner, 1982: 65).

Credit must be given to social psychology researchers who have gone further and attempted to verify experimentally this intuition derived from common sense. It has often been observed that persons, after having learnt each other's respective positions, try to align their viewpoints more closely. They veer towards the viewpoint which is the most neutral, the most frequent, the one from which they expect possible agreement to arise. Individuals who have ventured to express an extremist attitude rally to a more moderate choice. On the other hand, those who have remained over-cautious grow bolder and espouse the central tendency.

Sherif (1936) transformed this observation into a certainty in a series of experiments that constitute part of the classic legacy of the social sciences. He showed that individuals converge towards a norm of compromise, even in something so simple as looking at a luminous dot as small as a pinhead in a room completely in darkness. No one can locate the light with accuracy in the absence of any fixed object. Thus the dot seems to shift at variable distances, even if one knows with certainty that it is not moving at all. In these experiments Sherif asked the participants first to estimate the distance that the point of light was moving, until their judgement firmed up, each person forming his personal opinion as regards the distance it had allegedly covered. Then the participants were brought together in groups of three, each having decided on the extent of movement – one of 2 cm, the other of 4, yet another of 7 cm, etc. They were then invited to evaluate together and in public the supposed distance covered by the luminous point. What was observed? Without their being explicitly asked to do so, their assessments converged, after successive attempts, towards a judgement close to the average of their individual judgements. It was as if, since the participants had no reason to diverge from one another, they avoided doing so, making mutual concessions with the aim of arriving at a consensus. Since then this averaging effect has been held to be inherent in groups and the norms they set for themselves. It expresses a rule: they are already induced beforehand to converge, so as to draw closer to reality. The rule even allows one to calculate the concessions to be made in order to arrive at a possible line of agreement. It is one in which each individual acknowledges a certain merit in the position of others without being forced to repudiate his own.

On the whole, the classic theories postulate that rational and moderate characteristics of agreement go hand in hand. The free flow of information that each individual has at his disposal and that he can exchange at will with others normally leads him to end up with a compromise between individual positions. It represents the common denominator of all parties, and of the choices or opinions of group members, so that there is neither an increase in collective wisdom nor any loss of personal pride on the part of someone who has conceded to others more than he has received from them, as common sense requires. It is certainly true that perhaps individuals are so rash in making decisions that the consensus shifts away from a compromise towards an extreme position. This means that not only do positive or negative reactions run very high, but also that harmony between individuals depends greatly on a political and social climate favourable to the most radical positions. In any case, this may be seen an exception to the normal tendency, if not a failure of common sense. If it were neither an exception nor a breach of common sense, then all the deductions and theories elaborated concerning social behaviour, and even the process of how decisions leading to consensus are made, would have to be completely revised. However, let us rather look at it in the light of the facts, which are now abundant.

3

One revelation dominates all the rest. It was a shock, but not a surprise, to observe from evidence gleaned in the field that, as one suspected, these two postulates are not applicable together to reality. To be convinced of this it will suffice to consider two current reactions: abstention and, if we may so put it, combination, both very widespread in our societies, in the matter of decision-making. In fact, on the one hand, we have the reaction of those who do not exercise their right to vote and refuse to take part in the discussions of their associations, etc. It is true that every assembly, committee or jury, etc. comprises, in varying proportion, those who remain silent or indifferent. But to discover that those citizens who stay at home on election day are very many – in the United States, for example, half the registered voters – has caused disappointment. A dual question is posed: How does democracy function? Also, what is the value of the choices it makes? Those who abstain become spectators in deliberations that affect them intimately, and in consensuses that commit them. They are passive spectators, it might be added, of the practical abolition of values to which in theory they subscribe. Doubtless this large-scale abstention is ascribable to the social inequality of the most deprived, but it is also because of the communicative inequality of people bereft of the necessary ability to express themselves in public and to participate in community affairs. They are individuals and groups, sometimes dissenting groups, who may have something important to say but possess neither access to the media nor the appropriate know-how. It is dispiriting to end up by admitting that so many individuals abstain in a democracy, and even to acknowledge that there are advantages in this.

The person who complains of a distortion of principles does not grasp the fact that a certain level of abstention, and thus of inactivity, is compensated for because it makes consensus generally easier. By discouraging the convinced and the fanatics, by reducing the diversity of interests and arguments, it facilitates swifter convergence and an agreement appropriate to the just mean. This is not only because by decreasing the number of participants one is naturally reducing the sources of tension and instability. One is also avoiding having to take into account information and extreme options not asserted sufficiently forcibly, or indeed not asserted at all. To a certain extent this might lead to abandoning political, ethical or other decisions to experts possessing the necessary knowledge and time to devote to them. Thus in a democracy abstention could have the beneficial effect of allowing such experts to put forward optimum solutions most in accordance with reason. This might well be the case, as we shall see in a moment, had not the experts other handicaps that prevent them from exhibiting the mysterious virtues we attribute to them. The fear might arise that the less people participate in the consensus, the less what is established in their name is legitimate. Yet it is true that up to a certain point 'silence gives consent', and consequently this fear is not well founded. It denotes that partial exchanges and discussions, in the eyes of some running counter to rationality, in practice better ensure the viability of moderate solutions. It also ensures the viability of associations that, as the sociologist Max Weber observed, 'very often consist only in compromises between rival interests, where only a part of the occasion or means of conflict has been eliminated, or even an attempt has been made to do so. Hence, outside this area of compromise, the conflict of interests, with its attendant condition for supremacy, remains unchanged' (Weber, 1978: 42). Thus it is confidence that is most lacking in a democracy, because one does not know exactly what the various groups and individuals include or fail to include among the objects in dispute.

Moreover, this combination relates to the propensity of people to arrive at agreement on a solution that seems acceptable to them, since it allows them to avoid discussion and safeguards group cohesion. By conniving in their thinking and having a complicity of interests they strip their discussion of anything that risks damaging that cohesion. In a book that has since become famous, Janis (1972) described a number of fiascos suffered through cooperation between experts and politicians on US governmental committees.

Similar fiascos could be found in any other country. His remarks have attracted all the more attention because it has become commonplace to assert that to fall victim to biases and prejudices is a propensity of the masses, who are incapable of forming rationally considered opinions in the way that élites do. Yet it was indeed élites belonging to committees set up by American presidents who drew up decisions and arrived at agreement on choices, with results that, frankly speaking, were disastrous. To accept this, it is enough to familiarize oneself with a few of the cases studied, such as those occurring during the Second World War, the Korean War or in the preparations for the invasion of Cuba, etc. In all these cases history enlightens us as to how events unfolded.

In the early hours of 7 December 1941, a large part of the American Pacific fleet, based at Pearl Harbor, was destroyed by Japanese aircraft. But the American military authorities had judged that for technical and strategic reasons it was precisely at Pearl Harbor that the fleet would be safe from any attack. One reason advanced to justify this conviction was that enemy planes would be detected sufficiently early to prevent them from reaching their target. Now, historical research has since shown that Japanese submarines and unidentified aircraft had in fact been detected in the zone in question. However, intelligence reports, although received early enough to touch off a state of alert, were neglected by the General Staff. The conviction was so strong that the American fleet sheltering in this Pacific port was invulnerable that it led to the safe haven being transformed into a trap.

Another notable event occurred in the autumn of 1950. General MacArthur's troops crossed the 38th parallel separating South from North Korea, after having received the green light from a committee made up of the highest US political and military authorities. They thought that in this way the government of South Korea would be able to control North Korea. In reply, Chinese troops in their turn crossed the Korean frontier on 28 November. They reversed the fortunes of war and threatened to chase out MacArthur's army. Plainly the responsible American authorities had run the risk of being defeated by underestimating the likelihood of Chinese intervention.

We come to the last example. In January 1961, two days after his installation in the White House, President John Kennedy was informed that a plan for the invasion of Cuba had been prepared by Special Services, which had recruited and trained for it a brigade of Cuban exiles. We know how this brigade, with the logistical support of the US Army, on 17 April 1961 tried to land on the Cuban coast at the Bay of Pigs. It was a disaster. There is no doubt that during their meetings the authorities in Washington had played down the response capability of the Cuban Army and overestimated the chances that the brigade would receive a favourable welcome from opponents of the Castro regime. It so happens that this was not the only mistake committed by the committee of some ten experts. They did not leave open to the invaders the possibility of a retreat from the Bay of Pigs, nor did they reckon with the hostile reaction of world opinion.

How were competent people able to take such decisions? After examining the circumstances and the testimony given in the available documents, Janis deduced that the most important reason was the complicity between the members of these committees in order to arrive at the consensus expected of them, and so as to avoid any misgivings in their own minds or in those of others. Certain members set themselves up as 'mind-watchers' and scrupulously avoided any opportunity to discuss opinions opposed to their own, thus stifling at birth incipient disagreement. Whether one knuckles under out of loyalty or because of career prospects, the result is the same. It could be said that belief in the moral and intellectual infallibility of the committee, at the one extreme, and the will for a unanimous decision, at the other, limited its ability to contemplate possible alternatives, to examine the information available and to reassess solutions already rejected. This is how clever people neglect or sidetrack the patent signs of error in their arguments and conclusions. No matter how great the difficulty, what is sought first is to preserve unity and solidarity – in short, esprit de corps. Janis noted this when he wrote: 'The more amiability and esprit de corps among members of the policymaking groups, the greater the danger that independent critical thinking will be replaced by group think, which is likely to result in irrational and dehumanizing action against outgroups' (1972: 13). All in all, esprit de corps lowers the quality of the judgement and of decision-making, and the effect is to worsen the situations that it seeks to remedy.

A halt must be called to these observations, yet one further observation still appears necessary. The feeling 'My group, right or wrong', a loyalty that justifies every combination, which despite all the evidence stifles doubt and censures divergences, is most certainly responsible for such mistakes. Yet we should not confine ourselves to this observation alone, as it would be agreeable to do. This is because we have a representation of truth that presides over our discussions and exchanges: its sign is the *consensus omnium*, which all unhesitatingly obey. We sincerely believe ourselves obliged to behave with intolerance towards anyone who proves an obstacle to this consensus, since truth cannot be manifest so long as someone rejects it. We have all known such a situation, one in which the fear is that an idea of which one disapproves, but that the rest wish wholeheartedly to see triumph, may be rejected through one's own fault, thus we have not dared to contradict or denounce its iniquitous nature. It is most strange and disconcerting to see certain persons take that risk, whatever the consequences.

To characterize a historic decision as absolutely bad, after it has wreaked its effect, is always hazardous. What seems at first sight to be a total failure can, from another viewpoint, turn out to have been an unsuspected success. To assert also that the failure results from the conformist nature of collective thinking is an infallible recipe for the revival of old prejudices and the intoning of the old lament regarding the shortcomings of social psychology. However this may be, the paradox remains: individuals who in principle are logical and thoughtful, after having investigated and deliberated, and having available all the relevant information, can arrive at an agreement about a proposition that is neither well-thought out nor logical. It therefore seems nugatory to generalize about collective arguments and choices by using deductions drawn from the arguments and choices of individuals. It is not the qualities or knowledge they have available that are important, but the relationships of exchange and connivance between them, which lead them to avoid discord in order to satisfy their *esprit de corps*. In this respect abstention and combination highlight the confusion about the postulate of rationality on which our theories and practices both rest. On the one hand, we avoid agreement and, on the other, we avoid disagreement; on the one hand, we renounce the possibility of choice and, on the other, we renounce that of discussion; on the one hand, we withdraw from the search for consensus and, on the other, we shrink from becoming involved in conflict. In both, the first situation is hastily resolved by the submission of those who abstain and a resigned attitude by those who accept complicity, without subjecting the various positions to competition or truly reconciling them.

This is not the place to go back to the origins of this confusion and expose it. It doubtless springs from the fact that we allow ambiguity to preside over the meaning of rationality. To base it upon the amount of knowledge at our disposal arises from a healthy, although naïve, philosophy. It is, in the end, to imitate science and to treat the dilemmas of economics, politics and ethics as a scientist treats those of physics. But another meaning of rationality exists which takes account of the fact that we are individuals endowed with the power of speech, free to express ourselves and utilize all the resources of knowledge and experience to arrive at a solution, whether, in the eyes of the scientists, this is possible or not. What gives weight to this meaning, as it does to the rules of grammar or religious prayers by orators or believers, is its acceptance by others. We are not arguing as to whether the first meaning of rationality is more justified than the latter. We confine ourselves merely to saying that they are both employed without paying much heed to distinguishing between the rationality of a monologue and the rationality of a dialogue, which is directly social. The latter meaning represents a rationality which, in the light of the facts outlined, makes possible a consensus about the purpose of the discussion and is a modern mode of relationships. When, in a society, neither past traditions, nor the meaning of history, nor even the progressive values of science can suffice, only this rationality of dialogue leads the members of a group acting in concert to agreement.

4

The time has come to emphasize one important point. Let us for an instant suppose that we apply the first postulate of the classic theories: nobody abstains or combines in order to put an end to dissension; each participant in a committee, or gathering, or council of experts is even encouraged to express himself as fully as he desires, and to criticize his colleagues. Thus all can make plain their position, whether it is extreme or moderate, certain that it will be taken into account. It is this which constitutes an unconstrained choice, it is this which is democracy, yet also scientific debate. Does it follow that, under these conditions, consensus will, as we assume, turn out to be a compromise between the various positions? For reasons dealt with later, the answer is no. One can predict that the result will not be the 'average' of the various positions, but a specific response, produced by cooperation during debates between group members and proximate to the values they share. It is, to be precise, an extreme response. This view has been confirmed by a large range of experiments that have featured it as a major phenomenon.

It is none the less true that the tendency to take risks, and even betting in games of chance, had already shown that individuals are bolder in a group than in isolation. But this phenomenon, since termed *group polarization* (Moscovici and Zavalloni, 1969), manifests itself wherever people have to declare an attitude, make a choice, or resolve together a problem. It has been systematically demonstrated in the social psychology laboratory of the Paris École des Hautes Études en Sciences Sociales. Realizing a pretested scenario, the experiments brought together school students in groups of four. To begin with, the participants each expressed in isolation, on an opinion scale similar to one which surveys have made popular, their attitude towards General de Gaulle and towards Americans, as someone would in an opinion poll. The following is a typical statement in the questionnaire on de Gaulle: 'De Gaulle is too old to carry out such a difficult political task'; and another in the questionnaire relating to the Americans: 'American economic aid is always used for political pressure.' These statements were carefully chosen because, as might be expected, the attitude towards de Gaulle is somewhat favourable and towards Americans somewhat un-favourable. Once this was completed those participating in the experiment met together in groups and discussed each question until they agreed on a common, unanimous position. Whether it tended to be favourable or unfavourable is of no consequence. When consensus had been reached they dispersed, after expressing once more their individual view of de Gaulle and the Americans.

Examination of the results confirmed that the group members, during their discussion, arrived at an extremist consensus, and that after their discussion their individual attitude had become more extreme than it was previously. We predicted that the direction of this extreme response was foreshadowed in the original inclination of the participants. When the majority approved or disapproved of a certain person, a viewpoint or course of action, etc., afterwards they would individually approve or reject them more strongly. This is what occurred in our experiments: the participants became still more positive towards de Gaulle, still more negative towards the Americans.

It was evident that their attitudes had changed, and that those of the group had become the attitudes of each individual, since even in private they maintained the viewpoint adopted publicly. These results have been reproduced, using other sample populations, in a number of countries in relation to themes as diverse as peace, racism, ecology, moral dilemmas, etc., and the results have never been disproved (Doise, 1971). They demonstrate indisputably that an extremist consensus, far from being an exception, represents the norm.

5

The importance of such results resides partly in the fact that one might expect group discussion to cause individuals to round off the rough edges, smooth out their attitudes, moderate their choices, and so on. Now it appears, on the contrary, that the outcome is to make them more extreme. Thus up to recently it was believed that the individual tends to become extreme and the group moderate. We can see immediately that this idea must be turned on its head. It is not the only one either, since the idea that the consensus must be homologized to a compromise disappears and, by the same token, we can see arise the idea that the two are in opposition to one another. The fresh light shed on collective phenomena has been described in concrete terms by American colleagues:

> Whether members change before or after group decision, or as a result of discussion alone, the possibility of increased extremity in individual opinion excited considerable attention during the past decade. Called, perhaps inconveniently, *group polarization*, such an effect of group discussion ran counter to conventional wisdom, which, as we noted above, implied that group decision propositions should be moderate relative to the initial distribution of individual preferences. The group polarization effect was identified by Moscovici and Zavalloni (1969) who observed that French university students sometimes displayed more extreme attitudes following discussion than they had prior to the interaction. Originally associated with attitudes, the polarization effect has more recently been observed to apply to a wide range of judgement and decision tasks. The original Moscovici and Zavalloni report fitted easily in the political climate of the times in which student unrest was widespread and intense. Such results seemed to confirm the puzzling observations many had made informally – namely, that students sometimes were even more extreme in their opinions *after* what should have been moderating discussion. (Davis and Hisnz, 1982: 9, emphasis in original)

These remarks are entirely accurate and in accordance with a situation in which each participant, free from all constraint, is incited to defend a point of view about which he feels strongly. One can understand why, in certain circumstances and cultures, pressure is put on people to speak and arrive at a unanimous agreement. Is this so as to put one another in the picture, to form an objective position, or to facilitate eventual agreement? Most certainly not: it is in fact to make them converge towards a common position, and to ensure they embrace it wholeheartedly.

One can see where all these remarks are tending. More than one social science, and social psychology is no exception, deals implicitly with the effects of abstention and combination as if they did not require significant revisions of theory. Yet this is not so. For, if the quality of a decision leading to consensus depends not only on the possibility of receiving information on the subject and on taking part in the debates that lead up to it, then a limitation is placed on the first postulate that leaves open the question of what determines the consensus. It does not seem to have been understood that if one does not take account of the motivations for conflict, the rules for discussion or the meaning of truth, matters would remain as they are. In order to palliate these deficiencies, it is not sufficient to pride oneself on an improvement in communication, more widespread diffusion of knowledge, positive norms and the goodwill of all those concerned. To attempt to explain these facts without calling anything into question is to expose oneself to disappointment. Sooner or later one will discover similar facts, showing the rationality of decisions taken by default through the indifference or conformism of human beings.

One should doubtless resist the temptation to simplify that which is not simple. But this first postulate, when strictly and practically applied, leads to results that belie the second postulate. Close investigation of what usually occurs in a situation reveals that the attempts by individuals to reconcile in the group discordant choices or opposing opinions are spontaneously more successful when they arrive at an extreme solution rather than one nearer the mean. In reality we have tacitly accepted a convention. In essence, it presumed that social life moderated individual tendencies. Now, it would indeed appear that social life makes them more radical. The phenomenon of polarization does no more than demonstrate this and redefines what was assumed to be against nature as what is inherent in the nature of collective relationships.

6

In the chapters that follow, we shall propose a theory of decision-making that leads to consensus. We shall certainly preserve the first postulate concerning the rationality of decisions, although modifying it somewhat. We shall especially highlight the rules for dialogue and interaction as the vehicles of choice, and as more important than the sum of participant knowledge. In other words, the emphasis will move from the competence of individuals towards their relationships in a group. We shall, moreover, adopt a second postulate that may be enunciated as follows: consensus is normally established, if nothing hampers discussion or the exchange of views, at one of the extreme positions preferred by the group. The group is less inclined than individuals to tone down conflicts and avoid differences, but more disposed to devote the attention they require to criticisms and the various viewpoints expressed.

In order to make ourselves more readily understood, let us take an example. Some experts and politicians assert that agreement can be obtained on condition that those who advocate extreme viewpoints are excluded. In 1988 the Hungarian Prime Minister pronounced on the chances of an understanding between the Communist Party and the opposition in the following terms:

There are differences, but no opposition. I rule out the extremists on both sides, those on the right who wish to get rid completely of state ownership, and those on the left who contemplate getting rid of all private ownership. With the rest I believe it is possible to find points of agreement.[2]

Thus he implicitly admitted that a limit should be placed on dialogue and participation by one sector of society. Now we shall insist on envisaging the general case in which the extremists are included, and in which the limits of society are the subject of debate, and not a condition for it. In this way we can take in a more extended range of situations, instead of limiting ourselves to those very special ones concerning the preliminary conditions of balance and harmony that 'averaging' assumes.

But the essential point is that the new postulate as we have conceived it reverses our vision of the role that falls to consensus. Up to now emphasis has been put above all on its function as a remedy for the deficiencies in knowledge, by highlighting it as a means of avoiding or resolving conflicts when no process of calculation or experiment is possible. So long as its optimum remains compromise, it is expressed by the lowest common denominator among the opinions expressed, each one being partly right and partly wrong, and it reflects the contrast between opposing interests and ideas without modifying them. Thus, the status quo subsists. Even before negotiating, we know what the outcome will be, and negotiation leaves things as they were. A good example is given in coalitions between parties in Italy and Germany, where they are very necessary to form a government. The programme on which a coalition relies comprises a mixture of contrasting elements, liberal as regards the economy, socialist as regards work, Christian on school curricula, etc. This programme allows them to run affairs together, nevertheless without the parties or their doctrines drawing closer together. But, and this has been observed for a long while, these kinds of compromise inhibit decisiveness and the launching of the country on a precise course. *Mutatis mutandis*, these remarks are valid for any kind of group, party or collectivity.

Here, then, is the point where polarization introduces a difference. It proposes consensus as a means, and even a method, of changing the norms and rules of collective life. Its function is not to eliminate tensions or preserve an equilibrium between opposing propositions, but, on the contrary, to let them modify one another with the least amount of virulence, until a common element arises among them. Discord, far from representing failure or resistance, in the event, is the most valuable lever of change.

The excellence of modern democracy lies in the fact that it has institutionalized consensus in a number of domains. Viewed in this light, it implements the opposite of what it intends. So we note that the various committees and commissions entrusted with drawing up research programmes, providing ethical rules on abortion, the transplants of organs, and euthanasia, etc. have as their function to agree on a solution and to recommend it. Their true function, however, consists much less in reconciling opposing viewpoints than in fostering reflection, changing attitudes and time-hallowed rules, and of innovating in the habits and ideas of a reluctant public. This kind of innovation is still more unexpected, and even shocking, when it is a matter of discussing dilemmas that in principle are unresolvable, and making a choice between possibilities that are a priori impossible. Moreover, those persons coming together around a table, on a basis of equality, who are given the task of finding agreement, are scientists or representatives of churches or religions that would once have deemed such an eventuality absurd.

Henceforth, for them there is no alternative but to agree. This is something novel and disturbing, so that nobody is astonished when agreement is arrived at on an extreme position. It is as if there were incompatibility between the search for the golden mean and the attempt to change beliefs and practices of importance in the eyes of the general public. It would indeed seem that the role of consensus in modern societies is less to dispel uncertainty and tensions than to allow mind sets to evolve and transform norms and social bonds without destroying them. Far from stagnating, or falling into an insipid conformity, societies are permanently reinvigorated.

This is why this phenomenon, discovered some twenty years ago, shows groups changing their attitudes and decisions of their own accord, without any outside intervention. The phenomenon began with a theory of creativity and innovation as they were conceived of in collectivities in the process of growth. Since the theory was verified in relation to small groups, certain persons wanted to confine it to this. This would be a mistake, analogous to limiting the theory of hypnosis solely to relationships between doctor and patient, and not allowing it to enlighten us on the relationships between a leader and the masses. The pure theory explains the phenomena described, with no restrictions as to its extent, until there is proof to the contrary. It predicts facts that may be deduced from it, facts that clearly have significance for political science, economics or sociology, no less than for associations, commissions, juries, councils or committees whose practices relate very closely to it, if they were inspired by it. Thus we shall be able to disentangle the well-known difficulties that groups come up against as being due to the outmoded postulates that they share and the classic theories that nurture them. The best way of criticizing these latter postulates is still to put forward something that is new, and on a par with the old, and so replace them.

We shall expound the hypotheses behind our theory in such a way that they will be intelligible to everybody affected by them, not forgetting the specialists. But we can hardly hope to satisfy everybody. In social psychology, no more than in the other sciences, research does not carry equal acceptance: acceptance varies according to schools of thought and even continents. It may happen that the results of one investigation invalidate those of another. The certainty of being proved wrong sooner or later imparts to our explanations that air of the ephemeral that characterizes all scientific research. If this is a motive for questioning it, it should not be a reason for doubt, and even less a pretext for interpreting the facts in one's own way, without any reference to original notions. Such a mishap has struck us several times, so that, with astounding unconcern, certain people have arrogated to themselves the right to deal with it arbitrarily. We have written this book so as to reinstate the truth, so far as possible, and, by relating the facts to their theory, to mitigate the effect of their fragmentation.

As will be seen, what is in question is a coherent theory, sustained by a lengthy chain of conjectures relating to the psychological existence of groups, and one which stands the test of reality. It throws new light on many facts that were considered as taken for granted – a procedure essential for anyone who wishes to free himself from dependence on what is familiar. Moreover, a complete history of decisions leading to consensus in various societies and ages might hold the greatest interest for the social sciences. If, in spite of the difficulties of such an undertaking, loyal cooperation among numerous researchers were successful, the confrontation between the facts assembled, relating to very different situations, would illuminate a number of general ideas. These could even make comparative consensus the object of a separate science, and one of the most useful.

Notes

1 *Le Monde*, February 1988.
2 Ibid.

1

What Use Are Groups?

Reasons for the question

A brief preliminary sketch of decision theory as it relates to consensus, which will be expanded in the course of the following chapters, will at this stage be of help to the reader, even if it does not afford him all the clarity desirable. The notions put forward will also be better defined and refined later, so far as possible. In this summary we shall assume that the content of decisions, the relationships within and between groups, their rules and other factors are constant. This is in order to simplify the exposition, an expedient of which we shall be forced to deprive ourselves later.

Here then is the general line taken by our theory. How can one explain that the group comes to an agreement at an extreme position? In what way can we interpret its choice between one of the two possible extremes, which occurs spontaneously without any external constraint? Characteristic of the situation in which the decision is taken is that a number of individuals meet together and their combined presence raises the importance of the problem in the eyes of each one. By discussing it, additional meaning is given to it, the common aspects are emphasized as well as the contrasts. Yet, above all, the psychology of the individuals and of the groups is such that when the exchange of information and arguments, the debates on a significant subject, become intense, the involvement or the collective commitment (terms that we deem equivalent) likewise increases. In reality, the more a person is involved, the more a relationship or a problem that was almost a matter of indifference becomes significant or relevant for those discussing it. To an outside observer this disproportion between what is objectively at stake and the importance that participants attach to it is manifested in the numerous groups whose members at the outset hold different beliefs. A rivalry springing from familiarity accompanies the search for an agreement, each individual wholeheartedly wanting that agreement to be solid. Juries, promotion boards, resources allocation panels or parliamentary commissions: these are a few of the gatherings that come to mind. Their deliberations can be intense and even tumultuous, although the motives for this can occasionally seem trivial or even obscure, were it not for the degree of involvement that participants feel. At the same time one may assume such deliberations throw into relief the norms and attitudes to which all are attached.

However this may be, the hypothesis is put forward that collective involvement bears individuals and groups along in the direction determined by their norms, attitudes, etc., and thus, for example, towards greater clemency or greater pacifism, if these are the predominant ones among them. If we seek to understand why things happen in this way, we need only recognize that during discussion values become involved and each individual's attention is concentrated on a very limited range of arguments and knowledge relating to them. Moreover, the arguments and knowledge underpinning these values have more opportunity to circulate and be discussed. In other words, the arguments closest to the dominant values among the members of a group are collective ones, whereas the others are more or less individual. The discussion allows them to be identified and sorted out. This assumes that the attitudes, norms, etc. that are shared prefigure the shape of the agreement and at the same time the contours of the mutual involvement that emerges during the discussion.

Thus, given the propensity to overcome disagreement and the level of collective involvement, there will be one single decision leading to consensus compatible with these attitudes and norms: that which is closest to the dominant position. It is not a question of a shift that *diverges* from the mean, which is extremism, but a shift *towards* a predominant value, which is polarization. This is why one should not believe polarization is explained when extremism has been explained, nor should the two be confused, as happens in practice. Every extreme response in a society is not synonymous with extremism. If neither is possible, then the decision for consensus will tend to be a compromise. If no one, or almost no one, feels himself more closely involved through his relationships with others and discussion with them, and he is not alone in this, this is sufficient to produce such an effect. In that case, an agreement is reached to patch up differences, that is, to avoid discord and put the differences 'on hold', without their having been settled in the mind of each individual. This decision leading to consensus, from which classic theory has elaborated a model, is an optimal one, since no one gives up more than his neighbour. It suits a group whose members have no convictions or clear preferences. Yet it is only possible in the absence of deeply felt differences, where discussion is curtailed voluntarily, in order that no one should commit himself too much and take up passionately the problem under discussion. It is often repeatedly said that decisions taken coolly, with calm and detachment, are the best, although this has not been proven. What they are above all is more prudent, which can sometimes have advantages and sometimes drawbacks.

This summary clearly demonstrates that the theory of collective commitment conceives the decision leading up to a consensus as taking place in an ambiance where the group members participate and take sides, rather than in one where, as is often asserted, they 'can learn about other people's choices and opinions' (Pruitt, 1971: 355). The understanding reached rests much more on the force of the discussion and on arguments that highlight the hierarchy of values than on the information they glean from them or from listening to others. In short, the decision is taken in an atmosphere in which the persons become together effective actors rather than remaining detached observers. This is certainly a commonplace, but the consequences go well beyond practice, as we shall see later.

What characterizes the theory, the indispensable condition for explaining it, is, as you have perceived, to consider each step leading to consensus as a stage in a collective phenomenon. Clearly this phenomenon possesses autonomous properties, and one must rule out seeking to constitute it by superposing individual elements or by building a mosaic from them. There is nothing to prevent us from trying, save due respect for the nature of reality. This is because the phenomenon relates to a category of facts that assume, almost universally, a concerted effort on the part of everybody to figure in the consensus and to survive. Thus there exist languages, customs, rules for living, legislation, religious beliefs, the law itself, scientific theories, etc., whose value depends solely on usage and on the consensus of the greatest number. Nobody can organize them or modify them off his own bat without having sealed a contract with the other members of the collectivity. What Saussure wrote about language is applicable to all these examples: 'The collectivity is necessary in order to establish values whose sole reason for existence lies in usage and general consent; the individual by himself is incapable of prescribing any of them' (1972: 157). This is even more true of decisions aiming at a consensus, which constantly underpin this particular category of facts.

This brings in its train a series of errors, not the least of which is the little esteem accorded choices made in small groups or *en masse*. The most glaring difficulty is that the hypotheses deduced from the theory and verified by numerous experiments are impossible, if one clings to the prevailing conception. According to this, we should seek for hypotheses that account for the collective phenomenon being based solely on the knowledge of the reactions and thinking of individuals. Such a requirement is, in all good logic, a contradiction, given the impossibility of isolating *de facto* a reaction or a thought of this kind so as to make any sense. This is what many people forget who do not perceive they are avoiding the contradiction by separating these artificially. However, what is most serious is to impute to groups results that in reality would be prevented from occurring, and which, in the light of this conception, should turn out to be exactly the opposite. Since groups are held in such low esteem and can justify contrary results, it seems appropriate not to proceed further without having cleared up the question: what use are groups? This is because, in social psychology particularly, ideas as to the use of individuals appear firmly fixed.

Individuals and groups

1

We know that an individual does not behave in a crowd as he would if he were alone. In principle, he should always conduct himself according to reason, choosing what suits him after mature reflection and acting with full knowledge. He should only accept the opinions of others with that know- ledge, but after having, as it were, sifted them through, weighed up the pros and cons, without taking into account authority or numbers. Now, obser- vation would show that this no longer holds good as soon as he finds himself in the company of colleagues or close acquaintances, in a professional, party or church meeting, etc. Each individual accepts without a qualm the opinion of others. No action, not even a single step, can be taken without referring to the model they provide, even if his conscience demurs and his interests are opposed to it. Everything occurs as if he had changed and become a different person. But what are the effects of this metamorphosis? Why do individuals when gathered together act completely differently from how they would in isolation, so much so that one cannot predict their reactions once they are immersed in a crowd, or a political meeting, etc.? This is a puzzle that has not failed to astound ever since the origins of the social sciences.

The notion that once people meet in a group they are stripped of their characteristics is fundamental to the standard conception, and a solution that is widely accepted has been propounded. From mass psychology, from which it derived, according to this conception the level of the intelligence and reaction of the group is located at the mean, or, for most of the time, below it. This is drawn from the seafaring axiom: just as a naval convoy progresses at the speed of the slowest ship, the group is likewise forced to proceed at the pace of its most ignorant member. There are grounds for stating that thoughts and actions, far from improving when they are added together, tend towards mediocrity. Individuals as a group succeed less well than they do separately, whatever their education or wealth. They prevent one another from giving their best. What they all hold in common is therefore measured according to those who are the least well endowed in intelligence or force of character. This is very true: limited groups, like humanity *en masse*, are less creative and most certainly less effective (Freud, 1981; Tarde, 1910).

All peoples have thought the same thoughts, storing in the treasure-house of the collective memory proverbs, observations and maxims which all point in this direction. A socialist member of the French Parliament declared, regarding the 'Letter to the French' written by François Mitterrand on the occasion of his election to the presidency: 'The style will be all the more agreeable, because a personal pen is always better than a collective one.'[1] He was referring to the same evidence advanced by the economist von Hayek, who wrote:

> As anybody knows who has had the experience of working in a committee, its fecundity is limited to what the best mind among its members can master; if the results of the discussion are not in the end transformed into a coherent whole by one individual mind, they risk being inferior to what a single mind would have produced unaided. (1986: 140)

Here undoubtedly we have a few samples of a long litany of banalities. But the underlying idea comes across forcibly: in society we make less with more. We squander minds and abilities so that we arrive at solutions that have little originality, and are even incorrect. Crowd psychology has changed this litany into a theory which explains this loss as a phenomenon peculiar to society *en masse*. How does it come about that a normal person is caught up in the treadmill of action and uniformity of numbers even so far as to renounce his own singularity? The answer is that the individual, absorbed into the mass of human beings, as in any other group, undergoes a process of hypnosis. He implements what he is ordered to do without realizing it, and without being able to react against the contagion of thoughts and sentiments springing from others. A kind of mental unity is shaped which goes beyond him, shielding him from doubt, removing the spur of scruple and levelling down individuals by stressing the qualities they have in common at the expense of those possessed by each one individually. But if the mental faculties are dimmed, emotional reactions are exacerbated. Crowds 'go immediately to extremes' (Le Bon, 1963: 25), of violence and panic, of excitement and depression.

From this it would appear that people have lost their reason, are totally immoderate and wholly lacking in control. We can therefore see that in a collective situation the mechanisms of the intelligence are inhibited, and those of affectivity exaggerated. Although today such explanations appear somewhat outmoded, they have enjoyed considerable success (Moscovici, 1985). Crowd psychology associates the two in order to sketch out a conception of relationships between individuals and groups in society *en masse*. This is why we mention it here. Yet above all we wish to demonstrate just how much social psychology, in its contemporary version, remains faithful to this conception and to the evidence it assumes exists, in short, to almost everything save explanations. It is interesting to confirm this in detail, and this will retain our attention for longer.

2

So let us be more explicit. In the background to a great number of studies and theories of social psychology lies the conviction that they are not sufficient reasons for people meeting and associating. This is not a disagreeable conviction, but it is ineffectual. This at least should be the lesson from decades of years of research that have been centred upon how to discover in what ways several brains differ from one single brain. Above all, it is in order to learn why, on a practical plane, the performance of groups is inferior to that of the individuals that constitute them. Let us imagine the task of solving a mathematical, aesthetic or social problem. It possesses a correct answer, and usually the results obtained by a group of four or five persons working together are compared to those of the same number of individuals each working separately. A more decisive comparison consists in knowing whether the group solution is superior to that of the best member of the group. After going through a certain number of the results, one typical fact stands out: the group discovers many more solutions than do individuals. However, it is less effective than it would be if one considered the performance of members individually. Thus it would be more advantageous to let them work separately than to bring them together to cooperate on the same task, as is done on an assembly line, in a team or a committee.

It is generally deemed that this lesser effectiveness is due either to inhibitions arising from the presence of others, or to an under-use of personal ability when others are present. This is exactly what Davis and Restle (1963) observed when they suggested a series of problems as a task that had to be resolved in stages and could not be the object of any division of labour. It is true that their groups did solve more problems than the same number of individuals working in separate rooms, but the groups required more time and did not discover better solutions.

A few years earlier McCurdy and Lambert (1952) simulated in the laboratory a situation reminiscent of the assembly line in a car factory, in which one mistake made by a single group member entailed the failure of the whole group. Comparing the performances of the groups to those of individuals, they observed that the latter were more successful than the former. This may have come from the greater probability that the groups might include at least one member who made a mistake. The groups solved the problem more quickly than did the individuals, but few of the groups succeeded in doing so. On the same tack Taylor et al. (1958) sought to facilitate creativity by the well-known method of 'brain-storming', which encourages the unbridled association of ideas and allows them to be exchanged freely among group members. Bringing together their guinea-pigs in groups of four, they asked them to find as many answers as possible to a question, such as what would be the advantages and disadvantages that a person would have if born after a certain date if he had on each hand a second thumb on the opposite side to the one already there. As was expected, the groups suggested more answers, and of better quality, than did the average individual replying alone. But they produced neither more nor better ones than four persons chosen at random who had not worked together, and whose answers were totted up. The latter imagined more solutions, and of better quality, than did the groups.

On the other hand, in some rarer experiments (Einhorn et al., 1977; Shaw, 1932) it had been sought to show (and this proved to be the case) that groups are in every respect superior to individuals. Astoundingly, instead of investigating the conditions, efforts have been made to disprove the findings.[2] This was attempted by propounding that this superiority was due not to the way in which individuals worked in the collective situation, but to the fact that, among the group members, there was a greater chance of finding more gifted individuals. The conclusion, which is repeated like a leitmotiv, is well known: the collective situation turns out to 'improve the quantity but not the quality of mental performance' (Allport, 1924: 18). In brief, we reason more when we are together, but we reason less well. Less well, doubtless, and also less boldly. To support this deduction, Barnlund

(1959) thought up a series of experiments in which the participants had to choose between several conclusions for a series of logical syllogisms. Each syllogism was compiled in such a way that either the premise or the conclusion had a political or affective meaning. For example, one solution to a syllogism was '. . . therefore certain communists are conservative Republicans'. At the beginning each person, working alone, drew a conclusion of this kind from the list of thirty syllogisms he received. Then, eight weeks later, these same persons were brought together in a number of homogeneous groups and asked to solve a second series of analogous syllogisms. What was observed? As members of a group the same individuals exhibited prudence in their improved choices. According to the author of the experiment, they considered a broader range of ideas, gave themselves over to more attentive thinking and examined the conclusions more critically. The same fact emerged from a study by Zander and Medow (1963): working as a group, after some unexpected setback individuals modified their claims downwards more often than did individuals working alone.

The picture portrayed by this small sample of the research investigations has many nuances, and to claim that they are all of the same coloration would be to overlook what each one in particular brings to it. Reservations must be expressed so long as none definitively has the edge on the rest. However, the predominant tendency is to assert as accepted wisdom that the disadvantages of the group prevail over its advantages. Individual qualities of intelligence and creativity seem to lose their force and originality in the group. Put crudely in cost–benefit terms, more is gained by setting individuals to work separately than together. This conviction, which rests on proofs of known origin, is widespread in social psychology: collective thinking is held to be at a lower level, and impoverished compared to individual thinking. Collective thinking is described, more often than one might wish, as a string of vague prejudices, stereotypes and biases. It reasons on important social questions such as education, war, peace, the death penalty etc. by depending on special cases, and images and slogans to which one reacts more than reflects upon. When information is supplied as a basis for answering such questions, it is ignored, or distorted, or reduced to a few examples of doubtful value which impact upon the mind but do not open it up. Collective thought is therefore a kind of awkward copy of individual thought carried out by plagiarists devoid of any imagination, who tone down the colours and obliterate the original shapes with a layer of logic and heuristics of increasing crudity.

In reality this conception of thought and of humanity in the mass society continues to prevail. In one aspect it has been carried even further. This is because a number of theories and experiments (Jones and Gerard, 1967) were still able to add to it, redeeming its deficiencies in terms that remind one of Le Bon's hypnotized subject or Tarde's somnambulist. For example, an excellent textbook, expounding recent studies of social cognition, sums up their common viewpoint in the following terms: 'The view that more or less dominates the field . . . is the cognitive miser perspective, that is, the social perceiver often compromises the thorough, logical, normatively correct procedure that the naïve scientist would use' (Fiske and Taylor, 1984: 418). *Cognitive miser*, what a real gem to describe that common man having 'a lunatic disregard for external reality. . . . [A] fanatizer [sic] [who] seems to operate solely on whether convenient fictions are on his or her own hand' (1984: 415). The expression most certainly fits our vocabulary better than does the outmoded expression 'mass man'. However, a similarity subsists between the human types referred to and the prospective effects of the collectivity, which demean the individual. If the traditional viewpoint is enunciated in these terms, we have not much to object to in the experiments that illustrate it and the conclusions drawn from it, provided they are stripped of their exclusive character, by acknowledging that the facts depend on such a viewpoint being held, as does also their interpretation.

The basic human propensity to compromise

1

Let us now turn to the related question. Why do individuals participating in a decision or a solution to a problem take pains to avoid exaggeration, why do they look for the just mean? Ought not each individual wholeheartedly seek to shine in the presence of his neighbours, or his team, or with his colleagues, etc.? Yet it seems as if their presence, on the contrary, has the effect of blunting the intelligence and feelings. One might even say that, up to very recently, the most noticeable and outstanding social effect has been to turn us away from excess and point us towards moderation. Not surprisingly, this has been one of the first effects to have been verified in social psychology and is looked upon as a classic finding. On this subject, we may recall one of Moede's experiments (1920) in Germany.

The subjects of the experiment were submitted to auditory stimulations of varying intensity, at first individually, and then in a group situation, in which, however, they could not communicate with one another. For each participant a threshold of perception was determined for both situations. Moreover, the size of the group was varied – first two, then three, then six, and finally eight subjects. This was clearly to test the impact of group size, if this occurred, on individual performance. The results showed that in the group situation individual judgements drew closer together. Moreover, the impact of group size was characterized by a closer similarity of individual judgements when the group was larger. This might be explained by the variable degree of influence the group exercised upon its different members. Those who arrived at a better judgement in the individual situation did less well when they were in a group. On the contrary, those who showed up less well in isolation improved in a group situation. One might well believe that, even without his realizing it, each subject adjusted himself to the others in order not to do better nor to be bettered by them. Thus the overall result balances out at around the average.

What impels people to act in this way is the fear of standing out from the rest. It is roughly the same as when individuals feel ridiculous and embarrassed in the presence of other people and do not dare to be themselves, by making a bold gesture or uttering something audacious. A gesture, an idea, or an expression held to be extreme risks sparking off a negative assessment. Allport (1924) confirmed on several occasions this propensity to compromise on the part of individuals when they meet others. And, with the audacity proper to great theoretical minds, he did not see this as merely a fact, but as the very foundation of social psychology. 'There is', he writes,

> a basic human tendency to temper one's opinions and conduct by deference to the opinions and conduct of others. Early training and social contact have bred in us the avoidance of extremes of all sorts, whether of clothing, of manners, or of beliefs. This tendency is so fundamental that we are seldom conscious of it, yet we are seldom if ever without it. (1924: 278)

How can we account for it, except as obedience and conformity to established norms, or by the fear consequently of deviating from them, which leads us to wonder: 'Am I going too far? Am I too far removed from other people? The belief that our judgement risks differing greatly from that of our friends, our fellow-countrymen, etc. if we go too far rather than if we do not go far enough inclines us to prudence. In the end, to think or choose with other people is to submit to their standard.

It is undoubtedly this tendency that Sherif sought to highlight in the studies already mentioned. It is always this one finds in the very numerous investigations that have sought to discover how individuals cooperate together to take a decision aimed at resolving a problem, and whether they succeed better in association or in isolation. Kelley and Thibaut have summarized these observations very succinctly in a classic paper: 'While reacting with other persons, the person reacts to them . . . by tempering his judgement so as to avoid the possibility of being extremely different from others' (1954: 769). Over thirty years the propensity to compromise has become not only the postulate of the theory but also an experiential fact inherent in sociability, in whatever social area one looks at. It smooths over differences, suppresses excesses in interests and ideas, discourages eccentric behaviour, and in brief ensures that social life is lived without clashes. More energy is required to allow free rein to the forces in a collectivity, and overcome its inertia, than to tame them one by one, putting them in a uniform straitjacket.

2

As we know, it is wiser to interpret the real meaning of a fact according to the theories rather than to base oneself on the precise results that have preceded these theories or have confirmed them *ex post facto*. Now, from an examination of the theories themselves, detached from their alleged proofs, we can discern that the desire to resemble others and to achieve conformity accounts for everything. Let us, for example, imagine a situation in which there is a danger of producing conflict or disagreement. This is ascribed to the existence of one individual or an extremist minority, and thus deviant. This is why one can immediately see pressures arise for everybody, including the deviant individual or the extremist minority, for them to retract, and, from the majority, to force the minority to come closer to its view. If this does not occur, the minority is rejected. This is more than an act of revenge or a settling of accounts: it is a task of social integration.

Those who play the game in a team are generally appreciated; those who refuse to do so in order to play their own game are excluded. Stanley Schachter (1951) illustrated this in a well-known experiment, which we may here briefly recall. Each group was invited to discuss the case of a juvenile delinquent, Johnny Rocco. First of all, each group member was given this youngster's case history to read. After reading it, the group then met to discuss it and to suggest treatment, choosing the one considered appropriate on a graduated scale ranging from 'very mild' to 'very severe'. Thus it was a matter of the participants reaching a common decision, as would a committee or a jury. A typical group was made up of nine members: six were genuine students, and the other three protagonists appointed by the experimenter for this purpose. The confederates acted out in succession three roles they had carefully rehearsed before the discussion: the *modal* role, which adopted a position in conformity with the average position of the real students; the *deviate* role, which adopted a position diametrically opposed to the general tendency of the group; finally, the *slider* role, whose initial position was similar to that of the deviate but which, in the course of the discussion, gradually slid towards a moderate, conformist position.

Pressures were visibly exerted on the deviate to incite him to shift to a moderate position; hence the number of communications addressed to him. His reward would be the esteem of his fellows, the other participants, which meant that resistance to them was slight or non-existent, even if he had right on his side. It may be said that in such groups the one most esteemed is the modal person, who is preferred to the deviate. In everyday life, the same counsel for psychological well-being is followed as in the business world, as depicted by Keynes:

> Finally it is the long-term investor, he who most promotes the public interest, who will in practice come in for most criticism, wherever investment funds are managed by committees or boards or banks. For it is in the essence of his behaviour that he should be executive, unconventional and rash in the eyes of average opinion. If he is successful, that will only confirm the general belief in his rashness; and if in the short run he is unsuccessful, which is very likely, he will not receive much mercy. Worldly wisdom teaches us that it is better for reputation to fail conventionally than to succeed unconventionally. (1964: 158)

This observation has been verified on several occasions in the laboratory. Students, undoubtedly very clever ones, instead of following their judgement and winning, have been seen to follow the majority knowing that they would lose the rewards held out to those who remained independent. It is in no way surprising that the forces in social life are split. On the one hand, there are those which steer towards uniformity, ensuring the coherence and solidarity of groups. They are manifested in a similarity in thinking, a moderation in behaviour and a yearning to be like other people, which is the quintessence of most desires. They can be recognized in the logic expressed by Herbert Simon:

> For many purposes it is convenient to describe a group as though it were an aggregate which may be characterized by merely averaging or summing the individual characteristics of all its members. . . . Many of the propositions Festinger has formulated for group pressures belong to the first type; they are concerned entirely with aspects of group behaviour that can be treated as average aggregates for the group as a whole. (1957: 131)

On the other hand, the impulsion towards deviance, atypical behaviour and excessive reaction appears to be a sign of individuality, but one that is ill-adapted, disturbed and, in the final analysis, antisocial. Nothing points more clearly to this viewpoint than the many research investigations that classify extremism with pathological symptoms. Thus they serve to discredit anyone who cannot abandon extremism in order to rally, logically and convincingly, round a compromise. Moreover, it is natural that Allport was already speculating as to why individuals express atypical opinions. He of course discovered they are more assured and confident in what they think (Allport and Hartman, 1925). He nevertheless suggested that such opinions deviate from the mean and the norm because they are determined by the emotions rather than the reason. It is an interpretation doubtless drawn from mass psychology. By blending it afterwards with an uncharacteristic form of psychoanalysis, other authors continued this line of inquiry, seeking to show that intolerance, ambiguity, rigidity and various forms of frustration lead people to adopt extreme responses. Anxiety and neurosis are contributory factors. In a very searching study of a large population in Egypt, it was shown that adolescents, Christians – there in a minority – women and the petty bourgeoisie make more extreme choices than do adults, Muslims, men and the high-ranking bourgeoisie (Soueif, 1958). In other words, a certain level of maladjustment would explain this deviation from the median line chosen by the majority.

In the same vein, another study has compared normal individuals and individuals classed as abnormal, using questionnaires on motivation, anxiety, dogmatism, etc. (Brengelman, 1960). As was to be expected, the correlation between the sum total of extreme responses and rigidity was significant. Rigidity, in its turn, was linked to factors of anxiety and neurosis, which suggests, without its being proved, that rigid personalities will also be those who judge everything in terms of black and white. Another experiment went further, by comparing, using a scaled approach, the judgements of maladjusted groups (schizophrenics, maladjusted females and hospitalized children) and adjusted groups (normal males, adjusted females, children in good health). It was assumed that the first group would make use of extreme viewpoints more often than the latter, and the converse for moderate viewpoints. This was indeed what seems to have been observed *in toto* (Zax et al., 1964).

Making use of a whole battery of tests, study after study has shown how greatly extreme attitudes and judgements are linked to neurosis, deviance and a longing for certainty, or even to forms of social pathology such as authoritarianism and dogmatism. In contrast, they have highlighted how conformity and moderation are signs of social health. It is understandable that this viewpoint, taken to the extreme and recognized as a commonplace, incited the Sherifs to make a critical remark regretting it: 'Extremity of situation is frequently identified in this country as a signal of pathology' (Sherif and Sherif, 1967: 119). The remark is perhaps prejudiced, since the United States is not the only country where one thinks a sense of moderation is social and excess is antisocial.

It is precisely through compromise that the group can allegedly manage individuals and make them fit in to a common reality. Thus the forces that propel collective life towards uniformity and personal life towards difference and non-conformity complement one another. This notion appears so obvious that most of those investigating the riddle of sociability assent to it. One realizes by deduction that collective entities become incapable of intellectual creativity or epoch-making initiatives, but are abundantly prolific in the arts, the sciences and religions. How could they be otherwise, if everything that seems exceptional, mistaken or atypical is constrained, and, instead of blossoming, is inhibited by the majority? You may deem this a pessimistic view of social life, which levels us down so that we may associate with one another and makes us associate in order to level us down. All the rest, that is, creativity, is a matter for minorities and for leaders. In any case, for groups a conservative role is reserved; they serve to extinguish differences, positive or negative, between individuals, prevent their excesses and bring them back to the typical and habitual: as Bergson observes, 'We can opt out of it, but then we are drawn towards it, taken back to it, just as the pendulum shifts away from the vertical' (1976: 2). From the mass psychology where it arose right up to contemporary social psychology, which has codified it, this conception has been perpetuated – and this to such an extent that one may speak of a veritable paradigm, on which there is consensus within the academic community.

3

This can be discerned among its principal defenders. Yet, in order to appreciate it, in absolute fairness one needs to put a bizarre question. While collectivities moderate individuals, how does it come about that they act by taking extremist initiatives? Whether they opt out and withdraw to an inactive state, or combine forces and cherish illusions regarding the chances of success, they deviate from the golden mean that would otherwise be their norm. Like enthusiasm or panic, the alleged violence of crowds is the example usually cited. Whether crowds are manifesting their patriotic feelings or their religious convictions, it is always by their extremism and passion that they can be identified. Thus extremist opinions and choices are not infrequent. Since this psychology, epitomized in the mass situation, must be explained, a familiar model is required. In fact, when people meet together, anonymously mingling in the crowd, they feel less responsible for what they do and say. Left to their own devices, abandoned by their leaders, they are not bound to answer for actions and decisions that, although shared by all, belong to nobody. This is at least what crowd psychologists have maintained. Their views have broadly been followed in this respect ever since Gramsci adopted this explanation when he asserted that the masses are made up of 'people who are not bound by bonds of responsibility towards other people or groups of people, or to a concrete economic reality, a degradation that is counterbalanced by the abasement of the individual' (1953: 149).

Today it is not the extraordinary emotional intensity, or even the fear, that crowds display that has revived interest in such ideas. It is the opposite: for example, the none the less extraordinary apathy of thirty-eight New Yorkers watching a murder from the windows of their building, with not one of them intervening. The murderer took half an hour to commit his crime. Three times he walked away from Catherine Genovese, his victim, and then returned to her, but still not finishing her off. She dragged herself towards the door of the building, shouting that she was being murdered, but not one of her neighbours came to her rescue or called the police. No more than those living close by the concentration camps did statesmen or church dignitaries, having been alerted to the genocide being committed in them, lift a little finger to help the victims. In 1964 why did those witnessing the murder of Catherine Genovese likewise fail to do so, and thus became accomplices? Have the inhabitants of great cities become so anonymous, so insensitive – as is said – that they go so far as to ignore the distress of others? When the question was put to them, the onlookers declared they were overwhelmed and scared by this crime. How then to explain their lack of reaction?

Let us suppose that a stranger asks you for help: what considerations would motivate your behaviour? You find yourself with others and no one knows exactly what is happening. Everyone seizes upon scraps of information and believes that someone else will give help, or is already doing so. And so everybody is loath to intervene. By refraining from doing so, they are breaking the moral law of helping one's neighbour, but nobody is there to ensure that the law is enforced, or realizes that in enforcing it he or she would have done a good deed. In short, the victim receives no help because there are so many persons who can give it. Latané and Darley (1968, 1970), the American social psychologists, have postulated that, in every situation of this kind, the responsibility for doing so is spread among the crowd of onlookers and does not fall upon any one in particular. This is why someone in need of assistance will have more chance of receiving it if only one other person, rather than a group, is present.

This postulate was confirmed in a series of memorable experiments. Each experiment provided a scenario in which as spectator in an emergency situation there was either one person or a group. Next, a note was made of the frequency with which the victim received help in such circumstances. Mention of two situations will suffice to convey the idea. The first one brought together male students who were in a smoke-filled room that gave the impression a fire was starting. They were either isolated, or with two passive research associates, or in simple groups of three. It was observed that two out of three of the individuals in isolation drew attention to the smoke, whereas in the group it was only one out of the three. In the second experiment the participants were placed in separate rooms but could communicate with one another through microphones and earphones. They could hear one another speak but could not see one another. Once installed they were made to listen to a recording that gave the impression that one of the participants was having an epileptic fit. In one of the conditions each participant was led to believe that he was the sole person listening to what was happening. In another, the participants were informed that one or more persons were listening at the same time as they were. When the participants believed they were listening alone, 85 per cent rose and went to give help, as compared with only 31 per cent when they believed that five other persons were listening. It is consequently clear that diffusion of responsibility among the group brings about passivity.

One might say that individuals, fearing to renounce the comfort of anonymity, 'hid in the crowd', in order not to learn what was going on. Most of the witnesses to the murder of Catherine Genovese, questioned as to why they had not reacted, replied: 'I don't know.' Others explained they were 'afraid' or did not wish to become involved. But these reasons do not hold water. A mere telephone call to the police would have saved the life of the young woman, at no risk to the onlookers. They pretexted that since no one seemed to be doing anything or to be concerned, they deduced that nothing harmful was going on. They knew that in an anonymous assembly of people no one risks blame if he fails to do his duty, or will be praised if he performs it. One may assume that this dilution of responsibility 'happens to some extent in any group, but that it is an especially prominent feature of informal "leaderless" groups or of groups that lack formal organization' (Jones and Gerard, 1967: 623).

Such groups are as little required as they are dangerous for the survival of human beings. Without any play on words, one might say that they tend towards extreme moderation, in order not to attract attention through a natural gesture, if one is possible, which can appear inappropriate to some or precipitant to others. By remaining passive, paradoxically each individual makes plain he is anxious to preserve equality, since nobody feels more responsible than anyone else. In the same way it is not unusual to see the members of a political party hesitate when the chance presents itself to take power, for fear that this might divide them and some might lord it over the rest.

Up to now we have particularly envisaged the situation of a chance meeting where there is nothing to bind people to one another and where there are no exchanges between them. Let us now consider the other side of the coin, in a situation where links begin to develop, and exchanges of information and arguments. Shall we see there the same apathy and the same holding back? We are now arriving at the crucial point in these reflections, and the answer will be given by precise data. One of the most interesting moments in public life, in business transactions or legal negotiations is when a common decision is reached as to what degree of risk can be taken. People must always choose between long-term prospects which may yield big returns, and the more immediate, more certain solutions which may yield less. In the light of the classic theories, most of those who have studied organizations, businesses and even the behaviour of gamblers maintain that groups curb the boldness of individuals and are regulated by the least common denominator. In common parlance, a bird in the hand is worth two in the bush. This is why groups are deemed to be ineffective when an important problem is at stake, one which demands a creative initiative.

It was Stoner, a researcher little impressed by these theories or by the social psychology that flows from them, who discovered in 1961 at the Harvard Business School that, on the contrary, groups are bolder and advise the taking of greater risks than do individuals. Wanting to be more sure of this, Wallach and Kogan (1965) devised an easy, precise measuring tool. They conceived the 'choice dilemma questionnaire'. Its twelve items described a person who is faced with an obligatory choice between the terms of an alternative: one term is safe, but hardly attractive, the other term is more attractive but carries with it the risk of failure. The following is an example: A, an electrical engineer, married and the father of one child, has been working for an important firm since he completed his college course five years previously. He has the assurance of a job for life, at a modest but satisfactory salary, and a remunerative pension when he retires. On the other hand, he has little chance of seeing his salary rise much over his career. At a conference he is offered a post in a small firm that has just started up, but whose future is still very uncertain. It would bring him in a better salary from the start, and the possibility of acquiring a financial stake in the business, provided that it survives in the face of competition from more important firms. Imagine, therefore, that you have to advise A. A list of several conditions of the probability of the new business being financially sound has been drawn up. You are asked to tick the lowest probability that the person filling in the questionnaire would deem acceptable to make it worthwhile for A to accept this new post.

For each of the twelve persons described in the questionnaire, using the criterion of the probability of success, the subject had to advise the protagonist in the story to choose the alternative which was the most attractive and the most risky. The lower the probability indicated, the more risky the decision advised was judged to be. Each participant in the experiment was invited to indicate for each item the level of risk that he would accept before recommending the term of the alternative that appeared potentially preferable. Each one indicated his choices, first in private and then in groups of five during a discussion that ended in a unanimous consensus. This was achieved most frequently by settling for the riskiest alternative, but which was also more lucrative than the others. What was more, answering the questionnaire in private once again, the participants stuck to the consensus view, adopting it as their own, and did not revert to the individual choices they had previously made.

It is useful to emphasize the questionnaire and the way in which it was used, for most experiments in this field follow this model and illustrate a typical situation. It has been noticed every time that the spontaneous consensus of the group tends most frequently to the riskiest extreme rather than towards the prudent compromise. In this lies the interest of the experiments, but also the difficulty of evaluating their significance, if one holds the propensity to conformity to be of supreme importance. It is significant that Wallach and Kogan gave at the outset an explanation that presupposed a falling away from the norm in social life. As violent as the explanation pertaining to crowds, this did not take account of the realities. But, as distinct from that relating to crowds, it was marked by a consensus that should be more calculated and reflective, even in its extremes. The following is the reasoning they gave. If the individual takes a decision regarding the level of risk to be taken, he assumes responsibility for the consequences and is accountable for it both in his own eyes and in those of his friends and colleagues, etc. This inclines him to be moderate, for he is afraid of failure. However, when the individual is with others, and discusses and chooses with them, he feels less inhibited. It becomes less easy to identify the one advocating risk-taking, and no participant assumes more responsibility for it than does his neighbour. The one who is responsible could be anybody. So individuals feel less accountable as regards the outcome and no longer have the same fear of failure. Therefore their decisions when seeking consensus become more risky.

Undoubtedly this explanation presumes that the decisions are the effect of a notion of irresponsibility in groups, analogous to that of the masses just mentioned. Wallach and Kogan draw on this, believing that

> there exists a possibility of kinship between the apparently 'rational' deliberations of our experimental constituted small groups and the kind of mass or crowd phenomenon that one associates with extreme and violent actions. To speak of such a kinship is to imply that the mechanism at work consists of a diffusion of responsibility such that full participation and involvement in the decision process partially absolves the individual for possible failure. (1965: 2)

This comes down to stripping the decision and the group consensus of any rational character. This is because the group makes an extreme choice, whereas if the group had felt itself to be responsible, it would have made a choice approximating to the mean. The decision is allegedly determined by an exchange of arguments and the discussion of chances for and against one of the solutions proposed. But these are merely vehicles through which individuals have been brought closer, have intensified their emotions, and which have made them lose all sense of limitation, as occurs in any kind of collective assembly. Boldness arises from a complicity in fears and anonymity as regards the consequences.

In reality Wallach and Kogan explain the taking of risk in terms that Allport used regarding the psychology of crowds: 'The violence of actions in crowds is explained partly by social facilitation combined with the removal of individual responsibility' (1924: 318).

Half a century later, therefore, the wording has scarcely changed. It is very difficult to disabuse the human mind of this sophism. It springs from the belief that each person wishes to shrug off his responsibility, which is what otherwise makes him prudent and reflective. On the contrary, he desires nothing so much as to see his own responsibility recognized and associated with collective responsibility, which has very rightly existed from time immemorial, and is deeply rooted in us. It is just as arduous a task to eradicate the conclusions of this long series of studies in social psychology. They seek to demonstrate that the forms of collective life sap our moral fibre, and render superfluous our most precious personal qualities. Belonging to a group is a guarantee of mediocrity, because, as one can see, critical thinking is blunted and creativity diminished, knowledge under-used and responsibility lost, reducing the individual to the celebrated 'average person'.[3] One can well believe that this is the part pre-eminently played by the group and that it serves no other purpose than to remove from individuals all sense of responsibility, preventing them from helping anyone in distress when they form part of a group. This leads one to ask how natural selection has allowed such a disadvantageous organism to continue to exist, and even multiply.

In reality, this is no new conclusion. It follows inevitably from the logic of mass society, which is made up of anonymous, 'molecular' individuals, influenceable, and apathetic. Scorn of the masses is very widespread, whether it is expressed outright or mediated through the human sciences. This is some indication of the hold the conception exerts. It is true that mass psychology has presented it as something unique and in conformity with human nature. Not only has it been accepted by common sense, by statesmen, philosophers and teachers for over a century, but any conception that differed from it has only marginally survived. As the studies that we have outlined indicate, although present-day social psychology with one hand discreetly rejects the idea, with the other it accepts this view of the individual and the collectivity. More precisely, it adopts the viewpoint and deduces from it the hypotheses, verifying them in turn, completing what Le Bon (1963) and McDougall (1920) failed to complete. Examining the facts as such, removed from the context of any kind of doctrine and the laboured commentaries of individual psychology, one cannot assert that this orthodox conception is erroneous or even sterile. Nevertheless it remains limited to one aspect of social life by its insistence on the negative traits of the group, which only a failing on the part of the individual or the culture has made necessary. In a word, these are the characteristics of what may be termed 'mass man'.

If we emphasize this conception, it is in order better to clarify to what degree it conditions the hypotheses, the way in which the phenomena are viewed, and the weight that is given to one phenomenon rather than another. In addition, one may ask why social psychology insists so much on placing on the side of the individual everything that is negative and on that of the group everything that is positive, always tipping the balance in the one direction. This is doubtless because it is not concerned with reality, but rather with the segment of it it has opted to consider. In short, it has agreed to explain through the individual what functions, and by the group what acts dysfunctionally.

4

Yet groups are far from meriting all the evil said about them, or the way in which they are neglected in social psychology. On the one hand, nothing can lead more to error, nothing can fill the mind with more corrosive prejudices, exotic though they may be, than reading about these theories, which constantly intone the same litany: groups are less creative than individuals; they lower the effectiveness and initiative of each individual by inciting him to slackness; they produce conformity and obedience, and so on. On the other hand, one forgets that a second conception, which can occasionally be heard, has nevertheless shown how greatly groups are indispensable. This is precisely because they are needed to innovate as regards rules and norms and to change ingrained modes of behaviour. The conception sees in the association together of individuals a unique network having the power to stimulate and to overcome the inhibitions in their affective and intellectual qualities. Only when individuals come together are they able to lay down for themselves rules for living, to receive full and complete acknowledgement of what they are and what they do, and to give birth to something new. On this score Freud remarks, 'Moreover, we shall never know what the thinker and the poet in isolation owe to the stimulation of the crowd among whom they live, nor whether they do any more than round off a psychological process in which others have at the same time cooperated' (1981: 141). It is indeed because we shall never know this that it is pretentious to seek decisively to separate them.

Although there are not many, a certain number of studies are known that show that groups can act positively in some respects as well as negatively, succeeding better than their members in isolation (Collins and Guetzkow, 1964; Faucheux and Moscovici, 1960). But, instead of dwelling upon this kind of comparison between individuals and groups, let us ask why groups are the motors of change, an impossibility for individuals. Let us go straight to the most significant piece of research on this: that of Lewin on the change in eating habits in the United States during the Second World War.

Americans eat very little offal, which in the eyes of the middle classes passes for being an inferior quality food. Even a shortage of more 'noble' kinds of meat does not cause them to change their opinion. So the government launched a propaganda campaign in favour of the scorned offal, using the media available at that time, the radio and newspapers. The stress was put on its nutritional value, the proteins it provided and other dietary advantages. Advice was accompanied by recipes showing how offal could be tastily prepared. At the same time it was stressed that consumers who bought it were contributing to sustaining the US war effort. This propaganda attracted attention, as opinion surveys confirmed. The message had been got over, its recommendations approved, and many housewives declared themselves ready to buy offal, in the absence of other kinds of meat. But why did they not back their words with deeds? Without daring openly to admit it, persons questioned let it be understood that they deemed this kind of food barely good enough for the needy. In other words, they underwent the influence of the environment and conformed to the prevailing norms, for fear of incurring their neighbours' reprobation if they diverged from them.

We may compare their situation at this stage to that of smokers and certain alcoholics today. They know full well that tobacco and alcohol are harmful, and have a negative image of them. Yet they cannot stop smoking and drinking. They fail to match their words with deeds. Nowadays, just as before, very expensive press campaigns salve the conscience of govern-ments, give financial backing to the prestige of publicity organs with taxpayers' money, but the campaigns themselves remain a dead letter. This is not to mention various individual therapeutic treatments that succeed here and there but generally turn out to act no more than as a placebo.

Nevertheless, faced with these negative results, Lewin intervened and demonstrated the effects of group discussion. He brought together volun-teer groups of women belonging to the Red Cross. Some listened to a talk on the dietary advantages of offal. The others were invited to discuss them among themselves. The latter were invited to vote, by a show of hands, for or against offal, that is, to pledge themselves (or not) to buy and prepare it. Then women from the two groups were interviewed. It was discovered that in the discussion groups there was a much more marked disposition to take action and modify eating habits (Lewin, 1943).

An even more remarkable result was obtained among pregnant women in a rural maternity home, who before giving birth received advice on giving their infant orange juice and cod liver oil. Here also, two different procedures were followed. Certain mothers-to-be received this advice individually from specialist members of staff. The others, divided into groups of six, were given the same information on the value of these nutriments during a discussion, and then were asked to state what they intended to do. As one could foresee, there was a marked difference. After a fortnight, close to half the mothers who had taken part in the discussions were giving cod liver oil to their baby, whereas only one in five were doing so in the other group.

In this research and other later studies the method is clear: at a first stage, individuals are brought together around a common subject that may be concerning them; in a second phase they take part in a discussion during which they spell out their position; and in a final phase they take a decision after unanimous agreement. Naturally, they expect to be questioned later on to learn whether they have respected the agreement. There is of course a group leader, but his discreet presence is not a specific factor in the phenomena that occur. To what is due the greater effectiveness of, first, the discussion, and then the group decision that follows? Already before the war Lewin had suggested that the effectiveness a grouping in general exhibits derives from the fact that its members participate and become increasingly involved in the solution of vital tasks (Lewin, 1936). It is these same factors that he invokes later. Discussion and group decisions make individuals more active, in contrast to the passivity of those who listen to a talk or receive advice individually. 'The discussion, if conducted correctly, is likely to lead to a much higher degree of involvement. The procedure of group decision in this experiment follows a step by step method designed (a) to secure high involvement, (b) not to impede freedom of decision' (Lewin, 1943: 202).

The atmosphere in which exchanges take place weakens the pressure to conform. Pre-formed attitudes grow more flexible and the traditional view ceases to be the only one. Whereas there was no alternative – one only eats 'noble' meat, for example – now several possibilities are perceived. Where one expected uniformity – everyone prefers 'noble' meat – diversity is discovered. Extreme or deviant behaviour becomes more familiar, and it can be envisaged without apprehension in open discussion. According to Lewin, a member of such a group will sooner or later break the ice and express his willingness to give it a try. Since nobody reproaches him for this, others who share his viewpoint are emboldened to say so, and certain of those who were hesitant or hostile admit that offal, for example, is an acceptable dish. The consensus shown at the end of the discussion proves that the former attitude has ceased to predominate, giving way to a new one. Moreover, the consensus links the decision to the action. The individuals who accept it and as members of the group pledge themselves to respect the agreement will show a tendency to 'stick to the decision taken'. Saying or doing something in public makes it more difficult (costly) to depart from the line of action that one has promised to follow. As Simmel, the German sociologist, once wrote, 'When an extended group wishes to conduct its own affairs, it is indispensable that each one of its members understands and approves, to a certain degree the rules for action that it is following; they are condemned to a kind of triviality' (1896: 89).

Clearly, when the war was over, this exploratory research inspired others and an attempt was made to examine the phenomena more minutely. The role of the leader in the discussion, the hierarchy of the group that increases or decreases interaction between its members, the nature of the conflict, etc., were each examined in turn. In particular it was shown that groups whose members took opposite sides about a task arrived at a consensus when emphasis was placed on the factors favouring consensus. On the contrary, groups in which opposition is of an affective origin reach agreement when their members' attention is drawn to what is preventing them from arriving at a consensus. In short, when an objective case of conflict arises, it is more worthwhile to encourage what draws the parties together, and in the case of a subjective conflict, to combat what separates them. It is necessary, on the one hand, to accelerate, and, on the other, to take the brake off.

Moreover, studies have been carried out to determine the role of the various elements that lead to consensus: discussion, the choice, in public or in private, to commit oneself to something, and of course the decision itself, taken in common (Bennett, 1955). In certain aspects the role of discussion has been called into question, but the arguments put forward are not convincing. When a decision is made in public, it unquestionably has an effect on the action. The consensus determines the attitude towards the action. The participants rally round it so much more wholeheartedly when the consensus perceived among them is more complete. At the end of the day the principal point remains. Far from the decision to change behaviour and to act in concert against the prevailing norms being due to a diffused sense of irresponsibility, it results from a shared responsibility. In varying degrees the group commits its members to shape their own new attitude, one in which they can recognize themselves and by which they are recognized.

Societies have always deemed it useful to get their members to commit themselves through deliberation, through the swearing of oaths or through the vote. To bind them in this way has a purpose: to prohibit their remaining neutral or indifferent. Doubtless this is a condition for loyalty and change in general. The former President of the Soviet Union, Gorbachev, explained as self-evident that if previous reforms had failed it was, according to him, 'because these reforms did not rest on the main, decisive force, namely *the involvement of the people* [our emphasis] in the modernization of the country. We have drawn the lessons from the past, and this is why we insist so much on the development of the democratization process'.[4]

This agrees with all we know about the power of discussion, which melts away old attitudes and habits and prepares for a consensus on new ones. But does this occur around a compromise or around a somewhat extreme position? If we can trust a long tradition in social psychology there can be no doubt about the answer. How can one not be struck by the constant observation made in so many studies that to be committed goes hand in hand with clear, decisive choices? In the same way, we note repeatedly that the more a problem or an object acquires importance in the eyes of individuals, the more they are judged in extreme terms. Again, the fact that discussion occurs, or even the putting forward of arguments, has always the effect of causing alternatives to stand out and be better defined. Personal commitment provides an anchor mooring from which agreements or beliefs, attitudes and modes of behaviour are set out in a precise order. A kind of resistance sets up in us, preventing us from making concessions too easily and from accepting the boring position of the just mean. It is as if we refused to gain so little after having made so much personal mental effort. It would be to deprive the discussion of any meaning to finish up as a group at the point where we would have arrived without it.

For the moment we will not seek to explain this, but will content ourselves with registering the conclusion. This is: the more the members of a group adhere to an opinion or decision, the more they have confidence in it and in themselves, the less they are disposed to compromise, to add modifications that muddy the tracks leading to a clear-cut solution. Whether they are involved through the group situation or through the importance of a burning question – which comes down to the same thing – they resist pressures to moderate, to cut the pear in half or in quarters, a solution that would bring them back to the status quo.[5] In the same way they are less prone to hesitate when confronted with extreme attitudes, just as were those who had chosen to deviate from the norm and eat less 'noble' kinds of meat.

These first research studies by Lewin certainly discovered how far the group can be not an obligatory brake, but the necessary motor for change. By participating, people naturally become more active, but also capable of taking decisions as regards attitudes and modes of behaviour that go against accepted values, or, to be more precise, extreme decisions. This, however, does not warrant classing the group with the crowd, which is prey to over-enthusiasm and violence. It is rather the logical consequence of the fact of taking part in discussion and in a choice that concerns everyone. This logical conclusion has been established for a great variety of opinions and attitudes. Persons who are confident and involved always position them-selves close to one of the poles, either negative or positive, on the scale. How could this be viewed as a pathological symptom? Let us rather acknowledge it to be a sign of the meaning they ascribe to the adoption of attitudes or opinions for which they assume full responsibility. But we shall return to this point later.

5

It is as if the group tied the commitment of each member to its decision, taken in common and in public, in order to overcome the obstacles encountered in innovating. This is illustrated by a research project carried out in Iowa, which makes this plain. Its purpose was to induce property-owners to economize on energy. In the first stage the researchers advised them on tips on how to maintain the same temperature while burning less fuel, and asked them to put these into effect. The owners agreed, but consumption data over sixty-five households, taken after a month and then at the end of winter, showed no savings at all. The promise had not been kept.

Thus, in a second stage, following Lewin's example, the researchers contacted another group of owners and renewed their advice. This time it was accompanied by a proposal that the list of owners who were to take part in the fuel economy campaign would be published in the local newspapers. Each one gave a written commitment to allow his name to be published. Thus they would give an example of good citizenship. The repercussions were immediate. After one month it was found that the houseowners who had signed this pledge had indeed consumed less fuel, to a significant amount. In order to ensure that the publicity they were to be given had not affected them in any way, they were warned that in the end the list of names would not be published. This announcement had no negative effect; on the contrary, this group's fuel consumption continued to decrease throughout the winter.

In making this choice and commitment, the people concerned put themselves in a different situation and were borne along by its logic. Once converted, the householders began to see themselves as economizers leading a struggle against the waste of energy. They created new habits for themselves and sought to convince themselves that it was essential to reduce energy imports. In short, they acquired a different image of themselves and their way of life, and put a different gloss on their actions. This is why they respected the contract they had entered into, even if no publicity had been given to their gesture (Pallak et al., 1980).

Although we can have no absolute certainty regarding this, these explanations have the ring of truth. Thus they bring us closer to a different conception of the role of the group. This is, that it mobilizes the intellectual and affective potentialities of each one of its members by making them participate in a collective action, not in order to increase cohesion, but to allow them to breach together the barrier of norms from which, if faced alone, they would recoil. Such a 'mobilization' is observed in the ordinary course of social life, but is even more remarkable in the privileged fields of science and technology. Nowadays epistemology emphasizes the place of discussion and controversy in the choice of a research subject, of a method, or of the meaning assigned to the results. The researchers' interest in such and such a subject is measured by the 'gossip test' (Crick, 1990). By this is meant that the subject that absorbs them is the one occurring most frequently in conversations, when these take place between the greatest possible number of colleagues. Other subjects may well occupy their minds, but if they are not aired in such chatter, they arouse only little curiosity in the scientific community and do not engage its deepest attention. Hence those countless meetings, colloquia, seminars and talks, which it would be wrong to see as mere adjuncts to research. They are the energizing batteries designed to influence the choice of ideas or opposing facts.

Even if such permanent, shifting gatherings do not of themselves constitute a remedy for dissent, they are an indication that consensus is in the process of formation. This is what, within the scientific framework, gives them meaning. The formation of disagreements preparatory to forming an agreement appears to be a method for testing out new concepts. This is everyday practice. In any case it is one of the reasons invoked by Crick to explain the superiority of the team of which, with Watson at Cambridge, he was a member, over the London team, in the discovery of the genetic code:

> Our other advantage was that we had evolved unstated but fruitful methods of collaboration, something that was quite missing in the London group. If either of us suggested a new idea the other, while taking it seriously, would accept to demolish it in a candid but unhostile manner. This turned out to be quite crucial. (1990: 80).

The rule is therefore to carry to a conclusion intellectual and social polemics, avoiding personalizing them. This does not mean that they are not taken to heart and are not felt *ad hominem* secretly in the minds of the participants. In any case science today seems to be carried on by working through decisions transforming personal conjectures and disparate ideas into a common theory, sanctioned by a fresh agreement. If we examine closely the process whereby new science is produced, it turns out that scientists constantly link together choices between hypotheses on which they embark with the anticipated reactions of their colleagues, of scientific journals and laboratory rumours behind the scenes. Very appropriately, Knorr-Cetina, who has contributed much to revealing this view of scientific theory as a series of decisions taken in common, notes this reversal: 'The selections of the laboratory', she writes, 'are not linked to *individual* decision-making, but seen as outcomes of social *interaction* and *negotiation*. Consequently, we must reject such equations as that between the individual and innovation on one hand, and between social group and validation on the other, in a trivial sense' (1981: 13, emphasis in original). On the contrary, the terms of the equation change by virtue of the fact that most research in the exact sciences is carried on not by individuals but by groups. Moreover, the ideas and the products that are judged to be innovatory are collective events. They appear after discussions and detailed negotiations, and each individual, whether an ally or an adversary, is stimulated to participate in them.

Conclusion

We come now to the point where we shall conclude this chapter. If we wish to understand the nature of groups, it seems advisable to concentrate on the way in which they change, and in which they change individuals, rather than on their ability to aggregate individuals as parts of a whole. In the broader perspective we have just sketched out, which includes innovations in society as well as the discoveries of science, we are dealing with a process that is lasting and can take many forms. In the event, the danger lies less in anomie or disorder than in routine and apathy. In this respect we have highlighted the importance of participation, of the act of committing oneself with others. Everyone participates and becomes committed the more the task assumes significance in the eyes of each individual. Know-how and knowledge play a lesser part.

On the other hand, the prime condition must not be underestimated: that of a maximum difference in values among those participating. Let us, for example, suppose that several individuals have met to take a decision with a view to arriving at a consensus of a scientific nature. If all think that their judgements and those of others are of the same value, they quickly, and without hesitation, arrive at a consensus. If, on the other hand, a majority esteems that only its own judgements possess value, and those of the minority possess none, when that minority holds an opposing view, then it is clear they will never get together in a consensus. Each individual is talking to himself so as not to be heard by others, and the value of the judgements made has little chance of being modified. Complicity on the part of one side and blocking by the other side inhibits active involvement in the task to be undertaken. Whether it is a dialogue of the deaf or a dialogue of the dumb is of no consequence. For dialogue to stimulate both sides there must be a difference in values as regards the choices. This difference must in no way be too large to discourage people, but sufficient for them to discern what points they have in common, and allow them to try to persuade one another. It may be supposed that even the slightest involvement produces spectacular effects, insofar as it first prevents an automatic compromise, and then abstention.

Starting from this condition, we gave ourselves the task of exploring the function of the group to change and innovate. This is revealed in the decisions made in order to arrive at a consensus, indispensable in a society such as ours which is continually evolving, and in science, which has become a collective activity, as well as indispensable to numerous institutions. We have isolated the underlying phenomenon through experiments whose results we have indicated in the Introduction, but which it is now appropriate to set out in detail.

It was known that groups tend to take greater risks than individuals. This is undoubtedly an exception that proves embarrassing to the rule. But it could not be attributed either to the irresponsibility of some or to the emotions that overwhelm others in the course of a discussion, as with the crowd. Other experiments have taught us that groups are as prudent as individuals. Moreover, one can just concede that people, feeling themselves less responsible, are delivered from the fear of failure that tones down their opinions. Yet how can one explain the fact that, once consensus is reached, these same individuals, once more on their own, are not again smitten with fear, but continue to recommend risky choices, faithful to the position of the group of which for a while they formed part? They have manifestly changed and have adopted a different perspective, like those persons who opted for new types of food or made up their minds to economize on energy. We must certainly assume that something other than a dilution of responsibility is taking place and that people become involved in discussions and cling to their arguments, so that they end up by adopting a fresh viewpoint, which commits them and is binding upon them. Thus the exception becomes the rule, since the new opinion is necessarily extreme.

To assure ourselves of this, we needed to resort to topics and attitudes that carried with them no risk factor. Let us therefore resume the analysis of our experiment. Participants first answered separately a questionnaire of a political kind, consisting of statements such as: 'De Gaulle is too old to carry out such a difficult political task', and, 'American economic aid is always used for political pressure'. These are questions relevant to the group itself and to an outside group that was both admired and feared, both having profound significance for many Frenchmen. The subject had to express agreement or disagreement with each statement by marking a seven-point scale constructed on Likert's principles, which therefore has a neutral (zero) point.

In the next phase, four or five participants were sat round a table, the same questionnaire was handed to them and they were invited as a group to discuss each statement until they unanimously reached the same level of agreement or disagreement. Once this decision had been taken they were asked to express, once again in isolation, their opinion. By examining the difference between, on the one hand, the sum of the average choices on the scale before consensus ('pre-consensus'), and the sum of the consensuses, it was found that the group adopted more extreme attitudes than did the individual in isolation. Even in the third phase, when the participant in the test made a decision once more in isolation after the consensus ('post-consensus'), we found that the attitude remained extreme. The data thus clearly indicate that the attitudes exhibited by the members of the group after discussion are more extreme than those they held before the discussion. The direction in which this change proceeds is foreshadowed by the initial tendency of the group, which is either positive or negative. Moreover, this effect persists after the individuals have separated. Thus they privately endorse the judgement or opinion on which they agreed in public.

The question was posed whether this effect was due to the conformity of the group, or to participation by its members. To answer this, we compared groups the majority of whose members held the same position before discussion with those where such a majority did not exist. The former did not seem to polarize any more significantly than did the latter. Moreover, one conforms to the majority when its positions tend to move in the direction of the group norm, but much less if the positions are the opposite. It is as if, on a jury, a majority favouring clemency, which was the dominant value, had more impact than a majority of the same size whose positions tended towards severity. We can therefore dismiss the hypothesis of a conformity to numbers and to the authority they confer. Moreover, if these experiments have had an undoubted impact, it is certainly because they indicate that the group lays significant stress on the effect of non-conformity. In other words, the group deviates from the mean position, instead of swinging towards it (Brown, 1974). For this reason also the participants do not revert to their initial position nor react as if they had undergone some external pressure to follow the greatest number.

So long as this kind of effect was limited to the choice of risks to be taken, one could still retain the analogies with mass violence and ascribe them to a lack of responsibility. As soon as one perceives, according to our studies and subsequent ones, that a vast range of judgements, perceptions and attitudes become more extreme after having been discussed in the group, we find ourselves in a different situation. You know about this situation. The corpus of research in social psychology has particularly analysed the nature of the forces that explain cohesion and equilibrium around the group norm. Yet if these forces had the importance ascribed to them, we should not constantly observe a deviation from the mean, either positively or negatively. The analogy of the group with a certain perspective relating to the masses is profoundly undermined. Instead of a sociability whose ideal is to moderate the views of its members, we perceive another, which radicalizes them and keeps them far removed from the point of equilibrium. In fact, what is normal for the one becomes abnormal for the other, and what is individual for the former becomes collective for the latter. This is why the discovery of this phenomenon transfers the problem of decision from the practical plane to that of the concept of the group itself. This change was perceived at the outset:

> So long as the phenomenon was viewed as a risky shift, it was assumed to have mainly *practical* implications. The research seemed to imply that groups should be employed when risk taking is desired and individuals when caution is desired. . . . At the same time, and especially in the light of the discoveries about shift on non-risk-involving tasks, the phenomenon has begun to look more interesting from a *theoretical* viewpoint. (Pruitt, 1971: 340, emphasis in original)

Quite plainly there exists in social psychology a standard conception and a non-standard conception of the relationships between individuals and groups. The one puts the accent on the characteristic of the masses and the other on the characteristic of mutation in our society. These constitute the fund of hypotheses and facts that are brought together in a theory whenever that is possible. It would be vain to seek to decide in favour of the one or the other by means of observation or experiment. Choices in the matter depend – as is widely realized – more on ideological and cultural factors than on empirical data. However this may be, we shall not shrink from the task, in order to make the pendulum swing back in the reverse direction.

Just as the study of science until recently, the study of attitudes, beliefs, actions, etc. has been founded on that of the individual, isolated from his usual reference framework. We now know how these attitudes, etc. are formed and transformed during exchanges participated in by individuals meeting together. It is clear that explanation must from now on start with the group and be made in relation to it. In this way it will tackle problems concretely and, in the end, more heuristically. When do the relationships of members within a group have the effect of modifying them, when do they render them more extreme? Why are these members occasionally inhibited and rally to conformity, whereas in different circumstances they are stimulated and tend to innovate? From the above, it will be perceived that we shall be putting forward a theory associating these relationships with their outcomes, of which compromise or extremism are the symptoms. We shall make no display of modesty by repeating that the theory is provisional and calls for further research in depth. This goes without saying: no one has any illusions regarding the ephemeral nature of its hypotheses or regarding the quantum of uncertainty that the facts carry with them.

At the beginning, we shall indicate the reasons why, in the case of a dispute, whether it be personal, political or scientific, there is a spontaneous tendency to agree on an extreme position. Then we shall explore the conditions that limit this propensity. This will allow us better to understand the phenomenon of polarization itself. Finally we shall see how decisions leading to consensus at the same time transform categories of individual thinking into categories of social thinking. But, having so often made mention of the group, we must first of all examine its springs of action, what are its peculiarities, and what makes consensus generally necessary.

Notes

1 *Le Figaro*, 30 March 1988.

2 First Marquardt (1955), then Lorge and Solomon (1955), tried to show that in the final analysis everything depends on the quality of persons meeting together, and not on the way in which they cooperate in the task proposed.

3 An exposition of these studies is to be found in Collins and Guetzkow (1964) and Davis (1969).

4 *Le Monde*, 24 May 1988.

5 It is difficult to discover the origins of this tradition, and, because there are so many, to cite the most outstanding studies. Doubtless those of Charters and Newcomb (1952), Tajfel and Wilkes (1964) and Lemon (1968) have played an important role. But it is most certainly Sherif (1966) who is its most consistent theorist, as his numerous authoritative works demonstrate.

2

The Elementary Forms of Participation in Decisions and Consensuses

The need to participate

1

Acts of decision, as well as acts of consenting, are above all acts of participation. For various reasons their value springs from the bond that they create between individuals and from the impression each one receives that he counts in the eyes of everybody as soon as he begins to participate. We all know intuitively that this link, even if tenuous, is a preliminary condition for following a goal, fulfilling a political, religious or even an economic mission, or simply for giving meaning to the world in which we live. 'If people', Hegel wrote, 'are to take an interest in something, they must be able to participate actively in it', (1965: 105).

In fact they need to know that they are taking part in affairs, and that these depend on their energy and skill. In this way they acquire a feeling that this energy and skill are necessary and that their presence is appreciated. When we say 'in contact with', 'having a mission' or 'being in the know', we are expressing this sentiment. Its social truth is nowhere more subtly expressed than in the familiar phrases 'belonging' or 'not belonging'. It encapsulates the idea that being part of a family, a club, a gathering, or belonging to a social category is the obligatory preliminary condition for a form of choice and an understanding, and affords access to the exchanges that shape the public existence of each individual. Consequently much effort is expended to become a member of an association, to be elected to a committee, to have the right to meet together and communicate with certain people, and so on.

There seems no doubt that the motive for this must be sought in a basic need present in all of us. We mean the need to participate, which turns out to be a genuine need, but in the absence not only of any constraint but also of anything that might constrain the urge within us to associate with those like us and undertake action in common. No obstacle whatever can prevent this from manifesting itself in relationships with a number of others as well as in public life, uprooting the individual from apathy and indifference. 'Hence,' as Parsons rightly observes, 'it is the participation of an actor in a patterned interactive relationship which is for many purposes the most significant unit of a social system' (1952: 25).

Responding to this need, the group no longer appears as a datum or an outside association which holds individuals together, obliging them to fulfil a certain function or occupy a predetermined place. It is what they accomplish for themselves; it draws them closer and causes them to feel that everything they do together represents a choice. It is indeed true that the debased word 'participation' appropriately designates that elementary, immediate relationship in which one passes from a passive to an active state. Individuals no longer figure as pawns on a chess-board moved according to set rules, or as spectators at a play. They have the discretion to modify the rules and vary the play's dialogue or plot. Thus the group may surpass them as individuals, but at the same time they realize they are its originators, constantly contributing to its creation, so that their interests and energies converge on it. The individual and the collective are in some way synthesized within it, like oxygen and hydrogen in water, before they are identified and isolated. In his very fine diaries, published posthumously, Lévy-Bruhl observed that

> people are not first a given datum, and then enter into acts of participation. For them to be a given fact, for them to exist, there must be already acts of participation. An act of participation is not only one of fusion, mysterious and inexplicable, by human beings who at one and the same time lose and preserve their identity. It enters into their very constitution. Without participation, they would not be a 'given fact' in their experience, they would not exist. (1952: 250)

What meaning does participation assume for groups? What does it reveal regarding their status? We need to pose such questions if we want to understand the significance of this living notion, rich in history. Usage having made it a commonplace expression, it suffices for now to give it the narrow meaning of taking initiative, and the presence of individuals in political or social choices, for example, through the vote or through the right to express their interests. Yet participation extends much farther. Logically it defines an internal relationship between people who think, decide and act in the community when it spurs them on to do so, but for the sake of the community and in its name. Beyond this relationship a person has no identity. He belongs to nothing and nobody, and cannot be, in the incisive formula of Aristotle, either 'a brute or a god'. But there is no need for a detailed exposition of this point or reference to such an eminent authority in order to recognize its existence by pointing to what is most significant about it.

On the one hand, participation stimulates relationships that are more intense and more frequent than normal. In everyday existence, given over to looking after the family, to the requirements of an occupation, relationships between individuals become more distant and automatic. Contacts become more remote, indifference sets in and trust is eroded. By the mere fact of renewing contacts, and seeking out and increasing the number of exchanges, ties are revitalized. No one remains inactive, and in the same movement people draw closer together, stimulating one another. This can be observed in public places, cafés, bars and other familiar places where opinions are openly made and unmade. Beneath a façade of nonchalance, 'in congregating in public places,' according to A. Ryan as quoted by Hirschman,

> the French and English escape from their purely private activities, discuss all kinds of matters of public concern, from current sports and scandal to rising prices and the forthcoming elections, and thereby engage in action that has some bearing on the public interest. In flocking to their cafés and pubs, the French and the English are therefore not so much showing preference for pleasure over comfort as for public over private activities. (1979: 84).

Each individual is continually pressed to give his opinion, to indicate his preferences, to persuade or let himself be persuaded, occasionally unwittingly adopting the prevailing viewpoint. But contacts are clearly more frequent and intense at political meetings, religious ceremonies or large gatherings, during which individuals are in some way transformed. This is at least the case so long as individual voices seeking to communicate are not stifled, or are not mentally harassed in their discussion in order to press them to adopt some conclusion or other. Consequently arguments appear all the more fair, attitudes and values all the more true, when they have been fiercely disputed by the one side and defended by the other, preparatory to arriving at a common judgement. This is why in the last century a public vote was recommended as preferable to one by secret ballot. It incites everyone to participate more intensely, which 'involves exposing yourself to new influences, competitive views of the world, new demands on your capacities. It thus seems quite unlike shopping for policies in your interest; it is a – on the face of it gruelling – piece of social and political education' (A. Ryan quoted in Hirschman, 1979: 90).

The more numerous the modes of thinking set in train when this occurs, the more they enlarge the range of notions, the gamut of ideas, and the vocabulary of every individual. Yet they also strengthen convictions that have had to be defended on several fronts. Moreover, by drawing closer to one another, individuals draw closer to the group. Usually they see it as something distant and above them, impersonal and abstract, addressed in the third person. This is illustrated, for example, in a party whose members confine themselves to paying their subscription, or in a church where believers are not faithful worshippers, hardly attending its services, or yet again, in a parliament outside the election period. Yet as soon as people have a reason to come together, distances shrink, social life becomes fuller and its meaning becomes plain once more. It is often observed that, in the event, the first effect is the psychological phenomenon, whereby participation confers on each individual the sense of community, a feeling of effectiveness and involvement in the political or religious group, which becomes a concrete persona and receives a proper title.

Nevertheless this pressure must be resisted, and each person does so unconsciously. For the individual this consists in regaining command over himself when faced with a possible act of bonding, such as that of a child and its mother, or a crowd and its leader. Possession rituals or political meetings are so many examples of this. This fusion is tempting to the individual and threatens to deprive him of what is peculiar to him, as well as of his role as an actor, defined by the interests and opinions that he holds. It is a matter of responding negatively to this 'we', which decrees the sacrifice of the 'self' when choices and decisions are taken in common. For the collectivity it is imperative to overcome its consuming tendency to impose a uniformity upon individuals and encourage their inclination to follow the law of least effort and obey. It is true that by causing them to abandon their personal arguments and interests, the collectivity ensures, for its own benefit, that decisions are made easy. But this is at the price of a passivity that deprives it of the energy and active initiative of individuals. They have to struggle against themselves in order to form a living entity, and the entity has to struggle against itself in order to be made up of individuals. This is in fact the necessity noted by Pascal in his time: 'The multitude that is not reduced to a unity is confusion; the unity that does not depend upon the multitude is tyranny.' It is pointless to add to this, for every word rings true.

Participation has plainly only meaning if the plurality of group members is respected, and freedom of action and speech are guaranteed. If individuals were not distinct entities and acknowledged to be so, they would not feel it possible to re-establish the ties of belonging, nor discover what they hold in common. Ceremonies, images and signs suffice to manifest this. If they did not emerge from their isolation or seek to make themselves known to one another by taking part in public affairs, they would lack any certainty of their own worth. This is why each individual aspires to tread the theatre boards of society, as John Adams, one of the fathers of the American Revolution observed: 'Wherever are to be found men, women and children, whether old or young, rich or poor, noble or vile, wise or stupid, one perceives that each individual is motivated by a strong desire to be seen, heard, discussed, approved, and respected by the people around him and he knows' (1851: 12).

This feeling is an indication of the need to participate. By satisfying it we can hone those qualities of intelligence, initiative and speech that draw us to one another, and rectify the troubles caused by anonymity and loneliness in the crowd. Recently society has often been compared to the theatre, and has been described on this model. It must be emphasized that what individuals and actors share in common is not only that they are actors in a play, but also that they are participating in it. This is why the theories that have drawn inspiration from this source, although they have caused us to go on stage, have not allowed us to go behind the scenes.

2

Thus it is true for us that 'to be is to participate'. Through this we are from the beginning turned towards other people and public life. Whatever may be our egoistical tendencies and separate interests, participation, in the last analysis, aims at satisfying in individuals that need to decide and act in concert, which can be fobbed off but not suppressed. In practice it depends on the extent to which they first link up with one another, and then immerse themselves. Into the first factor there enters a certain empathy towards our peers that leads us to echo their sentiments, to think the selfsame thoughts and to act as they act. We are all the more successful in this because we are all involved together in events great and small – from an election to a natural catastrophe or a football match – which leave traces in the collective memory. Indeed we have all known a moment when we have felt that we counted for those who counted in our own eyes. Whether it be a gesture, a statement, or even a silent pledge, the individual making it, recognizing his attachment

> to the society of which he is a part, feels himself morally bound to share in its sadnesses and joys; to dissociate himself from them would be to break the bonds that unite him with the collectivity; it would be to give up wishing it to be so, to contradict himself. (Durkheim, 1978: 571)

Men and women are therefore right to base their relationships on the presumption that this attachment is lasting, despite the ups and downs caused by circumstances.

In many respects it is extremely difficult to fathom the meaning that the attachment takes on and understand the strength with which it is expressed in the supreme and joyous moments when the group is present *in corpore*, in flesh and blood. One is tempted to ascribe it to the consciousness of their own mortality, which only human beings as individuals possess. Yet as social animals belonging to a community they are immortal, just as is, so they imagine, that community itself. Thus their attachment to the group, a permanent one, moreover, delivers them from the consciousness of death and from fear of it. What assurance it gives to participate in a human entity – family, city or nation – promised to *de facto* immortality! In this sense to share in its events, its rituals and decisions, counterbalances the apathy and depression that man feels in solitude, and the boredom that haunts him in a society to which he feels himself bound. In almost all cultures a lone human being, without any attachments, is moreover considered as dead or condemned to be forgotten, which comes down to the same thing. When we touch on the reason for the bonds that bind us, we are close to dealing with depth psychology. Yet we are not obliged to stick to a 'surface' psychology, on the pretext that this is all we can observe, and what we can agree on without difficulty.

The second factor in participation is, of course, the need to invest our economic and psychological resources in order to associate with one another, to sustain an action once it has been decided upon in common, or even merely to remain together. These resources are the more precious, and even bring all the more satisfaction, if each individual sees in them a sacrifice or renunciation, etc. This is indeed what occurs for the individual who opts to join a group, initiating himself into its beliefs and practices, or to become a member of a union, to militate without thought of self in a political party, to be converted to a church, etc. He feels himself even more part of the group the more it demands from him. The participant responds to its demands all the more eagerly than if the group offered him something without demanding anything in return. One can better measure the results of such investment when one sees the distress of those who separate from a church or a party, or who leave their native city or country, abandoning that part of themselves they had given to it.

Let us look farther afield. A person who has begun to 'invest' even a small amount of time and resources must necessarily increase it. Not only is this so in order not to lose what he has committed, but also because by beginning to participate, he changes and acquires a new image, becoming in his own eyes someone different. How and why this occurs emerges from a fine study by Freedman and Fraser (1966), the American psychologists, which deals with a familiar situation. We see volunteers going from door to door to get householders to sign a petition whose purpose was 'to preserve the beauty of California'. Naturally, almost everyone signed it, since the beauty of the countryside, like child health or world peace, is a theme that strikes a chord. A fortnight later, these same people were asked to put up a board on their lawn: 'Drive carefully'. Almost half agreed to do so, whereas the figure would have been much lower if they had not signed the petition. In fact, they had made the first step and then took part in an action. The participants deemed themselves infused with civic spirit, and loyal to their principles. They acted in accordance with their beliefs and cooperated in a good cause. These investments would influence their future behaviour and imprint themselves favourably on their own self-image.

One thing is certain. For the individual to devote himself to a common action, whether voting or praying, whether he has to deliberate at a council meeting or on a jury, or attend events celebrated by the group to which he belongs, he is obliged to do it in his own time. Likewise the group has to use up a part of its resources in order to allow its members to play a role in it, just as the Greek and Roman cities paid the citizen summoned to public consultations. If these conditions are not fulfilled, an individual is deprived of her or his fellows. We may state that participation increases in direct proportion to the solicitations made by a collectivity and to the investments made by individuals in it, in contacts sufficiently lengthy to afford satisfaction to both. Plainly everything here depends on the passion and strength of the ideals that they embrace, and on the traditions of the social environment. Yet it also depends on the reward expected from it. One may indeed ask what kind of reward. Participation is peculiar in that it brings with it no reward in terms of profit and remuneration. It has, for example, nothing to do with the financial support brought by a capitalist to a firm. Rather it is related, as has long been noted, to human activities that concern the quest for community, the search after knowledge or after salvation. These are activities that bring their own reward, ones in which we sublimate very different impulses which still need to be better identified. 'Once this essential characteristic of participation in collective action for the public good is understood,' Hirschman comments, 'the severe limitations of the "economic" view about such participation, and about the obstacles to it, come immediately into view' (1981: 85).

This fact has been so often pointed out that one hesitates to recall it. Yet no observer of social life can do without it. Henry James, the great novelist, emphasized this in almost identical terms: 'If in consequence,' he wrote, 'to have a happy destiny consists in participating actively in life, sovereignly and not passively and narrowly, by mere sensibility and tolerance, happiness is all the greater when the faculty employed is vaster' (1987: 237).

There exists, of course, one benefit we expect from others, one which procures for us that happiness without which no individual can employ his faculties continuously. This is the social recognition of making the effort to play our part, to a significant degree, in the various tasks we pursue together. What use would it be to be a good citizen, a zealous worker, a talented artist, a devoted administrator, if no one noticed it, did not say so or did not take account of it? If one is not esteemed by one's peers, not to speak of receiving certain more tangible marks of respect – a decoration, election to some learned or artistic society – what good is it? Such a person, left out or pushed to one side, would be as non-existent as his action or his work: a citizen consulted by nobody, a book that nobody reads, a theory that is not adopted, a work that goes unnoticed, a picture on which the indifferent gaze does not linger. How many of the most solid characters have been broken by the indifference or the silence of their neighbours!

Nothing therefore stimulates one more to participate than this expectation, this need to be recognized by those to whom one is attached, and to be included in their world. This is true for the scholar who has made a valuable contribution to knowledge (Hagstrom, 1965) or the member of a sports club who wears its colours in every competition. Whoever hopes for this recognition sacrifices time and energy, personal affairs and tranquillity. He finds a certain reward already in the victory over himself represented in the act of shaking himself out of his inertia, and of forming frequent and intense relationships with others. But this victory would not be sufficient if it were not accompanied by visible signs that others had singled him out, or that they had all distinguished themselves together, like a football team or a team of researchers. The person who wants to obtain additional satisfaction and reward – reward from a larger number – tries to participate more frequently, to be among those who make decisions. Among such people are the secretary of an association, the professor who sits on every committee, the militant who does not miss a meeting, etc. Besides the satisfaction that success procures, they reckon upon the kudos being attributed to them, and upon the esteem accorded because of their contribution.

The reverse and obverse of decisions taken in common

1

Clearly when the members of a committee, a party or some temporary assembly 'invest' in these, they count upon having some say in them and influencing the course of events. They therefore hope to have an opportunity to present their viewpoint, to justify it as far as possible, and of course to be listened to. If this is conceded, at the same time one must concede that no obstacle should stand in the way for different viewpoints to be aired, and for these to conflict. At any moment, one may resort to violent means to re-establish tranquillity and harmony. Yet at the same time any pretension to consensus is abandoned, just as a government breaks off talks with its opponents in order to decree a state of emergency, simply requiring submission and waiting in silence. One set of views may be refused the right to take part in social matters, just as the British Parliament brushes aside one sector of opinion through the election law, so that only those may oppose who are already in agreement. This allows a consensus among unequal partners, contrary to the definition that assumes they are equal. In any case, the more the members of a collectivity 'invest' of themselves in it, and consequently justifiably believe they have strengthened their position, the more divergences increase in number and extent. It may be said that these are opportunities favourable to decisions aiming at change or innovation. This is exactly what was thought about some very outstanding successes in the moral and scientific fields, in an article appearing in 1864 with the provoking title, 'Antitheses as a method of social psychology', written by the scientist Cattaneo. According to him, they were the outcome of a series of disagreements, followed by agreement between persons seeking the same goal. One can see the reason why. It is extremely difficult for those convinced of the correctness of an idea or an interest to understand the reasons for differences with others, whether among a team of scientists, a jury or a religious community. Are they based on opposing convictions, a tendency to seek to be independent and different, or on motives of personal sympathy or antipathy – in short, on disagreement, rivalry or misunderstanding? Only by pursuing these divergences to the point of conflict, in a series of arguments for and against, or by the uncovering of a fact that proves or belies them, will the confusion be dispelled and fixed positions shaken. Moreover, this procedure makes one aware during the discussion of what is really at stake, of the common elements in various viewpoints, and above all of their merit. 'Only where there is conflict,' wrote Park, 'is behaviour conscious and self-conscious; only here are the conditions for rational conduct' (Park and Burgess, 1921: 56).

In this way the participants are borne along by a stream of controversy much stronger than their immediate preoccupations. Debating a particular fact or idea will provoke argument. To be stimulated to view things from several standpoints represents a breakthrough that no one could achieve by himself, if he were not confronted with minds not attuned to one another. An antithesis requires to be available, which people should be ready to espouse, and with which to confront others. Thus

> every objection provokes a response; every argument provokes a complementary argument that weaves opposing ideas together in an inseparable whole; from the viewpoint of the idea these are blacksmiths striking the same iron, blind instruments in a common enterprise. Each new effort adds a link to the chain that raises both sides upwards into the spiral of truth. (Cattaneo, 1864: 268)

Neither side can escape from this. This is all the more so because, like any individual who expects to meet someone different or opposed to him, they both feel a physical tension difficult to assuage.[1] This tension arises less from the content of the argument or the difference that exists between them than because the disagreement manifests itself through someone else, who has to be faced up to. Each one of us feels this kind of tension at a meeting where the impression is that, after the very first words have been spoken, hostility will be shown. Yet this fear acts as a spur, for each party is led to redefine its viewpoint, to see it through another's eyes, and weigh up the opposing viewpoint as it does its own. Thus picking a path through very many antitheses and differences causes the individual's thinking to be deflected towards the collective thinking. Even the innocent question 'What should we think of it?' alerts us to this. We know that it is not our answer alone that will be given, but it is an opening gambit to set in train a series of controversies 'in the rules of those who are involved with us in the common understanding of life' (Mead, 1964: 192).

Nothing is more appropriate for such an understanding than the social polemic. Yet how can it be contrived so that members of the group, disagreeing as to their choices, should nevertheless not be discouraged from making them? How can it be arranged so that they still agree to argue and yet remain always ready to search for an understanding? Without seeking to resolve this problem, let us note that participation, which sharpens conflicts in which we are immersed, at the same time fortifies the ties that exist. Thus, throughout controversies and counter-arguments, which resemble body-blows, the members of the group covertly exert upon one another an influence that emphasizes what can draw them closer. Between them can be observed a synchronized, imitative process which transforms every word into a signal, every gesture into a model, and every piece of information into an argument. All the forms of the rhetoric of mind and body become manoeuvres through which the distances between the participants grow smaller and the frictions between them are deadened. Behind the divisions, misunderstandings and the unrelenting polemic, a mental unity is reforged among the group. 'The hard task', as Mead also remarked, 'is the realization of the common value in the experience of conflicting groups and individuals' (1964: 365).

This dual dynamic of conflict and influence can be easily observed in any committee, jury, working group or gathering that meets to discuss. This is what we are simulating in our experiments. Indeed the persons we bring together in groups of four or five in a laboratory with the task of producing a unanimous decision have each their own attitude to the problem submitted to them. For the possibility of disagreement to arise we choose appropriate themes – peace, the emancipation of women, ecology, etc. It is certain that the conflicts are the more intense the more the theme is topical, concerns them closely, and when they are mandated to take part in the discussion, and thus become involved in exchanges with one another. The imperative to agree necessitates an exercise in persuasion and in breaking down differences until opinions and interests are synthesized. To escape from the unpleasantness that disagreements can cause, those involved might say, 'It's not a serious matter', 'It's nothing', 'No matter'. Yet the obligation to reach a consensus in spite of everything, and to accept it, blocks this escape route. Usually this aspect of the conflict (and being involved in a theory), which is omnipresent in social reality, is neglected. So the factor that distinguishes the judgement behind a decision is neglected. Abelson and Levi state: 'Not only does making a choice imply greater commitment and conflict than does making a judgement; it tends also to bring responsibility and regret into consideration' (1985: 235).

On the one hand, the divergence of opinions, and, on the other, the need to arrive at agreement link the conflict to the reciprocal influence we have just mentioned. Thus we may deduce that heterogeneous groups change and polarize more than do homogeneous groups. This is even more so when the subject on which the decision is to be taken is sufficiently novel and important to afford meat for ample discussion. For, as Thibaut and Kelley found through observation, 'much of the unclarity that members have about prospective goals may be reduced by group discussion, with a maximum participation throughout the group' (1967: 261). But they do not know why this lack of clarity melts away and brings out extreme attitudes. We have just given a few indications as to this.

2

The example most constantly offered us of this need to participate lies perhaps in the rituals that societies have devised to cope with it. They could not leave to chance the circumstances in which people publicly manifest their attachment, nor could they leave arbitrary just how many resources and how much time should be invested in the collectivity. They have therefore instituted rules and periodic ceremonies designed to satisfy this need that each individual possesses. It is beyond our purpose to go through the list of rituals, which range from sacrifice and the swearing of oaths to exercising the vote. Let us confine ourselves to the most widespread one, which concerns us most nearly – discussion, and with it the deliberation of issues and adversarial debate, where people speak after having reflected on a matter. If discussion did not occur, it would be useless to propose problems and suggest solutions, because the latter would not have any profound influence. Most people indeed see in discussion a form of exchange, one where, instead of things, information is bartered, just as in judicial interrogations or technical committees, in order to resolve a difficulty or to clarify what remains vague. It is mainly a communication rite bringing members of groups together periodically in an appropriate place – a drawing-room, café or market – in accordance with set rules. This link with participation appears in its most distinct form in the Greek art of politics just as it does in the French art of conversation, that form of dialogue of no apparent utility where apparently one speaks above all for the sake of speaking, for pleasure or as a game. But most frequently, by the very fact of being called upon to discuss, each individual feels himself to be an actor in the ritual and a member of the group instituting it. In this way group cohesion is reinforced at regular intervals. The appropriate words pronounced in a suitable tone of voice and at the prescribed moment have this effect, whatever may be the piece of information they are communicating.

Atkinson and Heritage have observed, 'There is a bias to many aspects of the organization of talk which is generally favourable to the maintenance of bonds of solidarity between actors and which promotes the avoidance of conflicts,' (1984: 265). What is more, debate involves an effort of control and expansion, through speech, of the rivalries that come to the surface. This is why all political institutions, and scientific and religious communities, are careful to summon their members on more or less fixed dates to meetings where they can speak out, renew their beliefs and common practices, by taking part in public discussions. We cannot therefore consider discussion between people, even in a laboratory and in a temporary situation, as *any* kind of activity. Can one perhaps liken it to a physical channel through which flow arguments relevant to the solution of a problem? Should one see it as a social channel in which mingle and accumulate individual opinions to form a collective opinion? This would be to leave out of account the essential element that constitutes the symbolic, unconscious strength of an institution, in which what is visible has always less importance than what is invisible: France, in the three colours of its flag, equality through the ballot paper, or the sentiment of the divine in prayer.

However, we must not depart from the framework of social psychology. Let us consider discussion as an institution giving to each individual an opportunity to take part in the affairs of the group, and as the emblem of consensus. It already has this meaning, even before the first words have been uttered. To sit round a table is to carry on a conflict, and also to commit oneself to conclude it by other means. If this meaning is dissipated, it can only be seen as a useless waste, gossiping lacking any spiritual content, or as a bureaucratic ceremony, to which one must bow, as one does to many other things. This at least is what is often heard said regarding public discussions and debates, and of any ritual that has lost its prestige and fails to find an echo in the minds of those who take part in it.

From consensual participation to standardized participation

1

The detractors of discussion are doubtless wrong. But if we try to pinpoint their error, we perceive it is not so easy as may be supposed. It would perhaps be best to see in it a symptom of a more general tendency. Let us begin with the observation of Hannah Arendt, the political philosopher:

> Human plurality, the basic condition of action and speech, has the twofold characteristic of equality and distinction. If men were not equal, they could neither understand each other and those who came before them nor plan for the future and foresee the needs of those who will come after them. If men were not distinct, each human being distinguished from any other who is, was or ever will be, they would need neither speech nor action to make themselves understood. Signs and sounds to communicate immediate identical needs and wants would be enough (1983: 92–3).

Now if we examine these two characteristics, we find in fact that equality leaves the field free for a multiplicity of conflicts, and distinctiveness opens the way to mutual influences, and to tactics of persuasion with the aim of uniting. How then can they be combined so that the various alternatives which arise from disagreement are limited or prevented from proliferating, to the benefit of a norm to which consent is possible? Let us remember that a note of dissent and disagreement is a sign of an increased will to win over, in the interest of the group, those holding an opposite viewpoint. Numerous studies justify the assertion that people are more disposed to start out on that painful intellectual and affective path when they have to deal with opposing arguments coming from several sources rather than from one source alone. It is as if a group speaking with several voices were more conspicuous and offered greater room for manoeuvre than a group with only one voice. This is not to dismiss the satisfaction felt by all parties, which Tocqueville noted in the United States, where 'to become involved in the government of society and to talk about it, is the greatest matter and, so to speak, the sole pleasure the American knows' (1961: I, 254).

A striking example is precisely that provided by democracies as opposed to monarchies and dictatorships. In the latter, consensus is a show, since opponents are either in prison or in exile. In them speech is not a pleasurable experience, even though remaining mute is hurtful. By contrast, democratic consensus regards silence as blameworthy, and everyone is encouraged to speak. The best proof of the reality of consensus is that it can still be called into question, as can be seen when the opposition becomes the majority and vice versa. A higher level of consensus is reached when disagreements are expressed more vigorously, just as with friends who calm down and become more deeply reconciled after having quarrelled, placed their friendship in jeopardy and risked losing it. This is no imaginary possibility. Machiavelli observed it in his analysis of Roman public life. He wrote:

> Those who condemn the quarrels between the nobles and the plebs seem to be cavilling at the very things that were the primary causes of Rome's retaining her

freedom, and that they pay more attention to the noise and clamours resulting from such commotions than to what resulted from them, that is, to the good effects they produced. (1950, vol. 1: 218).

For in the end – and this is the paradox we encounter – consensus serves more to tolerate conflicts than to suppress them, something that can be done by many other means, which are those of authority. Only a static and individual conception produces an agreement that avoids discord and dissension, whereas a dynamic conception identifies in these an agreement that transforms them. Under its aegis, they can be developed to change, and to stimulate collective action, carrying individuals along when reality so requires. Protests and disputes are, as it were, the criteria of the human vitality of the group, and measure the degree to which each individual is attached to it.[2] Although it is said, without reason but as a kind of shorthand, that union gives strength, it is rather the disunion which measures strength and stimulates it. In any case, as French noted after meticulous observation, groups with greater cohesion have more conflicts than do less cohesive groups and, he added,

> The probability of such conflict depends not only on the degree of interdependence within the group, but also the extent of involvement of the individual in the group. If only a small peripheral segment of members' personality is involved, the conflict is slight. If on the other hand, many of the individual's goals are involved in his relations to the group, some conflict is almost inevitable, inasmuch as individual differences make it very unlikely that all individuals would agree on all goals and on the best path for attaining each. (1941: 369)

This common-sense observation, if ever there was one, leads us to ask why individuals are sometimes more involved, sometimes less involved in the group. Conflict appears intense in one case, slight in another. In this connection we can only put forward conjectures supported by no more than a few observations.

Everything depends on the way in which participation develops, since this is what motivates the desire to 'invest' and choose, and the extent to which one can put up with differences and justify one's options. We know two elementary forms of this, two phases through which it alternates. The first, *consensual participation*, develops in a way that maintains an equal balance between individuals, without conferring any advantage to the majority or disadvantage to the minority, who can clearly express themselves regardless of any prescribed rules. It reaches a peak when opinions and desires, interests and prejudices are fully exposed to the light of day, without encountering any external limitations, save those of resources, and of places for discussion, for which societies can plan in advance. Whatever the reasons, a seeming incoherence and disorder is manifest. It is as if all societies were convinced that only effervescing, uninhibited reactions, born of tension and improvisation, can reveal their creative forms and fight every tendency to error. Gramsci has written that for many social organisms, this was

> a vital question, not passive and indirect consensus, but an active and direct consensus, and this through the participation of individuals, even if it gives rise to a

semblance of disintegration and disorder. A collective consciousness is in fact a living organism, formed only after the multitude has become unified through the activity of individuals . . . an orchestra that is rehearsing, with each instrument playing individually, gives the impression of being a horrible cacophony, and yet rehearsals are the sine qua non that give life to the orchestra performing as one single instrument. (1953: 143)

In such situations, where opposing forces are in equilibrium, the individual feels not only an invitation but also an obligation to address himself to the collectivity, since he regards himself as one of its organs. In this way he incorporates himself in it as well as making it his own, expressing himself without fear of being censured or excluded. This is because 'whenever strong commitments to values are expected, the rational calculation of punishments and rewards is regarded as an improper way of making decisions' (Hagstrom, 1965: 112). Each individual displays a kind of boldness in the controversies and discussions, in order to be given recognition. It is assumed that, if the inner dialogues of self are turned inside out like a glove in the course of the vast external dialogue, it is undoubtedly because they enliven the most intimate corners of social life. What we are getting at can, for example, be found in the energy that is expended in group discussion to such a degree that Coleman, the American sociologist, at the conclusion of a study of conflict, states that this discussion 'is such an important phenomenon that in the case studies most descriptions of behaviour during the intense part of the controversy were descriptions of discussions and of attempts to persuade or reinforce opinion' (1973: 18).

In theory the discussion should be pursued without anyone being able to restrain or halt it, even for so-called objective reasons, so that each person gains the impression that he is contributing to the consensus and to its renewal. To identify with it and the better to adhere to it, without letting himself be the prisoner of personal interests, judgements or choices, the participation of every single individual is desirable. Individuals then allegedly realize where their own advantage lies, what representations they have in common, and feel justified to one another. A German sociologist has written that to this end, to communicate and to engage in polemical argument is

an act which is irreducibly pragmatic, and this precisely because it is not an act of *reason*, but an act of the *will*, an act of collective *choice*. The problem we are confronted with is not a problem of *justification*, but of the *participation* in power, of who is to make decisions about what is permitted and what not. (Tugendhat, in Habermas, 1990: 73, emphasis in original)

Thus the individual emerges from the closed domain of his individual power and enters into the collective power of participating in choices, in the formation of the consensus that he makes his own, and for which he assumes the consequences. Through stirring meetings, referenda, festivities in which the social roles are reversed, or solemn gatherings, societies have preserved these moments in which each individual can acknowledge himself and be acknowledged in them. Some societies, such as the Greek city-states, made this compulsory. Lycurgus required each citizen to take part in the debates and deliberations of the *polis*. He even made a law which prohibited citizens from remaining neutral in civil disputes.

In the other form of participation, which may be described as *normalized*, it is the existing hierarchy that regulates how members of the group enter into the discussion and participate in the consensus. Thus they are singled out by the relative standing accorded each individual, the extent to which they can 'invest' in the communication process and the concluding of an agreement. Within this framework everything that poses a problem or requires a decision, whether it is a matter for litigation or of an action to be undertaken, proceeds from the base to the summit, for the decision to be made.

By this procedure, to some extent differences are sifted out and controversies diluted by gradually lowering the temperature of the debate. In this way the opportunities to participate in decisions are limited by eliminating any alternative that cannot be absorbed. Not that it is judged to be of no importance or that people are indifferent to it: it is simply left out of the public discussion. Under such conditions clearly people feel reticent about formulating their thoughts and wishes, as if they feared the hostility of their peers. By keeping silent, they give consent. It is even more the case that, if they possess lower status or belong to a minority, they are wary of expressing judgements that pit them against those of individuals of a higher status or belonging to what they assume to be the majority. In fact, the former are afraid to be considered adversaries, have the impression that they are not following the correct rules for communicating, or procedures framed precisely to create a reluctance to participate, and where disagreements are censured. In general, as an American social psychologist has noted, an individual hesitates to express an opinion that conflicts with that of another, for fear that the latter will feel offended or will hold it against him. (Torrance, 1954).

Decisions taken are the outcome of a series of unequal concessions that converge towards a position that gives the advantage to the majority and disadvantages the minority. This has been confirmed in the laboratory with small groups, but in society as well, with those other small groups on which the destiny of people depends. Is it not significant that the testimony of a highly-placed person regarding the form of participation in the meetings of the Soviet Politburo caught the attention of the international press? Is it not also significant that this form was put forward as a benchmark to denote the contrast between the previous state of affairs and the state of the reforms and of 'glasnost'?

> Previously they [the meetings] were prepared and concluded within the hour. Now they occasionally last ten hours. Much discussion goes on in them. Almost all the members express their opinion practically every time. Yet there is virtually no disagreement within the Politburo. We never take a vote since after we have attempted to formulate a joint view there are no longer any objectors.[3]

In other words, emerging from stagnation and embarking on change, the Politburo, in taking its decisions, was moving from a normalized form of participation to a consensual form. In contrast to the consensual form, we can understand that the normalized form, which gives only a subordinate role to some members of the group, creates a certain distance, causing the group not to loom so large in the life and consciousness of individuals, so that in the end it appears strange and abstract. Immediately the participants become detached from one another, and instead of being actors become mere spectators in the discussions.

In concluding his own observations on the life of trade unions, Coleman, the sociologist, sums up this evolution as follows:

> When trade unions play an important part in their members' lives, one finds active internal politics, with lively fractional fights, internal disputes, and challenges from the ranks. 'Business unions', on the other hand, which do no more than carry on wage negotiations, and whose members are little involved, are quiet, stable bureaucracies with little internal discord. Even more extreme in their bureaucracy and mass apathy are such voluntary organizations as consumers' cooperatives, automobile clubs, professional societies, business associations, and veterans' groups. (1973: 3)

Since controversy is in proportion to the participation of members, few conflicts are observed, unless it be in the ranks of the leaders. It is as if individuals tended to minimize their 'investment' and their attachment to the collectivity, remaining aloof from intrigues, and, so far as possible, conforming to the opinions and actions that were suggested to them.

Without pushing speculation too far, it can be seen that decisions leading to a consensus are obtained differently, depending on the form participation takes. The first form, in which no one individual is advantaged in comparison with the rest, offers the possibility of participants being able to confront one another and state their views in the course of discussion, without constraint or time limits. The agreement at which they arrive transforms the conflict inasmuch as respective positions become alternatives in relation to the same purpose or problem, which is conceived of in an identical way. The second form of participation establishes relationships between certain individuals holding specific trump cards, but according to a certain procedure. This first defines the conflict between them as tolerable and then steers the discussions so as to favour a hierarchy of opinions corresponding to a hierarchy of persons. In this way the Babel of imperfectly discussed propositions and counter-propositions is halted, by means of a forced consent, there being no other way to achieve it. The choice between a consensual form of participation and the normalized form is a question not of preferences, but of circumstances.

Although the one satisfies the need to participate in a more intense way, and one of which people cannot be deprived for long, the other at least provides a substitute for it. This is what happens at American conventions over those few days when the delegates take the floor, compensating for the years of apathy and silence. This does not imply that to satisfy this need is an unmixed blessing, when we think of relationships, as tense as jangling chords, that exist in gatherings or in crowds, or in the anarchy of swarming masses of people participating in street demonstrations. It is true that, from the utilitarian viewpoint,[4] to participate in any shape or form appears superfluous, a drain on resources and time which deserve to be more worthily employed. However, in any society, whether in former times or the present day, the whole action by people depends on this 'superfluity' being put to work.

2

The present discussion assuredly does not rely on the customary certainty of scientists who know they can base it on indisputable premises. Rather these are conjectures, and of a kind into which one does not venture without reservations, but which one cannot do without. To synthesize them, we shall state that they show us why the social fact of participating has as its psychological outcome the collective involvement of individuals in all matters that concern the group. Now, this involvement, or commitment – its equivalent – is, and we have insisted on this several times, a force that moves individuals closer to others in any decision that leads to a consensus. We know, moreover, just how much 'the most obvious candidate for a motivational variable constraining effective decision-making is psychological commitment to a prior decision. By commitment is meant some public behaviour on behalf of a position, making it more or less irrevocable because change is costly, socially awkward, damaging to self-esteem, or personally dangerous' (Abelson and Levi, 1985: 289). It is entirely normal, as we shall see, for a force which both checks and stabilizes to be one that sweeps people along, and modifies.

This does not explain everything, but reminds us that, for those who actively participate, ordinary situations or minor problems acquire importance and are of deep concern to them. Thus the general question of hunger in the world, or that of nuclear accidents, can grip us when we read a newspaper article on Chernobyl, when we argue with our neighbours or as members of an association that is mounting a campaign. Clearly the degree to which we are involved grows. Knowledge of such happenings, at first greeted with intellectual detachment, becomes a preoccupation and causes us to reflect anxiously on what might happen to ourselves, to our children or our country. In other words, our interest increases according to how far we include ourselves as participants in the activities relating to the events described or imagined. When events acquire this living presence, they mobilize all our interests, stir up a wealth of discussion and instigate meetings in which individuals unrestrainedly expound their sentiments and opinions. Continual discussion multiplies points of contact, inclines towards agreement and motivates people to discover the arguments tending in that direction. In reality these point them towards what they feel to lie behind the ideas and attitudes of each individual.

An intensified consensus is usually prepared for by a substantial number of exchanges between the members of the group, and by emphasizing the reactions and positions that go well together. There can scarcely be any doubt that, by meeting and talking together, a group's members bring out the values predominant among them, ones to which they are attached. In some way their substance is given shape, so that what we hold in common, but is concealed, becomes manifest. In the same way we see patriotism, normally dormant, aroused and dominating the sentiments and attitudes of everybody during the Olympic Games, or when some political threat arises. The outcome is a closer attachment, a firmer degree of consent, and one even more extreme. In the event the majority seeks to draw closer to the minority, while the participating minority takes a step in the direction of the majority, impelled by the same necessity. This convergence alone makes the decision leading to consensus something other than a compromise. It is therefore shaped by some affective element. It cannot be denied any more than it can be avoided, in spite of efforts expended to stand aloof. Like any institution in society, it cannot be delineated by, or identified with, solely intellectual factors. Asch, the American sociologist, rightly asserts that 'there must be a degree of affective consensus with respect to the aims and needs of the participants' (1959: 373).

From these conjectures can be deduced a certain number of predictions which will be submitted to the test of facts. In general, as we have just seen, consensual participation probably has the effect of raising the level of collective involvement, whereas normative participation lowers it. One may conclude that the former polarizes the decisions leading to consensus, whereas the latter modifies them. The former causes the members of the group to converge on the pole of values already shared by them before they took part in the decision, and the latter towards the just mean. In what follows we shall present the experiments carried out in the light of these conjectures and others that can be called upon to back them. It is not a matter of describing and observing each one of these ideas, something that no theory can succeed in doing, and that no science can claim to do. Moreover, if it were necessary to limit ourselves to those that are described and observed directly, as certain persons have asked us to do, we would only be studying the most crude and most superficial of them. But first we shall spell out these hypotheses, which, together, cast light on the phenomena that matter to us. They will be better judged from their effects.

Notes

1 The relationship between the level of conflict in a group and the psycho-physical activity has been studied by Bogdanoff et al. (1964), Gerard (1961), Shapiro and Crider (1969), Smith (1936), and by a number of other researchers.

2 One can find interesting details on the conditions for the validity of this proposition in the studies of Guetzkow and Gyr (1954) and Coleman (1973).

3 *Le Monde* 30 March 1988.

4 To associate participation above all with effectiveness or productivity reduces considerably its significance. It is a question of principle that moral philosophers have been discussing for a long time as regards its role in political and legal decisions. Their analyses are of the greatest interest for social psychology, in particular those of Rawls (1971) which refer to it.

3

Extreme Conflicts and Consensuses

Which groups are liable to polarize?

1

A group tends towards a consensus, which will sometimes be a compromise, and sometimes an extremism. It arrives at one or the other by manipulating the two levers it has available: conflict and influence. Like any generality, this observation requires to be adapted to the realities of each situation and environment. This is all the more the case because we know, with sure, mathematical knowledge, that there exists no automatic rule giving an indication as to which will be the collective choice of a group of individuals who have differing, and even opposing, interests and preferences. Majority rule itself, so important in a democracy, may well have more qualities than other forms of government, but it represents a pressure to conform and not in any way to come to agreement. It has been the main contribution of mathematics in this respect to demonstrate the indispensable character of discussion and interaction in the taking of a decision that leads to consensus. Seen in this light, the attention paid to them for so long begins to make sense. Discussions are not skirmishes, nor embroidering on words that one delights in for their form and artistry. What is really at stake is the reason for the group's very existence. Let us realize this and plunge into the heart of the theory.

Like any theory, ours must first enunciate a hypothesis on the magnitude of the effect produced by the cause – here, the displacement of the consensus towards an extreme – and then another hypothesis concerning the direction that this effect takes. We should be modest about this, particularly as regards the magnitude, for it is very difficult to measure precisely. Save in exceptional cases, we have few means of determining exactly, for example, the magnitude of a conflict between the choices of individuals, the degree of discordance between two ideas, or the level of involvement of the members of a group. Consequently hypotheses can only predict the order of size and the circumstances in which the effect has the most chance of manifesting itself. Thus all that we can say is that by intensifying the conflicts and discussions in which group members participate, their collective involvement is heightened. By involvement, we mean here a relationship that increases for each individual the importance given to a problem and to the agreements reached regarding it. This is why agreements should be concluded under appropriate conditions and, in particular, allow contributions to be made fairly to the distribution of information, to the exchange of arguments for or against a solution, and to the expression of opinions. No true involvement, no rational decision, no understanding, are possible if these conditions are not fulfilled. They lead spontaneously to a consensus that is extreme, even more extreme to the extent that the participants have become involved in the controversies that have arisen from their disagreements. Thus, as a hypothesis concerning the polarization of groups, it may be concluded that the consensus reached will be the more extreme:

(a) when individuals participate more directly in the discussions;
(b) when the differences between them, their knowledge and their opinions are more marked;
(c) when what is at stake in the discussions is perceived by them as valuable.

Coming closer to reality, we must assume these relationships vary from being disjointed. Just as a quantum of discontinuous energy is needed for an electron to move from a stationary state, where it does not radiate, to a stimulated state in which it does, so doubtless a discontinuous amount of conflict and discussion is required for members of a group to shift from a state of indifference, in which nothing can be observed, to a state of involvement in which they polarize. However, as opposed to the physicist who can measure this amount, the social psychologist must be content with assuming it, in order not to draw false conclusions, if he can find no continuous relationship between the magnitude of the cause and that of the effect.

2

Discussion, as we have emphasized on several occasions, is a preliminary condition. But we can speculate on what importance to give to the particular subject content about which it revolves. We can wonder whether it engenders a general atmosphere that induces a shift in opinions and judgements tending spontaneously in an extreme direction. If this were the case, one could be talking disconnectedly about anything at all, in the way in which one imagines that matters proceed among crowds, with the result that the attitudes of the participants become extreme. To express it differently, is it discussion in general that turns groups towards extremes, or do they only become extreme by taking decisions on particular problems that have been fiercely debated? Such questions are legitimate when one recalls the very widely held belief that a gathering becomes extremist on all counts once it has begun to be so on one particular point. It is concluded that such decisions are by definition irrational, as are those of any group, and for the selfsame reason.

However, the majority of experiments belie this. Discussions provoke a change only in the problems about which group members have to inform themselves and make up their minds together. This is reassuring, for a certain degree of rationality is maintained. In any case we cannot assert that, if a group adopts an opinion or takes a specific action, it has become, or will definitively become, extremist. Several studies have elaborated on this observation. Let us start with the very moderate study by Alker and Kogan (1968) on risk-taking. The authors asked those who had been brought together for the first experiment to read accounts of fictitious situatons which described one protagonist faced with a choice between two terms of an alternative, with one of the actions that he had to undertake being more risky and more attractive than the other. After having decided separately between the more risky solutions and those that were less so, they were requested to take part in a group discussion about their preferences as consumers. It was made clear that they need not necessarily arrive at an agreement, since it concerned a matter of taste. The discussion was in fact about fashion: they were presented with colour photographs of hats, dresses, slacks, shoes and hair-styles selected from recent issues of periodicals such as *Vogue, Mademoiselle, Hairtrends,* etc.

After having discussed each set of models, participants had to select in private the four colour photographs they preferred. They were also asked to reply to a questionnaire on risk-taking (which they had not discussed). The results were clear-cut. The group discussion, centring on questions that bore no relationship to risk-taking, brought about no shift in individual choices concerning risks.

Although prudence is advisable, it clearly seems that debate about a problem that concerns us intimately has a limited effect on the question itself. This emerges, moreover, from one of the studies by Myers (1975) where the researcher tested out the results we had obtained in France. His method consisted in putting forward a questionnaire in which three items described a good university professor and three others a bad one. For instance, stress was laid upon his qualities as a teacher, the care taken to prepare his course, the time he devoted to students in personal discussions, and the success he achieved. Participants in the experiment had to evaluate each member of the imaginary academic staff according to these criteria, on a scale ranging from 0 for the deplorable professor, to 10 for the excellent professor.

Two scenarios were prepared. In the first the participants judged the professors described, and they were asked, each individually, to recommend a distribution of salary increases for these six fictitious professors. After all participants had finished the test they were assembled in so-called assessment committees to discuss each case and the salary increase they would suggest. The person conducting the experiment gave them to understand that during the period for discussion they would perhaps arrive at a unanimous group decision. Once the period for discussion was over, the participants received an instruction to indicate the salary increase they would recommend, in the case where they had not done so all together. All in all, the situation was a fairly concrete one, not only because in certain universities students do evaluate their professors, but also because even where they do not do so officially, discussions on the subject are very frequent.

The second scenario was in every respect similar to the first, but with the exception that participants devoted the discussion time to talking about subjects that had nothing to do with the test. At the end of it, they were requested to reply to the questions on salary increases and attitudes towards the professors. As was foreseen, it was found that the bad university teachers were evaluated more negatively after the discussion, and the good ones more positively. The effect was significantly more marked in the first scenario than in the second. A similar tendency was noted concerning salary increases, the distribution of which became more extreme after discussion than before it, but this tendency was less strong than might have been expected. However, the discussion in the simulated academic committee significantly polarized judgements about the fictitious professors, and even more so when the debate was related to the test than when it related to any subject. Plainly, there is no halo effect of discussion on questions that are not included in it.[1]

3

Having established the exact significance of discussion, we can now examine more closely the hypothesis put forward. It is postulated that the conflict arising from the gap between the choices and the opinions of members of the group is all the more apparent when the differences between them are more marked. More precisely, this occurs when the individuals concerned, initially forming a very diverse and heterogeneous group, hold positions about a particular problem that are then far removed from one another, and in the end when information concerning it is unevenly distributed among them. Since, if they were already homogeneous, on the same wavelength and possessed the same amount of information, the occasions for disagreement and argument would be reduced to a minimum, as would also the chances of becoming involved. Fewer shifts in attitudes or judgements tending towards extreme poles would occur, or even none at all. In such a case the tendency to compromise would carry the day.

The following demonstrates this. In the experiment relating to attitudes towards de Gaulle and the Americans previously described (Moscovici and Zavalloni, 1969), we assumed that where discussion had created tension, shifts in the direction of a consensus should be more frequent. To verify this, the distance was measured between the two individuals whose opinions diverged most before the beginning of the discussion. A distance of 1 meant that these two opinions were separated by one point on a seven-point attitude scale. The opinions of the others, whether identical or not among themselves, were located between those of the two individuals who differed most. In the same way a distance of 6 meant that one of the individuals in the group was located at the favourable pole and another at the unfavourable pole. Thus they were opposites; the opinions of the rest were distributed between these poles. It is here, where conflict was greatest, that the maximum polarization should be recorded. In fact, the shifts towards an extreme consensus turned out to be more frequent in the groups when the gap was more than three points than when it was below that figure.

It is often claimed that in situations where there is marked disagreement, the consensus is less stable. Individuals allegedly tend to revert to their original opinion after a group discussion. Our theory maintains the opposite is true. When the participants become more involved in a more intense discussion, polarization should be more marked. We verified this. In groups where the distance between individuals is great, after consensus individual opinions remain more extreme than when this distance is small. Rather than converging on an average value, groups made up of individuals with very different attitudes and judgements, and even entirely opposing ones, will manifest a strong propensity to polarize.

The awkward fact about such experiments is not that these data are true or false. It is that they may be *almost* true, but not entirely so. In fact, the data were collected in conditions not devised expressly to verify the hypothesis. One might obtain such results, but, on the other hand, one might not. But this would have changed nothing about our knowledge of the phenomenon. This is why we must take this into account. Yet it is preferable to consider other experiments in which the researchers constituted their groups in order to study the effects. For instance, let us deal with the size of the group. Let us assume that one wishes indirectly to sharpen the conflict by increasing the chances of including in it heterogeneous individuals. Some experiments have tried this out, the most well known being that of Teger and Pruitt (1967), who constituted groups of three to five persons. The task proposed consisted in resolving the difficulties of a protagonist by opting for a solution that carried with it a more or less high risk. We need not recall it in detail, since the reader is already familiar with it. The researchers asked the groups to agree on a prudent or a bold alternative, comparing their opinions either by reflecting in silence, or by discussing them aloud.

The finding was simple: the common choices were much more extreme in the groups of five than in those of four, which themselves were more extreme than those in the groups of three. Moreover, they polarized more when they engaged in discussion among themselves than when they proceeded to a silent exchange of notes.

Another experiment (Vidmar and Burdeny, 1971) supports the hypothesis that an extended group must statistically include a wider range of opinions rather than a more limited one. Hence the probability of encountering an extreme opinion that sharpens tensions. This in turn is evinced by firm attempts to iron out differences through more intense discussions in which each individual becomes more heavily involved. The result inherent in this procedure indicates that decisions are polarized. Conversely, this result can be expressed as follows: by reducing the number and variety of the participants in the public debate, the chances of arriving at moderation and a compromise are enhanced.

We have available more direct evidence of what we have just propounded. Instead of relying on numbers to increase the diversity, it suffices to make up heterogeneous groups having the desired qualities. Resorting to the same type of questionnaire on decisions concerning risks, Vidmar (1970) classified individuals according to the high, medium or low level of risk they would take. Thus, as you might expect, he formed them into groups of five, some 'pure', that is, comprised of individuals who favoured the same level of risk (all 'daring' or all 'prudent'), the others mixed, made up, for instance, of two 'daring' persons, one taker of moderate risks and two 'prudent' persons. Once the group had been set up it discussed the various dilemmas concerning the risk that a given person should be advised to take, and it agreed on one of the possible solutions. Surprisingly, it was the mixed groups that chose the most risky solutions, whereas the 'pure' groups did not shift and converged towards a kind of mean.

The danger of extremism, so often mentioned, arises not, if these observations are accurate, from the extremist and excessive opinions of individuals, but merely from the differences that separate them. It is precisely to exorcize this remote danger that societies have created and laid down military and religious codes of discipline. These have the purpose not of suppressing deviant, excessive types, as has been claimed, but of organizing the difficult task of creating simulacra of one type, whether extreme or moderate is of no consequence. Is this a vague, gratuitous statement? We shall make a judgement on this, without being discouraged by studies that proved to be barren. Let us therefore consider the parallel established between the tendency to take risks and the interactions of members of a group. This is: the greater the number of times the discussion is relaunched, the more times high risks are taken. This is a perfectly reasonable proposition, one confirmed several times over. Thus, using the procedure described, Willems and Clark (1971) constituted mixed and pure groups gathered together under two different conditions. In the first, individuals exchanged information regarding their respective positions; in the second, they discussed together. Using the same material as the researchers previously mentioned, Willems and Clark observed that the mixed, more varied groups opted for more extreme choices under both conditions than did the pure groups. The result seems to have been fairly well established, so that the researchers could suggest 'that the degree of diversity of opinions in a group is, in fact, a necessary condition for the shift towards risk observed in groups. When group members agree, no shift is found, but when group members differ substantially, a substantial risky shift is found' (1971: 309).

We would subscribe more readily to such a conclusion if we were more sure that the absence of diversity leads to a compromise. English researchers have found this to be the case. They used similar material and constituted groups by matching members who all had the same level of risk-taking when they judged matters separately. Once matched in this way, they were gathered together and asked to discuss and come to a unanimous agreement on the level of risk to be taken. The person in charge of the experiment then withdrew from the room and, at the end of the session, each group reported its decision to him. Certain changes occurred within the groups, but these were not significant. In any case the existence of a certain diversity is an accepted precondition. 'Nevertheless,' the authors wrote, 'the startling number of cases among the experimental groups where no shift at all occurs after group discussion must surely point to the importance of heterogeneity of group membership that has hitherto been standard in precipitating the risky shift' (Ellis et al., 1969: 338).

Is the heterogeneity of the group indeed the dominant factor? One might well doubt these effects when one sees them echo one another with such regularity. It would be normal to think that behind this heterogeneity of opinions is hidden a heterogeneity of power. This last form of heterogeneity might well in reality be more determining than the former one. In other words, why not assume that the presence of an individual more powerful than the other members of the group suffices to bring about a more extreme form of consensus? In a fine, very realistic experiment, Siegel and Zajonc (1967) invalidated what common sense affirms. To this end they brought together eleven groups, each containing a psychiatrist, a psychologist and a social worker, who were accustomed to working together. Two of these groups were exclusively male, three comprised two women and one man, and the six others one woman and two men. The researchers asked them to go through a questionnaire containing items with a clinical content and others with no clinical content. The purpose of this was to assess their tendency to counsel a risky or a prudent action. Each person replied separately. Then the participants were assembled in groups of three as indicated above, and invited to arrive at a common decision after discussing the items of the questionnaire. A marked shift towards the most risky action was noted. However, it did not appear that the presumed authority of the psychiatrist had played the determining role. This affords an excellent illustration of the fact that it is the exchanges occurring between the different members of the group that shape the outcome of their decision, much more than their individual authority. There is hardly need to add that these results corroborate the majority of the studies about which the reader has just been informed.

4

What remained to be done was to create groups that expressed their disagreements under a reduced pressure to conform. Knowing that this pressure is all the greater when social cohesion is increased, Dion et al. (1971) merely varied the quantum of cohesion between group members. The higher the level of cohesion, the more individuals feel bound to one another, exerting on each other a pressure to behave and think in the same way, even if nobody demands it of them and the situation does not require it. It is expressed either in the restraint exercised by each individual or in censorship of propositions that might fuel dissension, and even by eliminating the most daring ones. This is sufficient to tone them down, and to give priority to compromise solutions. Groups having less cohesion, however, are less inclined to avoid divergences of views and risky options, which have more chance of being voiced. To use a metaphor, a country such as Switzerland, where compromise is a method of government, should be less receptive to the extreme decisions taken than a country such as France, where compromise is repugnant. The authors of this study therefore varied the degree of cohesion in the groups formed in their laboratory, whose task was to reach an agreement on the risks to be recommended to the fictitious persons of the questionnaire with which we are now very familiar. The results obtained were in conformity with expectations. It turned out that groups having less cohesion recommended daring options, and groups having more cohesion prudent ones. According to the former groups, the fictitious persons would jump at the chance of changing their job and lifestyle; according to the latter groups, they would be content with their present lot. At the same time it was discovered that groups conscious of their cohesion were little subject to tensions and contradictions; this means that their members showed more esteem for their group and desired more strongly to be together than did members of groups possessing less cohesion. They also declared that agreement was reached with their fellows in greater personal intimacy and in a more favourable atmosphere. These are indications that they have done everything to maintain harmony and minimize the differences between them by avoiding factors leading to discord. In short, as the long-standing theory of Festinger (1950) had predicted, cohesion increases the pressure to conform and leads to the search for a compromise in the group.

However, we must not lose sight of an evident reality that we often experience. Whatever may be the committee, assembly, colloquium, etc. in which the individual is participating, he hesitates to speak, to question and even more to express an idea that he believes is personal to him, or to voice an extreme opinion. It is as if he feared a rebuff, a negative judgement or even a hostile reaction from other people. Hence that puzzling silence of pupils in the classroom, or of an audience at the end of a lecture, whereas one might expect questions to be sparked off and an animated discussion to ensue. It is not at all because they have nothing to say that people remain silent in public, but, on the contrary, because they have too much to say, yet fear they will unleash an argument or provoke the rejoinders of others. What causes them to fail to express their thoughts is less their personal judgement than the shared conviction that opinions held in common are more important than those peculiar to the few, which do not merit being aired in public. Seen from this viewpoint, cohesion is an exhortation to conform to others and to defend oneself against still more people. But from another standpoint it can be seen as a bond of trust, a line of credit that the group extends to its members, allowing them to act as they think fit while at the same time relying on their loyalty. It creates a favourable climate and reassures those participating, helping them to overcome the fear of being rejected by others. In this atmosphere relationships favour diversity and the clash and play of argument as adversarial as one could wish.

What interests us here is to observe that one can end up with a more extreme consensus than in a less confident climate in which compromise carries the day. Nevertheless, Moscovici and Zaleska (Zaleska, 1982), in order to ascertain this beyond doubt, brought together in the University of Rouen six groups of four students, none of whom knew each other previously. They pretended to halve the participants – groups they termed 'friendly' – that they had assembled because in examining the questionnaire they had filled in beforehand they had found a commonality of thought among them and a desire to understand one another. To the other half of the group, termed 'neutral', made up in the same way, nothing like this was said. But the main point was that in the attitude and tone adopted by the researchers the former groups were reassured, whereas with the latter groups they showed themselves as merely behaving correctly. Once this atmosphere had been created, the students were invited to discuss a number of questions on their attitude regarding life at the university and to adopt a common position.

As we anticipated, the friendly groups leaned towards a polarized consensus, and the neutral groups towards a moderate consensus. Second, this consensus was interiorized to a greater degree by the members of the former groups than by those of the latter groups. This was observed by comparing the percentage of responses given in private by students, once the discussions leading to a consensus were over. Just as we discovered above that the more a group is composed of extreme individuals, the more they embrace consensus, so here this was likewise true (Figure 3.1). It can be seen that the more an extreme attitude was chosen initially, the more this was adhered to in the friendly groups. In the moderate groups, however, the converse was true, as if their members were less involved through the group discussions.

Figure 3.1 clearly shows that the stability of responses increases with the extremism of the opinion in the friendly groups, and decreases in the neutral groups.

It is no mere play on words to state that two facets of cohesion exist. The one prohibits discussion and dissension, the other permits and even favours them. The former is turned against threats of deviance, the latter against those of uniformity. They are manifested in the effort that collectivities make from time to time to prove their tolerance by encouraging their members to speak out loud what they are secretly thinking. They are also apparent in certain psychological or even pedagogical techniques, which try to combat the very widespread fear of opening one's mouth, or the repugnance felt by those who dare to do so at saying anything other than what they think is acceptable – in substance, commonplaces. This is not so

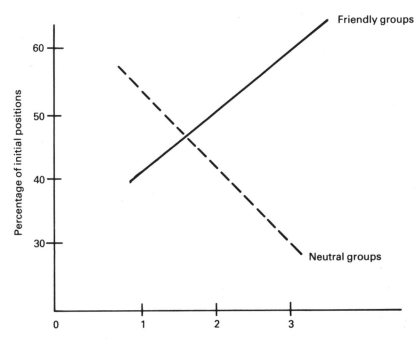

Figure 3.1   *Stability of positions in friendly and neutral groups as a function of initial extreme positions*

much in order to modify consensus as to get group members to exteriorize it. It is as if the more one has the possibility of manifesting individual differences, the more one is imbued with the rules and norms, which one revitalizes and even contributes to establishing. What at the beginning serves to express individuality is in the long run changed into the cement of sociability. One conclusion should be kept in mind because it throws an astonishing light on one of the most general phenomena: it is through difference and disagreement that their antonyms penetrate most deeply the human personality – the opposites of similarity and an understanding with others. Aragon, the poet and novelist, described this phenomenon with great delicacy in *La Semaine Sainte*, regarding a gathering of anti-monarchists:

> Even these verbal challenges, this refusal on the part of some to have confidence in the rest, seemed to express the will of everybody to find something in common – precisely what, was not known, but in any case it was a truth infinitely precious to each individual, but which hitherto had eluded them all. (1958: 328)

However, this is not our main conclusion. We have highlighted it in order to show the constancy with which the same effort is repeated. After all, there is no lack of historical examples, or even those of the laboratory, to indicate that societies that have sown harmony and agreement at any price have reaped discord and seen the disavowal of individuals. Indeed it appears that Gorbachev was referring to an outcome of this kind when he declared:

> Today we have no need of a kind of unity in order to show off, for this unity is both useless and impossible. True unity can only be obtained on condition that the Party guarantees freedom of discussion, and freedom of debate on the basis of alternatives for problems of party policy.[2]

Indeed, in order to avoid unanimity being arrived at beforehand, and artificially, differences must not be stifled and conflicts repressed, but should be left to develop.

Our main conclusion is that, without prejudice to any verdict on facts yet to come to light, our hypothesis is on the way to being verified. Clearly, by favouring divergence, and then debate, through the heterogeneous nature of individuals, through their belonging to different professions, through the distance between individual positions, through a lesser cohesiveness in groups or increased trust among their members, consensus is polarized. Moreover, is it not characteristic of such a consensus for common choices not to be decided in advance by a majority rule or compromise, but discovered during adequate discussion? With this as a basis they are rooted in the collectivity as much as in individuals. This is why those who meet together have an interest in not resembling one another. And yet it is true that birds of a feather flock together. All our collective relationships hinge on this paradox.

The division of cognitive labour

People are constantly talking about what their colleagues or teachers, parents or priests, and books or newspapers have taught them. Thus it is knowledge gleaned from several sources that fuels discussion among them. They are the cornerstones of a well-informed society, a collective organism that is endowed with the power of thought. But the organism shares out among individuals the task of selecting and exploiting the various kinds of knowledge, as well as the job of imparting meaning to words (Putnam, 1979). Like other divisions of labour, this division becomes a source of tension and controversy, and therefore of polarization of decisions. In fact it supposes that each section of the group is in possession of a fraction of knowledge, a fraction that differs in quantity and nature from all others. Thus, for example, each section can readily perceive a number of reasons for committing the fictitious person in our questionnaire to take risks or to exercise prudence. Certain members will think up more reasons than others: practitioners of different professions – as economists, judges, insurance officials, etc. – they will put forward distinctive reasons of their own. We find this, for example, in the ethical committees that bring together scientists, ecclesiastics, administrators and representatives of the family. Their deliberations are likely to be more animated and their arguments more solid since the participants have to decide on a solution to which everybody will assent. Consequently, the division of cognitive labour, by multiplying the opportunities for polemical argument and by involving the participants, contributes in polarizing their consensus on a solution that initially aroused controversy and induced them to try to convince one another.

The same explanation, looked at from another angle, can be illustrated in detail from the very fine study by Kaplan and Miller (1977). They set up fictitious juries of six people to whom they played a recording that dealt with thirty-six proofs in a judgement concerning an assault, presented in different ways. In half the groups all their members listened to the proofs in the same order; in the other half, each member listened to them set out in a special order that differed for each member. The first set of information was homogeneous, the second heterogeneous. Moreover, twelve juries listened to proofs that inculpated the accused, and the twelve others to proofs that exculpated him. According to the usual procedure, after listening in court to the facts presented, the jurors assessed separately the degree of guilt of the accused. Then, meeting together as a jury, they discussed the case before evaluating once more separately the degree of guilt. Here we are very close to a real life situation; hence the great significance of the findings.

The following is what emerged: consultation together, yet again, led to more decisive verdicts. The difference was even more marked in the groups where each juror heard the proofs in a different order than in those which listened to them in the same order. In other words, when the task of cognition is divided up, the groups polarize more than when the task is uniform. One consequence among others is the following. It is often recommended that jurors should be selected from people whose social origins and intellectual training are as diverse as possible, that is, based on reality, in order to ensure fairer verdicts. The suspicion is that in this way they may be either more clement or more severe. In any case, the analysis of the discussions themselves showed that those jurors who had listened to the proofs presented in a different order mentioned a wider variety of facts than did the others, particularly towards the end of their discussion. They had therefore made better use of the information provided and had engaged in exchanges that were more concentrated and more varied. On the whole, a correlation could be discerned between the number of facts recalled and the variety of facts brought up in the course of the discussion, and a shift by these makeshift juries towards the extreme limit when judging the degree of guilt. Yet they resemble in many respects real jurors, or at least that section of the public which is enthused by great trials and debates the possible verdict wherever they meet others, or within the family. One might deduce that the desire to know and mull over all the facts and evidence in order, as they say, to shed light upon justice has the desired effect of objectivity. It also has an effect that was not sought after, which is to make the verdict either more clement or more severe depending on the way the jurors order the elements for discussion. This is doubtless too hasty a conclusion. But it is one that practitioners would lose nothing by reflecting upon, and one which would merit testing against the facts, with which they are much more acquainted than we are.

Meanwhile, all of these studies appear to militate in favour of the hypothesis put forward. The essential factor is one of difference, whether in points of view or of ability to argue, and in the system of knowledge or positions within a group. Just as a heat machine needs a hot source and a cold one, so the range of difference sparks off discussion, feeds opposition and stimulates controversy by inciting everyone to participate. Where there is convergence, this is almost always at a point above or below the mean. We may make a very simple observation, but one not without importance. It is not through the exchange of items of information and through combining these according to mathematical rules that this convergence is arrived at. On the contrary, each individual must seek to defend his choice, to convince his colleagues and commit himself for or against a particular solution. It is those arguments, which appeal more to ethics and sensibility than to reason, that carry the day and make the decision an extreme one. In fact on this point – but is it the only one? – we come across Keynes' advice to keep in mind

> that human decisions affecting the future, whether personal, or political, or economic, cannot depend on strict mathematical expectations, since the basis for making such calculations does not exist; and that it is our innate urge to activity which makes the wheels go round, our rational selves choosing between the alternatives as best we are able, calculating where we can, but often falling back for our motive on whim or sentiment or chance. (1964: 63)

We ask the reader to take this into account, without hastening to plump for one or other of the causes on which compromise or polarization depends.[3] For the moment it will suffice to take note of the concordance of so many studies based on such differing facts as an encouraging sign for the theory, but nothing more.

Notes

1 This conclusion is backed up in many other studies, among which those of Gaskell et al. (1973), Horne and Long (1972), Madaras and Bem (1968), Marquis (1962) and Rettig and Turoff (1967) are the most categoric on this point.

2 *Le Monde*, July 1989.

3 Today, there is agreement to give priority to the processes of information. On this, numerous articles setting out convincing arguments exist, particularly those of Anderson and Graesser (1976) and Kaplan and Miller (1985).

4

The Effects of Private or Public Discussions

Groups in the flesh and 'canned' groups

1

This first look at our hypothesis was designed to give some idea of its validity. We were intent on showing the relationship that exists between, on the one hand, the conflict of opinions and differences in information and, on the other, the eyeball confrontations that lead to consensus. It is now appropriate to continue with our study of the one factor in decision which we know to be the most constant and the most general: that is, discussion. It can be considered as a way of exchanging information, of airing conflicts and differences, just as much as a means of negotiating them. Yet it also has other purposes as a rite of participation in social life and an effective vehicle of persuasion. It is consequently the most powerful agent for propagating feelings and ideas, for causing people to adhere to values, and for stimulating them to imitate each other. Above all it affords them the pleasure of expressing themselves, of taking part together in something that is of importance to them. In reality, all cultures establish a profound relationship between speaking and arriving at agreement. This is because if one is talking one is not fighting – or not yet: Shakespeare said, 'Words before blows'. Moreover, if one is fighting in words in fact one is preparing for an agreement and even guaranteeing one. To give one's word often concludes an agreement and obliges one to respect it.

In the same way, in our experiments the participants pledge themselves as soon as they opt for a common position. But discussion is also a powerful agent for effecting changes in opinions, rules and social representations that it causes to circulate among the members of a group. It creates a focus of attention that highlights certain aspects of the question under discussion, leaving other aspects obscure, and confers authenticity on the opinions and viewpoints that are exchanged. These thereby acquire a greater depth than do other human relationships. Tarde, who devoted to these dialogues and conversations a study that is still relevant, wrote:

> There is a close link between the way a conversation functions and changes in opinion, on which depend the vicissitudes of power. Where opinion changes little, slowly, and remains almost immovable, it is because conversations are rare and timid, revolving round idle small talk. Where opinion is swift-changing, heated,

oscillating from one extreme to the other, it is because conversations are frequent, outspoken and freely expressed. (1910: 33)

They are the critical factor which, as we have discovered, produces a consensus that in fact shifts to an extreme. The mere presence of other people already produces a movement in this direction. It is hardly surprising that, through looking at and listening to them, one becomes a participant in the dialogue, engaging within oneself in one of those imaginary conversations with which we are all familiar. This is sufficient to spark off a 'fictitious polemic' with our friends or superiors, in which we argue with them, and which on occasion leads us to modify our attitudes or choices. This most certainly happens less when the polemic is effective, with friends or superiors expounding their arguments realistically and intensely. This certainly occurs to a lesser extent when the argument is a real one, with friends or superiors expounding their arguments in an intense and real fashion. This should therefore be taken into account even more urgently than in the fictitious situation in which one was, after all, both judge and a party to the action. It is assumed that changes in opinion, if they occur, are more radical.

It is self-evidently practical to distinguish between two modes of discussion, namely between passive and active communication. Passive communication consists in observing, of informing oneself about the opinions that are circulating, in overhearing unexpectedly the conversations of others or reading a message that is addressed to them, etc. Apparently a mere spectator, one is participating in a mild way, without being fully stimulated by the actions or words of other people. Active communication is on another note, and lively in a completely different way, since each individual is both the source and the target for the opinions and information that are circulating. In this true state of communication, tensions and dissonances are continuously modifying ideas and perceptions, until they converge.

We can unhesitatingly subscribe to Hannah Arendt's remark:

> The power of judgement rests on a potential agreement with others, and the thinking process which is active in judging something is not, like the thought process of our reasoning, a dialogue between me and myself, but finds itself, always and primarily, even if I am quite alone in making up my mind, in an anticipated communication with others with whom I know I must finally come to some agreement. From this potential agreement judgement derives its specific validity. This means, on the one hand, that such judgement must liberate itself from the 'subjective private conditions', that is, from the idiosyncrasies which naturally determine the outlook of each individual in his privacy and are legitimate as long as they are only privately held opinions but which are not fit to enter the market place, and lack all validity in the public realm. And this enlarged way of thinking, which as judgement knows how to transcend its individual limitations, cannot function in strict isolation or solitude; it needs the presence of others 'in whose place' it must think, whose perspectives it must take into consideration, and without whom it never has the opportunity to operate at all. (1961: 21)

It is indisputable that to engage in dialogue produces good results, directing old ways of thinking into new channels. One can feel carried along further than one would wish, but one would hate even more to lag behind, a prisoner of subjective routines and remaining apart from others. As if moved by the need to find themselves once more on the same wavelength after being engaged in confrontation, opponents move towards a fresh understanding, which temporarily puts an end to the numerous misunderstandings, real or imaginary, that divided them. As a specialist has remarked, 'The converging process seems to require more active involvement in communication with other members of the group' (Scheidel, 1986: 122).

We are fully convinced of this. With this as our starting point we can formulate another version of our hypothesis. The conflicts or differences between members of the group are normally resolved by convergence towards an extreme position. Yet, depending on whether the discussion is public or private, or the dialogue exterior or interior, the convergence will be more, or less, close to that position. In other words, discussion, in its current meaning, depending on whether the individuals involved are active or passive, determines the extent to which the decision will become polarized. Certainly this is a mere tendency, since the appropriate means for measuring it are so very limited.

2

If we admit this, even with reservations, we can call upon a lengthy series of studies that verify it. Most of these use the same material and throw up similar problems. We may briefly recall that they deal with a choice that depends upon the degree of risk that the group has to advise a fictitious person to take. Some ten or a dozen imaginary situations are put forward on which the group has to exercise its judgement. Each situation depicts the person concerned as being faced with an alternative in which he has the choice between two possible actions, one of which is more attractive but which has less chance of being successful than the other. The participants' task is to advise the person, pointing out the minimum possibility of success in the most risky action so as to make it attractive. The level of risk taken varies on a scale running from 1 to 10 (that is, a one in ten chance of success), 5 in 10, 7 in 10, up to 9 in 10. Finally the participant has the possibility of advising against the choice of the most risky solution, whatever the chances of success.

We are reminded that the experiment took place in three stages. First, the participants indicated separately and in isolation their preferences in relation to the risk to be taken in each situation. They then met in discussion groups and were invited to arrive at a unanimous consensus, that is, to advise one single solution for each fictitious situation. The group was then disbanded and usually the participants were asked separately to indicate once more the level of risk they would propose in the selfsame situations. In this way it was possible to assess, first, the shift in risk-taking that had occurred as a result of discussion, and, then, how far the group decision had committed each of its members and how far each one of them had adopted it.

New studies set up a situation that was almost identical, for one very simple reason. Their authors set out to prove that an individual who learns of the opinions and choices of a group 'polarizes' in the same way as the members of that group. Consequently neither the act of discussion, nor its content, were needed for the effect we are studying to take place. This is why these experiments laid down in varying forms opposing conditions: in the one, the participants were separated without being able to communicate with one another, and, in the other, they could discuss. Their authors believed they were contrasting an individual reaction with a collective one. In the event, the illusory belief was that when the participants were separated they were made passive, and this changed the state within the groups to which they belonged. This is not an artificial situation; on the contrary, it is a very familiar one. For belonging to a flesh and blood group gives way to belonging to an artificial ('canned') one. The situation resembles television viewers seeing a programme in which the comic gestures and quips of the actors are emphasized by 'canned' laughter off, and the comments of an invisible 'manipulator' of the audience. Television makes use of this 'canned' laughter and commentary because studies have shown that they make the viewers laugh more often and longer, as if they themselves were part of the prefabricated applause. The consequence is that they feel themselves at one with a wider public. In these studies, therefore, a comparison is being made between the decisions taken by members of the group in, so to speak, the 'canned' situation and members of a flesh and blood group. This is a comparison of above all practical importance.

Let us now take a closer look at these studies.[1] The first question posed is the very precisely formulated one by Wallach and Kogan (1965): it is to discover whether active communication is indeed a necessary condition, and whether it plays a more crucial role than does consensus. 'To ask a group to achieve a consensus', they write, 'concerning a matter of risk-taking, is to provide a request that may influence the type of commitment made by the group members. The requirement that a consensus be reached may engender a feeling to the group as a unit' (1965: 4). They therefore put before the participants the questionnaire we have just described, this time according to three scenarios. In the first, after having replied to the questionnaire separately, individuals had to discuss it together and arrive at a unanimous decision for each fictitious situation outlined in it. Once the group had come to an agreement on all the situations, the participants were asked to reconsider them and make a fresh decision, each of them separately. In the second scenario, the participants' choices were written up on a blackboard and, by a succession of votes, but with no discussion, they were asked to come to an agreement on one choice. If disagreement persisted, they had the possibility of making a different choice, which in turn was written up on the blackboard. They voted once more, and so on, until agreement was reached. As you are well aware, it is a method used by numerous committees, juries and similar institutions. Once this stage was over, the participants were asked to express in private their individual choice. The third scenario, that of discussion with no consensus, in which a 'diversity of opinion' was encouraged, resembled the first, to the extent that after five minutes discussion was halted without requiring any consensus.

It was noted that in the first and third scenarios, where there was discussion, the decisions became more extreme, that is, more risky, whereas, when there was no discussion, decisions stayed around the mean, so the consensus tended towards compromise. Discussion, whether consensus was required or not, polarized the decision taken collectively. Moreover, in both cases there was a strong temptation to play down the variety of positions, which supposes that the group members influenced one another more strongly. This is of course true if one interprets the results literally. All the same, whenever consensus was not required, this did not prevent an implicit consensus from emerging.

It is not without interest, at least anecdotally, to know whether the discussion had to be face to face, or whether it was sufficient merely to hear the sound of the others' voices, and what this might conjure up. In a series of studies of dialogues we were able to show (Moscovici, 1967) that, provided those involved communicated aloud, the fact of being able to see one another or not did not modify the language used. Kogan and Wallach (1967b) wanted to check whether this fact had any impact on the group's decisions. Their experiment was almost similar to the one above. The participants were asked to discuss various hypothetical situations that carried with them a risk; sometimes they were asked to arrive at a consensus, and sometimes not. The difference in this variation of the experiment was that they were placed in separate cabins and communicated by telephone. The network was organized so as to allow for entirely spontaneous discussion between group members, who could speak without seeing one another. The results obtained were similar to those of the preceding experiment, no matter what condition was stipulated; this is in no way astonishing.

The explanation may be as follows. Whether people can see one another or not has indeed physical importance. But discussion is not diminished through it, since 'the speakers react upon one another very closely, through their tone of voice, their gaze, their physiognomy, the magnetism of the gestures they make, and not only through the language' (Tarde, 1910: 85). The presence of any one of these elements suffices for one person to represent to himself the personality of the others, producing the same feelings and ideas. Although isolated, friends, relations or colleagues can easily imagine they are engaged in a face-to-face dialogue as if they were all assembled in one room. Everyone can easily verify this now that the telephone has become part of our way of life.

3

It is tempting to simplify matters. This can be done by considering discussion as serving solely for the exchange of information concerning the choices and positions of members of the group, and thus as passive communication that scarcely commits them and does not cause them to participate, in the full sense of the word, in the decision-making process. Can one then expect that a change in opinion or preference, or the taking of risk, is of the same magnitude as in a situation of active communication? One must assume that the latter situation includes not only an exchange of information regarding opinions and preferences but also an exchange of arguments designed to justify the options taken and to secure backing for them, in the course of subtle negotiations leading to a unanimous agreement. This exchange of arguments is reduced to the minimum in passive communication, which unfolds in a neutral atmosphere, making impersonal the various attitudes relating to the purpose of the decision. Undoubtedly it favours moderation and compromise rather than the taking of high risk or any other extreme choice.

Several remarkable studies have proved the correctness of this way of looking at things, among them particularly the one already mentioned by Teger and Pruitt (1967). They did indeed compare active communication, in which the participants discuss, to passive communication, in which the group merely exchanges information in silence. Imagine a room in which individuals come together after having answered in isolation a question about risk-taking, and are seated at tables in groups of three to five, each with his fellow team members clearly visible. But the participants do not speak to each other. Each has received a set of cards that indicate the various possible choices in figures, such as one out of ten, three out of ten and so on. One after the other they have to hold up the card that shows their precise choice in the question posed, just as do judges in an athletics or skating competition. Yet, unlike these judges, after having compared the various figures, each individual can opt for another choice and indicate his new position. They go round the table in this way three complete times. They have been informed there is no need to arrive at a consensus. Naturally the experimenters compare this situation with another in which, for a predetermined length of time, a spontaneous discussion takes place.

Let us therefore look at the results. In both situations the groups tended to polarize, but in the second situation the tendency was more marked than in the first. In fact between them was found a significant difference in the shift towards risk-taking (F = 8.58; $p < .01$). This does indeed indicate that the shift towards risk-taking is more considerable where discussion is possible than where only an exchange of information on individual choices is allowed. Moreover, it is normal to think that collective involvement leads to convergence, this being because of the stronger influence exerted by members of the group on one another. Teger and Pruitt hit upon the happy idea of calculating, in this same experiment, how far group members were in agreement on the answer to a question. This can quite properly be described as a convergence. They took as their yardstick the estimated variation on the initial choice, minus the estimated variation on the subsequent choice. This indicated how nearly the group approached implicit consensus in relation to a given question. Now, as was to be expected, groups whose members made a decision during a discussion arrived at positions closer to one another. Thus they converged more significantly than those who had confined themselves to comparing the marks in silence.

In all logic a discussion should be all the more clear and efficient when more clear-cut decisions, and we would add, more significant ones, are expected from it. We may assume both that the exchange of arguments will be more substantial and that the participants will feel themselves more involved by virtue of the results that are expected. In the experiment we are about to describe (Clark and Willems, 1969) risk-taking was measured with the assistance of a questionnaire identical to those already used. The respondent was intended in theory to serve as adviser to a principal character, choosing the lowest probability of success he would deem acceptable for this character to adopt the solution that appeared to him to be both the most attractive and the most risky. Clearly such a brief directs the individual and the group in discussion towards positively desiring risk-taking. What would occur if the direction was not evident, and the same were true for the discussion, when no precise value was indicated; that is, when the discussion becomes more neutral and consequently more objective? To bring this about, half the participants were given the instruction as outlined above, containing the expression 'the lowest probability', while the other half received one more neutral: 'Please tick the *probability* you would judge *acceptable* for the option in question.' In reality the experiment was more complicated, for the participants were split up in such a way that they had to perform the task under three different conditions: some discussed aloud their choices and decisions; others exchanged information, holding up three times cards indicating their positions; finally, the last sub-group listened to a recorded discussion of the same question.

In accordance with expectations – and we shall return to this finding and interpret it more fully later – those subjects whose task was defined in neutral terms tended towards compromise, without changing their opinion or their preference. Only those who had to commit themselves in a clear direction tended to shift towards a more extreme risk. But this depended on the condition. This propensity was manifested in the groups which discussed as well as those which exchanged information. However, the result is not surprising: to discuss involves the group more deeply than merely to exchange information. Thus when they were asked to confront their viewpoints they 'polarized' more than when they were content to show their options on the cards and to compare them. Under the condition where they listened to a discussion, nothing like this was observed. Here we are dealing with a substantial phenomenon that has been verified on several occasions,[2] which justifies the confidence we have in it. It shows, if it needed to be shown, that what is important is not the information – what some learn about the positions of others – but in fact the framework of interaction in which it occurs. To discover whether our fellow group members are more or less rash, more or less favourable towards an option, affects us relatively little. On the other hand, we are affected by the circumstances in which we discover this, and our reactions reflect this fact.

This has been observed beyond all doubt in a study (Clark et al., 1971) in which groups were constituted with participants known to be either rash or moderate. As in preceding experiments, the same questionnaire was used, varying the conditions under which subjects had to make their decisions. Certain of them were invited to discuss and defend their position, others merely exchanged information regarding their position. Finally those subjected to a third condition had solely to give their arguments in favour of various solutions, without disclosing their personal position. Under the two 'discussion' conditions, judgements clearly shifted significantly towards risk-taking; in that where there was merely an exchange of information the subjects tended towards a compromise. Revealing or concealing personal choice before entering into discussion or the public exchange of information had hardly any influence on the extreme or moderate nature of the final decision.

Here we should note that the very idea of an exchange of information prevents the discussion being conceived of as participation or a social relationship. It not only deprives us of the pleasure of paying tribute to the art of rhetoric and the dialogue devoted to it, but even robs us of the very pleasure, very fashionable today, of practising such arts and in observing their concrete effects. Moreover, this idea of exchange of information creates the illusion that these can be foregone and that the decision-makers are like experts resolving a problem. From this viewpoint it would matter little whether the character of the exchange were personal or impersonal. Yet we suppose the opposite to be true: discussion in which there enters an ingredient of personal involvement tends more towards polarization than one in which this ingredient is missing.

A study by Goethals and Zanna (1979) allows us in fact to verify this proposition. Participants were invited to answer individually four questions relating to risk-taking situations, and also a questionnaire concerning their abilities and creativity. They were then divided up according to four scenarios. In the first they discussed fictitious situations and again answered individually. In the second they communicated passively, each one holding up a card indicating his personal position. In the third they did the same, but in addition revealed how each of them had evaluated himself in the questionnaire on his abilities and creativity. As was to be expected, every individual judged himself to be above average. In the fourth scenario the participants had ten minutes in which to look again at the four fictitious situations, after which they made a fresh appraisal.

On the whole the groups polarized and tended towards boldness in risk-taking. But the tendency towards this was more marked when they communicated actively and advertised their personal qualities than when the communication remained passive and impersonal.

We have gathered together studies conceived on the same principle, and often bearing upon the same questions, in order to facilitate comparison.

They justify our stating that active communication between group members entails more extreme decisions, while passive communication leads to less extreme decisions and occasionally to compromises. We have been asked, 'Why is this not always so?' It is clearly because simply to inform oneself about the position of others involves and associates us with them. Likewise in groups in a 'canned' situation, although we may well know that the laughter and commentary is prefabricated, we are nevertheless affected by it. In general, no one remains entirely passive when faced with what emanates from other people. They are approved of, or argued with in one of those interior dialogues, those silent conversations, in which the group with whom we are communicating is no longer outside us but within us – which is what 'thinking' means. Arguments are adopted because they are better formulated, or because we believe we have discovered them ourselves, although we are often repeating, without being aware of it, those we have heard at the time. And when we exclaim 'I've always thought so, but I didn't dare say it,' or, 'I've always said so, that's plain,' it matters little whether we are sincere or not. It is a cry for recognition by the group.

Thus the consensus of the great majority of the groups undergoes a polarization effect. The effect is weak when communication is carried on passively and impersonally, but grows stronger as soon as communication becomes intense and touches people personally. This signifies that the convergence observable in a group depends more on the level of participation and on reciprocal action between its members than on their individual qualities. This finding confirms, if confirmation were needed, the viewpoint we adopted in our explanation of collective decisions. By emphasizing the part played by social interaction, are we stressing a social cause at the expense of psychological causes? One might believe this to be so, since a specialist on the subject has reproached those that do so in the following terms: 'They are concerned more with identifying the social process that produces the effect [of polarization] . . . than with the psychological mechanism involved (e.g. affective or cognitive)' (Vinokur, 1971: 239).

This is a curious way of looking at things and certainly not the most enlightened one from the viewpoint of scientific logic. It neglects the plain fact that, on the contrary, interactions must be taken into account to contrive the transfer of social mechanisms to psychological ones, and vice versa. What would be the sense of a social psychology that would include one set of mechanisms and exclude the others, including the individual aspects and not the collective ones? Above all, we are forgetting that opting for the psychological mechanism to explain a phenomenon depends on the conception one has of the social process, just as the choice of a chemical mechanism depends on the conception one has of the physical process in space and time. In the case we are considering, it is how we envisage what a group is that enabled us to recognize that the risk-taking phenomenon is ascribable not to a diffusion of responsibility but to the involvement of the group members. It is therefore a special case of the polarization phenomenon. However this may be, our conjectures seek to understand its individual as well as its collective aspects. Those conjectures aim at identifying the social process and the psychological mechanisms that correspond to it. Moreover, they are reasonable enough to account for facts already known and to foresee those unknown, for which they cannot be reproached – on the contrary.

Two aspects of communication and sociability

The greatest experiment ever undertaken in this field is taking place here and now. This is not in the laboratory, but in rooms, in hospitals and in the streets. Here the researchers are not social psychologists but doctors and social workers dealing in condoms and little bottles of disinfectant. The purpose of the experiment is to halt the onward march of the AIDS epidemic by modifying the habits of thousands of people. We are seeking to get drug-users to disinfect their needles when they go in search of heroin, and to discourage homosexuals from continually changing their partners and to accustom them to use condoms when having sexual intercourse. It is therefore a matter of tackling deeply ingrained patterns of behaviour and of stimulating people to make the decision to change them when they enter upon a sexual relationship or stick a needle in their arm.

However, no matter how strongly one has been warned against the dire consequences of a particular mode of conduct, knowledge scarcely suffices to bring about a decision to modify it. The information remains a dead letter, and most of the campaigns financed by government fail. First, they are not teaching anything new to the persons concerned, who know full well what is at stake – just as smokers have been warned long ago about the toxic effect of cigarettes and have heard time and again that it is in their interest to stop smoking. Nevertheless the decision goes against habits that hitherto have been in accordance with the norms and have been socially approved, but which have suddenly become deviant and are frowned upon. Now, individuals by themselves cannot change a norm, no more than they can change a grammatical rule, the value of a currency, or the traffic direction. To jump from one extreme to the other, and to consider abnormal what up to then was deemed to be normal, a concerted effort must be made by the group as a whole.

However, important changes have taken place in those cities where the AIDS epidemic has decimated vast groups of homosexuals. In San Francisco, for example, the use of condoms has become common practice. Likewise drug-users are no longer reluctant to disinfect their syringes and their material in order to avoid passing on contaminated blood to others. In other words, it has become socially commendable to offer a disinfected needle, or to carry a condom when starting up a sexual relationship with a stranger. In this way group beliefs are modified, innovations are adopted and a new consensus is established. One may presume that commitment to a habit or routine gives way to commitment to the group whose individual members share the new norms. This imparts a real, immediate and imminent character to the need to change.

Let us venture further, and observe how a decision changes existing attitudes and conduct. On the one hand, we know that the person joining a discussion group assumes that everyone has a certain point of view and shares an opinion. He will therefore hesitate to formulate openly an opinion or choice that he assumes is personal to him, and different. For example, if he is against sexual equality he will make the assumption that all the rest, each to some extent, are for it. It is symptomatic of this generalized prejudice that causes us to believe that all Englishmen are fair-haired, Protestant and reserved, etc. – in brief, we are mindful of the uniformity, but forget the diversity. To avoid tension, such a person will therefore not express with frankness his own opinions. Each individual reasons similarly until discussion gets under way. This leads participants to discover the multiplicity of opinions and the absence of certainty. They then become aware that their freedom of manoeuvre is much greater than they imagined. This opens up for them the possibility of expressing their own viewpoint and even envisaging the likelihood of persuading others. The pressure to conform brought to bear is in reality weaker than anticipated. Thus discussion with other members of the group carries with it less risk for the person who propounds an alternative solution to the question posed, and he perceives a chance of causing it to prevail. So divergences have the effect of opening up perspectives formerly believed to be closed. Hence their major role when it comes to modifying known attitudes and common modes of behaviour.

Moreover, much more effectively than does passive communication, active communication favours the uncovering of information germane to the problem, and shows its usefulness in seeking a solution. It is true that such knowledge is unevenly distributed among the members of a group. Each member has at his disposal his own special segment of it, depending upon his origins, education or social status. But the cognitive division of labour that follows from this, like all division of labour, separates out individual characters at the same time as it emphasizes collective relationships. It highlights what members of the group communicate to one another, the segments of information that overlap, their opinions and values, and organizes all these according to a principle. To revert to the example of tobacco-smoking, no smoker is ignorant of the risks he runs, which range from infection of the gums to circulation troubles. But each smoker believes that his constitution, his way of life or his personal history protects him more than his neighbour. It seems likely that when they come together they discover just how far these various items of information weigh in the balance as compared with the medical information of which they become aware. It is therefore not at all astonishing that the experiments we have reported show that those involved in an active discussion are more likely to modify their viewpoint, if necessary, in a direction previously held to be extreme.

The marked divergences that emerge in the process of communication, the interest each individual has in participating in the decision-making, are not so simple as they appear. In reality these make demands, and consequently involve, as we have emphasized, most of those associated with them. The consequences are not inconsiderable. We know that people deeply immersed in a problem weigh up more carefully information that has been gleaned regarding it, have a clearer idea of the alternatives and can work out more arguments. Their judgement is usually more sure, whereas at the same time they tend to become more extreme in matters of opinion, just as, on the other hand, persons holding an extreme viewpoint are more sure, confident and ready to defend it (Miller, 1965). Yet does what has been demonstrated as being so often valid for individuals still hold good for groups? Can we rely on it, as regards decisions they make leading to a consensus? An attempt has been made to answer these questions, which are not easy when tackled empirically, by using several methods. One consists in asking individuals to express a subjective choice.

In the original experiment in which this phenomenon was brought to light it was expected that individuals would feel more involved when they expressed their own viewpoint than if they appeared to give an objective response. Participants were therefore invited to express and discuss their opinions on de Gaulle and the Americans. They had to decide to what extent they approved or disapproved a proposition relating, for example, to the age of de Gaulle, and another relating to the policy of the Americans. In a second scenario we asked other participants to determine whether a judgement passed on de Gaulle was favourable or unfavourable to him, regardless of whether they approved of its content. To ascertain this we asked them to record their decisions on what are known as the Thurstone scales, ranging numerically from one to seven. This was the very condition for using these scales, one stressed by their inventor, who declared, 'If the scale is to be recognized as valid, the scale should not be affected by the opinion of people who help to construct it' (Thurstone and Chave, 1929: 92). The proviso is valid. When the participants expressed their viewpoints, they arrived at a more extreme consensus than when they were asked to make an effort to bring an objective judgement to bear on a problem (Moscovici and Zavalloni, 1969).

This result allows us to understand that, during the discussion of a proposition, to present it in one form rather than another influences the outcome more than the content of it. This is not a one-off finding. In a study carried out in Germany (Lamm et al., 1980) participants were presented with a fictitious situation that varied according to the groups, but which each time presented two persons, one of whom was seeking to obtain something from the other – for example, an employee wanting promotion, a father exhorting his child to study harder, etc. For each of these behaviour models destined to lead to the desired result (promise, warning, etc.) participants had to indicate on a scale the chance that the person in question had of success in his endeavour. Alternatively, they had to indicate their own ability to utilize this behaviour model successfully. Thus, on the one hand, there was an objective judgement, and, on the other, a subjective one. The participants first replied separately, then they discussed in groups of three, and finally replied separately once more. The aim was to measure their degree of optimism or pessimism. Discussion in the group resulted in making everybody more pessimistic, particularly when they made a subjective decision. When deciding objectively they remained close to the average. It is revealing that a situation in which one has to choose in a personal fashion renders the judgements and choices more extreme, whereas a situation demanding an impersonal choice favours compromise, or almost does.

We can already divine the other way of strengthening the degree of involvement. It consists in choosing problems in such a way that they take on social significance. In the initial experiments to illustrate this we asked participants to judge the characteristics of a young man of English or Anglo origin whose photograph they were given. Their judgement involved twenty characteristics, ten of which were considered important by the great majority of individuals, and the ten others as relatively unimportant. After they had answered separately, they were brought together in groups of four and were invited to discuss and, in a common judgement, to arrive at a consensus on the same characteristics and the same photographs (Moscovici, Zavalloni and Weinberger, 1972). A shift of the consensus towards the extreme was noted, but only for the important characteristics of the young man, and, on the other hand, a tendency to compromise for those not important. It was as if the latter did not merit any expenditure of energy in discussion about them.

We should bear in mind that all this related to the portrait of no one young man in particular. What would happen now if the participants were presented with photographs of familiar people, socially typical, such as workers or intellectuals? Inasmuch as their characteristics stand out more and attitudes towards them are more marked, it might be expected that the results might be more extreme. This was indeed the case. After the group discussion it turned out that judgements on the characteristics became more extreme, even on the less important ones. Other studies have likewise demonstrated the same thing, with convergent findings.[3]

It is encouraging to note how far studies made in the laboratory allow us to magnify and observe as through a microscope what takes place during a host of debates, whether silent or spoken. The mere fact of inviting people to explain themselves in public, thereby most certainly exposing themselves to contradiction, sets in train a whole armoury of facial expressions, arguments and defensive body movements, which attract the attention of others, or, on the contrary, reduces their participation to a minimum, it being limited to taking up a position. In both cases the outcome is predictable, as we have already noted: conflict in the group, the possibility of active communication, and the degree to which the participants are involved – these determine just how extreme the consensus is. In the case where these factors are reversed, it swings back towards the average. The hypothesis we formulated allows us to understand why. It would be superfluous to dwell upon the considerable agreement between the results obtained by other researchers and ourselves.

It is as if there were two kinds of sociability. One aims at radicalizing and changing individuals, the other at moderating and normalizing them. It could not be said that the former is more spontaneous and preferable to the latter, just as it could not be said that a strong currency is always preferable to a weak one. Everything depends upon the circumstances and the goal one is pursuing. Nevertheless it is certain that the line of thinking set in train by Allport gives pride of place to the form of sociability whose model is compromise and maintains the equilibrium of individuals by making them moderate and similar to one another. Through these studies we can uncover another line of thinking in which sociability is recognized according to a model of difference, one of expression with no restriction on opinions and continuous debate. Here the first rule is not to take a decision unless one is convinced of its value and unless one has convinced others.

We would have, on the one hand, a *mimetic* sociability, and, on the other, a *cathartic* sociability. But once more this is an antinomy that depends upon circumstances and upon human nature. If we mention here both lines of thinking it is not in order to plead for one rather than the other, but to put both in perspective. This will allow us to broaden the horizon opened up by those facts that are of interest to us. It is an horizon that one often tries to limit to the first line of thinking, which emerged three-quarters of a century ago, and neglect the second line.

One illustration of this could be the opposition between America and European nations. Made up of heretics and immigrants from every country, the American nation has always been anxious to make them all alike, to make them speak the same language and to melt them into an integral and balanced whole. The American is not a model fashioned by thousands of years. He has been shaped according to circumstances, by combining elements of diversity that clearly do not rule out unity. By contrast the European nations, made up of small homogeneous groups, bound together by their own traditions and languages, have always been held in check by powerful bonds in their efforts to unite. They are open to history, but each one wishes to shape it in its own way, according to its own particular model. The resistance met with by the idea of a common European currency or a European government speak volumes on this. Insofar as the sciences seek to resolve problems posed by the immediate social reality, it can be understood why American social psychology is interested in factors of balance, similarity and conformity, whereas European social psychology raises questions of difference and change. There are distinct sociabilities at work in both cases, as well as different viewpoints. More is to be gained by taking account of them together than by seeking to reduce them to only one.

Notes

1 Several authors have tackled the question of emotional bonding. See especially the article by Clark (1971) and the chapter in Jones and Gerard's textbook (1967).

2 See especially the studies by Bell and Jamieson (1970), Brim (1955), Cantril (1946), Castore (1972), Hermann and Kogan (1968), Hoyt and Stoner (1968), Lemon (1968), Myers and Bishop (1971), Willems and Clark (1969).

3 See in particular the studies by McLachlan (1986), Moscovici and Nève (1973), Moscovici, Zavalloni and Louis-Guérin (1972), Nève and Moscovici (1982), Nève and Gautier (1978), Vinokur and Burnstein (1978).

5

Conflicts and Extreme Consensuses: The Role of Values

Which comes first?

1

Since we have just touched on the relationship of conflict to consensus we should investigate further its primary origins. This is certainly essential, even if there is no need to go back to the circumstances in which these consensuses generally arise. However, we may note that when we participate in the circle of discussion and debate, we already have readily available a large number of formulas for decision-making and an ample fund of know-how indicating which of them has the greatest chance of being accepted, or, on the other hand, of being rejected. Likewise the convictions and arguments that we bring to bear represent our experiences in previous groups in which we have participated. Each individual comes to the task with a capital of knowledge and methods on which he can draw in fresh discussions and in negotiations with others. In this capital, values in particular are included, some of which we have acquired, but the majority of which have been inculcated in us almost without our being aware of it. They have been imbibed, as the saying goes, with our mother's milk. This is why individuals, like groups, choose with the help of what they have not chosen. In fact, we sense that these values – and we shall realize this better later – are like moulds in which is shaped the mental space in which decisions take place, just as physical space is shaped by vectors. The values contain privileged directives for communication and establish a hierarchy of opinions and practices for the members of the group. They profoundly shape the relationships between them, colouring their ideas and words, and filtering everything that comes from the outside.

In principle we tacitly agree to fall back upon a convention of leaving values outside our decisions and choices, save when there is a specific reason to bring them in. Hence we stick solely to the facts, and to neutral information regarding objective reality. Theories of decision leading to consensus, whether in psychology or social psychology, respect this convention and often seek to explain the phenomena observed by minimizing the role played by the values of those who take part. It may be said of these theories what Grice, the philosopher, said of theories of meaning:

'What has been left out has in fact been left out because it is something which everyone regards with horror, at least when in a scientific or theoretical frame of mind: the notion of value' (1982: 237). One goes even further: one ceases to be concerned by the notion, which, once it has been marginalized, becomes accessory. However, the convention means that it is implicitly admitted that values do indeed orientate the mental space of the decision, which is considered superficially to be homogeneous and neutral. It is a question of appreciation. Yet when we seek to account for phenomena we have to acknowledge that any alternative proposed in order to solve a common problem, and about which there is discussion, presents these two inseparable aspects, like the front and back of a sheet of paper.

Among problems at present being debated there figure, for example, the use of nuclear energy, organ transplants and health expenditure. On the one hand, information is gathered in order to evaluate the human consequences, political costs and benefits, and economic interests. This is done for each of the alternatives suggested. On the other hand, the various alternatives are compared, and one assesses how each one, ranked in a hierarchy, is superior or inferior to the others from the standpoint of principle. In this hierarchy one realizes the hold exerted by values and norms, according to whether one ranks higher or lower safeguarding the environment, the quality of life, technical progress, risk-taking, or any other value that society can envisage. Even the everyday language in which these alternatives are argued is replete with values and norms. They are the *ratio decidendi*, that is, the very criterion for ranking these alternatives against an ideal model from the political, economic or moral viewpoint.

We very often invoke juries in our research and everyone knows that a jury must deliver its verdict by taking into account the proofs presented to it, the evidence obtained and the pleadings that have been put forward. Nevertheless its judgement on a case and the punishment for the crime committed are not aimed at establishing the truth, nor do they claim to explain it. The jury judges whether the person who has committed the crime is innocent or guilty in the eyes of the law. The legal viewpoint does not depend on any authority of truth but on the authority of justice; if it were otherwise it would be confused with science. The same holds good for most of our committees, meetings and colloquia, etc., which usually assess before making a calculation and agreeing upon an option. This is especially true when they are dealing with social questions, in which values most often determine what is to be known and even the desire to know it. It is because research incurs the risk of harming morality and its results transgress what people believe is forbidden that it arouses protest. 'They fear', wrote one observer of these processes,

> that science may change the normal state of nature, alter the genetic structure of mankind, or related deeply held belief about free will and self-determination. A major source of concern with respect to recombinant DNA research, for example, is the potential for removing the obstacles to genetic engineering by allowing scientists to transfer hereditary characteristics from one strain to another. This

evokes images of eugenics and leads directly to questions about the wisdom of seeking certain kinds of knowledge at all. (Nelkin, 1979: 13)

It is to the indignation aroused by sexual or racial discrimination, for example, that we indeed owe the host of studies on feminism or prejudice. Social reality clashes to such an extent with stated ideals that certain people feel themselves obliged to react through the medium of science just as others do so through the medium of religion or politics. We have been prey to many illusions in believing that the realm of knowledge would expand while that of values would contract; in the social sphere and beyond they both stretch along parallel paths. Putnam was right to say that 'a person without values would have no deeds either' (1981: 201). This sounds like provocation, but sums up a psychological truth which it would be wise to cling to firmly.

2

For anyone participating in a decision, it is, as we know, not enough to have chosen and voiced his position. He must still persuade others to adopt it. Each person individually is in this way forced to take into account the direction to which the group is oriented – is it 'pro' or 'anti', on the left or the right, etc.? How are preferences distributed between its members, how much do they cling to them? This is appraised without being aware of it or calculating it, by seeking to grasp that common element around which the majority converges. When people meet together, even in a public place or a café, they often light upon this element as if groping in the dark, even if only from a desire to express themselves and reach an agreement. The more they speak, the more they recount to one another, the more this element is revealed and is made explicit. Without it they remain an amorphous entity, and their conversation mere chatter.

Thus any group whose members assess the information given, and discuss, attempting to bind themselves to one another in an agreement, seek the common element that will help them to understand one another and to persuade one another. To take a concrete example, when Lewin (1943) brought American housewives together to discuss, they already knew that to cook the less choice portions of meat – tripe, liver and the rest – was one way of contributing to the war effort. Yet this knowledge was not sufficient to induce them to change their habits. Only their meeting as a group could emphasize the patriotic aspect of the change and strengthen the norms they shared. In one way, everything was already in place. And in another way, everything had to be discovered, that is, just how far this norm was common to them and met with their unanimous approval. If people often dislike meeting and discussing, it is less because speaking is a sheer waste of time than because of the fear of not finding what they want in participating, that is, what they share in common and what binds them to one another.

This is an enormous question, one too far removed from our present discourse to be able to deal with it here as it deserves. But it is evident that these common elements belong to the order of values and norms. The more discussion there is, the more these are thrown into relief, and the more they govern the arguments which seek to convince, filter the information available and stimulate the desire to seek out more of it. At the same time, the more precise the information, the less the field is left free for differences and individual positions. Gradually these are supplanted by collective positions in the consciousness of group members. If the members continue for long enough, the consensus approximates to these values, just as a house under construction does to the architect's plan.

Let us take an elementary example. Individuals taking part in a movement of opinion can come to blows over any kind of problem whatsoever – racism, the death penalty or social security, for example. Numerous differences can subsist among them, real differences that could turn them into enemies. But when, for one reason or another, they rally round a principle such as the Rights of Man, as we observed in the bicentenary year of the French Revolution, some of these differences are hidden away. Forces are mobilized for an agreement to take shape around this principle, the Rights of Man providing the content for consensus and collective action. These rights give meaning to the various views on political or moral discourse, and filter the arguments and the information that sustains a consensus in movements of opinion.

There would really be no need to insist on this close relationship between communication and values when decisions are taken in the group if some did not seek to separate the two, and even to restrict the role of values in social psychology. For motives difficult to grasp they proceed as if the presence of values or 'norms' removed from phenomena their rational character, limiting objective information to a secondary role. In reality, values and norms enhance this role by throwing a more penetrating light on what in social life is rational. In many respects they are a determining element in group psychology, if not psychology in general. This is because, as Grice again states,

> I have strong suspicions that the most fruitful idea is the idea that a rational creature is a creature which evaluates, and that the other possible characteriz-ations may turn out to be co-extensive with this, though in some sense less leading. I don't know whether it follows from this, but at any rate I think it is true, that all naturalistic attempts at the characterization of rationality are doomed to failure. (1982: 238)

Without subscribing to so categoric an assertion, we are struck to see that a thinker whose theory of communication has had such profound reper-cussions in the human sciences believed it necessary to spell it out. It justifies our emphasizing how obsolete are the distinctions between factual and value judgements, the one exercising an informative influence, and the other a normative influence. Yet others continue to adhere to these distinctions.

However this may be, if we stick to what we observe and not what we should observe, values not only introduce order into the alternatives that exist within a group, and give meaning to communication between its members, but also afford a relatively secure haven for their opinions, judgements and knowledge. It is from this common perspective that they discuss and compare them, accepting or rejecting the various alternatives. This is continually being done when one states that a piece of information is useful or not, a solution is prudent or risky, a political measure favourable or unfavourable to the country, a jury's verdict is fair or unfair, and a scientific theory valid or invalid. Each time the assessment is arrived at by ordering the terms on a scale, one of whose poles has in our eyes greater importance than the other. It is in relation to this pole that we place persons, things or ideas.

We may go further. We can say that a clear assessment defines a class of situations in which every position or attitude which is close to one of the poles of the hierarchy of values, the one to which society clings – equality, justice, democracy, etc. – takes precedence in the eyes of the individual and guides his conduct. These situations are ones that favour a shift towards an extreme position and disfavour one tending towards the mean. In a social environment, as soon as this hierarchy becomes explicit, individuals and groups clearly move towards the dominant pole. They seek to become more than they were, and this more so than others: more loyal, more courageous, more tolerant, more patriotic, more modern, and so on. This occurs particularly in novel circumstances, where experience does not relativize values or the image individuals wish to have of themselves. This is most certainly very apparent nowadays, where the value assigned to novelty, to being avant-garde, to the fact of being different, is very high. Now, this category of situations is important and 'has not been represented adequately in the literature. The problem of learning from groups how to manifest in concrete situations the virtues and values one holds is important, timely, and perfectly continuous with social psychology generally' (Brown, 1974: 469). The remark is absolutely relevant. Even if the problem has found no solution in most of the previous theories, as described by Brown it is indeed the one that concerns us. It concerns us insofar as it consists not in the manner in which individuals learn, but in the way that together they recreate values and virtues according to the circumstances. We shall see later what these circumstances are.

For the moment, we are concerned with this plain fact: values are the indispensable germ for consensus. They begin to loom large as a common element during discussion. Finally they become an anchor point for opinions and judgements in a situation that favours extreme positions at the expense of average positions. Now, the evidence we have summarized in this way justifies what we call the normative hypothesis of the theory. This is, that the tendency defined by the dominant values and attitudes is accentuated during the discussions, meetings, etc., and determines the directional shift of the decisions that lead to group consensus.

Let us reiterate that the hypothesis predicts, for example, that a group in which individuals having leanings towards pacifism will become even more pacifist after discussion. Those who are against tobacco-smoking will agree on a measure that condemns even more than usual the smoking habit, and so on. We realize that here a number of these values are fated to be fiercely contested. But once they are shared by a sufficient number of people, and are spelt out, they become as categorical as other undisputed values. To sum up: it may seem strange that groups spontaneously swing away from the just mean and the conformity they should adhere to. But they do not do so regardless of the direction, which is towards the norm to which they all adhere. This is why one can scarcely ask whether a consensus is going in the right or the wrong direction, without asking on what basis it has been established and by whom. Stated in statistical terms, this hypothesis predicts that the mean of the choices on which the group members reach agreement is closer to the dominant pole of its scale of values than the mean of the initial choices made by each one of them separately.

In many respects this hypothesis is the most important one. It indicates how greatly the direction taken by collective opinions and judgements is predetermined, no matter what one does. Thus they are predetermined by the store of previous knowledge and values, and up to a certain point by the collective memory that all share before they meet, and which are all ingrained in them. Observations made of numerous groups with whom we have worked justify our view that the hypothesis correctly explains the evolution of decisions from the moment when groups first meet in order to decide up to that when they interiorize the decision as being properly their own.

The role of values in decision-making

1

Very often a hypothesis, once it is accepted as a fact and commonly used, creates the feeling that it is self-evident. This is all the more so since words like values and norms give it a familiar air, as if it can be taken for granted. Yet if we do not proceed further, what it defines becomes blunted, because we no longer recognize whether what it states is specific, nor what are its limits. Yet a hypothesis that excludes nothing is not a necessary hypothesis. Its necessity is demonstrated when it uncovers facts that counter-hypotheses exclude. By this its uniqueness is manifested, and justifies the experiments devoted to it. Now, the hypothesis put forward is the opposite of others and modifies certain others to which, in spite of everything, people continue to subscribe. First, it is a hypothesis that is widely current, one shared by science and common sense. It enunciates that in a collective situation, if the conditions lend themselves to it, people react in an excessive, immoderate way. Moreover, this does not depend on the moral rules and attitudes that have been inculcated in them previously. It is as if, when they are together, they become the antithesis of what they were in isolation. We often express this when we say that crowds are violent or cowardly, collective reactions are aggressive or apathetic, and individuals assembled together are intolerant or conservative. It could be said that this is a property inherent in collectivities in general, which we attribute to the numbers assembled, to their being crowded together, to the relaxation of discipline and other like causes. This is not to take into account their composition, the values they share or the aims they are pursuing.

As we know, a large number of studies have been undertaken in the light of such a hypothesis, which tends to prove that groups take greater risks and are bolder than individuals. In all these studies it was anticipated that the gamble taken and the choice made in common would be extreme, regardless of whether the individual members of the group were daring or timid. This is the essence of the phenomenon known as *risky shift*: on every occasion groups opt for risk rather than prudence. Although this has been regularly observed, no less frequently there is noted what, according to this hypothesis, is a double anomaly, which one tries to dismiss because it should not exist.

On the one hand, certain dilemmas in the questionnaire on risk-taking that we have described regularly brought about a shift in choices towards prudence, instead of risk, as one might expect. On the other hand, on several occasions it was noted that groups were less bold than individuals, without the reason for this being understood. Always an *ad hoc* explanation is given. One wishes to know why these groups do not take risky decisions and why they are less bold than their individual members, as if this were a defect. But this is instead of posing the converse question: why do they take prudent decisions? Why are they timorous? This leads, as one might well believe, to artificial explanations valid in one particular case and belied in the next one. This is always so if there is no reference back to the hypothesis but a mere attempt to correct the facts. The belief is that one can hold to the rule and try to justify the exceptions.

These exceptions are due to how the groups and the relationships between their members are conceived, as if there were no values that held them together and determined their actions. As soon as one acknowledges the power they possess to mould the social space and the decisions taken by the group, what one takes for an exception is no longer one. It seems miraculous, if not incomprehensible, that consensus tends more to risk than to prudence. There is nothing to justify our stating that, by the mere fact of being together, the tendency should be more in one direction than in the opposing one; that is, unless the tendency was not already present without being visible or prominent. Otherwise one would find oneself faced with a kind of spontaneous generation in society, similar to the one already assumed for a long time to exist in nature.

The hypothesis put forward emphasizes that there exist values that are shared and implicit, and it is these that are exposed and highlighted in order to increase the chances of agreement. There is no tendency towards any kind of extreme whatsoever, but towards the one that appears to exist in potential. In short, people coming together do not become this or that, violent or fearful, or bold or more intolerant, etc. They merely become *more* this or *more* that, more bold or more intolerant, etc. Contrary to what has been often asserted, they rarely swing from one extreme to another, unless the climate of the times or force constrains them to do so. This is the difference between the phenomenon of extremism, which has been studied sporadically, and the phenomenon of polarization, the meaning of which has been precise ever since it was discovered (Moscovici and Zavalloni, 1969). Thus this latter phenomenon is more exactly defined than the first, and consequently more difficult to accomplish.

In any case, granted the hypothesis, it becomes futile to impute to groups propensities that do not exist in a population made up of individuals. It is useless to seek to explain why individuals should be violent, aggressive, competitive, etc., because in the end these kinds of assertion are meaningless. Everywhere it seems that the so-called anomalies are not ones. It is just as normal to see groups coming down in favour of a bold solution to the various dilemmas as in favour of a prudent one, if individuals tend towards one or the other. This argument, arrived at by Fraser together with Billig and Gouge, his colleagues at the University of Bristol, once put to the test experimentally, has enabled us to clarify the meaning of our hypothesis. Harking back to previous studies, they wrote:

> In all cases they found that group decisions resulted in shifts towards the extreme of the scale, and these shifts they described as polarization effects. Moscovici and his colleagues explicitly related their work to research on group risk-taking by suggesting that the reported shift to risk was one example of a more general polarization effect which could occur in groups. Thus, perhaps for the first time a content-free account of group risk-taking was proposed. (Fraser et al., 1971: 17)

For their part, they demonstrated this in a very simple way. On the one hand, they devised a questionnaire with choice dilemmas analogous to that used by the American social psychologists. Four dilemmas brought into play risk values; four others called for prudence values. But they changed the method of answering by using – as we did – a graduated seven-point scale. This read as follows: 1: strongly recommend *x*, the risky solution; up to 7: strongly recommend the prudent solution; with 4 as the neutral point at which both solutions appear of equal value.

The scale provides a measure of the tendency of the group, indicating unambiguously whether the average of the attitudes of its members at the beginning was located on the side of prudence or of risk. In order to verify the hypothesis, consensuses must be polarized in the direction of the initial values prevailing before the discussion, that is, they should not go beyond the neutral point, crossing the invisible Rubicon of risk towards prudence, or vice versa. The answer can therefore easily be given, since this neutral point expresses indecision or psychological indifference. It is clear that in most cases the groups have polarized, if one makes the comparison between the consensuses or final decisions and the initial decisions. Very rarely did they go beyond this neutral point in the opposite direction to that which their members had tended at the outset. If these members were bold, the shift took place in the direction of risk, and if they were prudent at the beginning, they became even more so. One cannot speak of any special propensity of the group, even if the number of shifts towards risk observed in this study is superior to the number of shifts towards prudence.

In this we have an entirely practical indication of what must take place every time people meet to choose or judge as a group. It has been verified in a number of studies – for example, in that of Gouge and Fraser (1972), which, instead of choice dilemmas, proposed to the groups that they debate a great variety of problems ranging from drugs to sexuality, and including racism, suicide, etc. With one single exception, consensus accentuated the initial tendency of attitudes and judgements. Those propositions about which participants were already in agreement separately secured even greater agreement after discussion. Those that met with moderate agreement from individuals separately produced a more extreme agreement when they assembled in a group. That is, group discussion and consensus crystallized the range of attitudes then dominant among the Bristol students who were the subject of this inquiry.

From studies of this kind it emerges that although polarization is a general attribute of groups, as we seem at least to have discovered, extremism is not one. The direction tending towards risk, violence and aggressiveness – and there is a long list – is not inherent in them, contrary to what has been believed, and is by no means general. Everything depends on the distribution of values among those participating in social decision-making at any given moment. We can never insist enough on the importance of this distribution for determining our way of acting, and of looking at social phenomena, because up to now no one has learnt to recognize it.

2

Next, following the logic of the hypothesis, we arrive at an apparent contradiction in an essential notion of our theory, if the theory is not sufficiently spelt out. The time has come to do so. In studying the role of values we must acknowledge that their consequence is to involve or commit people collectively, and this goes beyond the effect of mere discussion. In a kind of snowball effect, as soon as groups begin to recognize these values, and then debate and give prominence to them, they end up by subscribing to them, just as do individuals who follow the same course. Thus they become the goal, a kind of sheet-anchor for their opinions and arguments, as can be seen with party militants or believers belonging to a church. Few are capable of maintaining an uncommitted and neutral attitude under these conditions, even supposing they wished to do so. For, as Goffman, the American sociologist noted, 'The individual's actions must happen to satisfy his involvement obligations, but in a certain sense he cannot act *in order* to satisfy these obligations, for such an effort would require him to shift his attention from the topic of conversation to the problem of being spontaneously involved in it' (1967: 115, emphasis in original). Moreover, he emphasizes that in any relationship resulting from interaction 'the engrossment and involvement of the participants . . . is critical' (1983: 3).

It is therefore incumbent upon us to detail with the greatest care the meaning of this critical factor. We may state that if the collective involvement to which our theory refers were not different from individual involvement, at least there would follow one consequence that our hypothesis rules out or that would be deemed highly improbable. This is as follows. In classic studies such as those of Sherif and Hovland (1961) and Kiesler (1969), it is supposed that the more a person is involved in a problem, the more he is committed to an opinion and adopts a firm stance, and the more he withstands persuasion and anything that might cause him to change his mind. It is thought that he rates more negatively any fresh communication that expounds a novel viewpoint, and rejects most of the messages or interventions communicated. This would, for instance, be the case of a practising Catholic participating in a round table with women in favour of abortion, or an inveterate smoker who is the recipient of pamphlets inveighing against tobacco-poisoning.

The conclusion on this point might be formulated by stating that the more one is personally involved, the less one is likely to change and act with the others; or, put differently, making common values explicit prevents ending up with a consensus. And this may be expressed even more concretely: extremist individuals who are generally more committed and more sure of their opinions stand firm on their position. Only moderate individuals, normally less involved, and more uncertain, modify their opinion in order to draw closer to one another. In short, those holding extreme opinions resist; those who have average opinions change.

The human fact that constitutes involvement in participating in ordinary collective relationships is, it seems to us, too widely and too deeply rooted for us not to take account of it. Yet, in the light of the hypothesis, it is postulated that it matters little whether group members are extreme or moderate. They change, or do not change, they converge towards the opinions of others or the latter converge towards theirs, depending on whether they are further from or nearer to the common value. Thus this is according to the distance from the dominant pole, which in everybody's eyes represents the norm. In a nutshell, it is the relationship to others and not to the object that determines who shifts his viewpoint and who does not. This is what distinguishes collective involvement from personal involvement and makes it psychologically specific.

The empirical problem raised here in order to bring out this distinction is as follows: do extremist individuals shift less than do moderate individuals, and is there less chance of their converging after discussion? Or indeed, as we suppose, will this convergence come about by a shift on the part of the group members furthest away from the pole of reference towards those who are closest to it – regardless or whether they are committed to an extreme position or a moderate one? Let us suppose, in order to make the alternative more concrete, groups made up of feminists, anti-feminists and 'neutrals', who have to come to an agreement about certain common claims they are putting forward. According to the first premise of the alternative, only the neutrals will shift during the discussion; since the feminists and anti-feminists, deeply entrenched in their positions, do not succeed in reconciling their viewpoints, any attempt at agreement will fail. The second premise of the alternative supposes that, in the population, at the time when the meeting occurs, the tendency, for example, is rather in favour of feminism. The involvement of the group collectively in the discussion will mean that not only will the neutrals change but that the anti-feminists will change still more in order to find common ground for an agreement.

In a series of very elegant research projects Zaleska (1982) decided between the two eventualities. She examined the results collected from twenty-six studies. Some related to individual attitudes; these concluded that personalities holding extreme positions possibly change their opinions less after discussion than do those with moderate positions. Zaleska compared these results with our conjecture. Having drawn up the statistics relating to the opinions, she found that the percentage of changes in responses was greater for moderate opinions than for extreme opinions. This chimes with current theory as well as common sense.

However, a closer look reveals that, depending on whether individuals are nearer or further away from the dominant pole of the scale, things proceed differently. When nearer to it, the extremists maintain their position, shifting less than do the moderates. This arises because the extremists can move only in a direction running counter to the norms, which is an eventuality ruled out, whereas the moderates can shift closer to this pole. As regards the other pole, it is the extremists who change more than do the moderates ($p < .001$). They are comparatively more numerous than the latter (70 per cent as against 59 per cent) in linking up with the predominant norm in the population. Moreover, their greater distance from the norm has the result that after the discussion not only do they change in greater proportion, but also this change occurs to a significant degree.

Thus our predictions are verified and the hypothesis holds good, provided it is made clear that it is collective involvement that increases in the interaction, and not individual involvement in the objective under discussion. More precisely, what counts is the fact that each individual is involved not as being extremist or moderate and as an individual, but as a member of the group, through the trend in society and the drift of opinion. As Zaleska correctly writes,

> Thus initial disagreement with a dominant tendency results not only in a greater proportion of change. This difference is not surprising. As pointed out elsewhere . . . the responses which are most frequently chosen by a population of individuals are more likely to gain wider acceptance following discussion than responses which are relatively infrequent. (1982: 171)

In these same research projects the French social psychologist wanted to convince herself that these results held good on a larger scale, in conditions close to reality, given the importance of what was at stake. She examined a whole series of experiments carried out in Germany at Augsburg. There the participants followed a discussion between two or three people, on radio or television. The discussants always expressed the same number of arguments for or against a proposition. When there was a third party participating he adopted a neutral stance. The discussions dealt with two topical problems: access of members of left-wing parties into the German civil service, and the severity of the punishment imposed for possessing drugs. The participants were students and inhabitants of Augsburg drawn at random from the telephone directory. Their number varied between 100 and 300 for each one of the six experiments, and thus was very high.

It is interesting to observe that here, too, after having followed a radio or television debate between persons defending opposing viewpoints, individuals changed their opinion, and this occurred all the more frequently when they adhered to a position closer to the non-dominant pole. Those students who advocated exclusion from the civil service of a member of a left-wing party were more inclined to modify their position than were students opposed to such an exclusion. By contrast the inhabitants of Augsburg maintained their position and continued to demand exclusion. Very clearly one may think that persons who have been subjected to different arguments are more receptive to those arguments that suit their inclinations than to those which go against them, especially if these arguments chime with the dominant values of the population being studied.

The Augsburg observations agree with the Paris experiment, inasmuch as they reveal a similar relationship between the scale of values shared at the outset by members of a group and their involvement during a debate which ends with an agreement. In this the notion that we are employing – and Zaleska provides the arguments for it – predicts special consequences that can be verified. The notion must be divorced from any notion of personal involvement, the merits of which are indisputable if values are not taken into account. Such a notion is better known, for it has existed for a long time.

We arrive at a definite viewpoint by excluding any inherent tendency in collectivities towards a special form of extremism: violence, aggressiveness, risk, etc. On the other hand, our conjecture is applicable only to situations in which a decision arrived at favouring an agreement is formed by a norm. Given the fact that this is the most common situation in society, the bounds are comparatively widely set. In fact, after a short period of time, what is natural, that is, the sum of received ideas, generally reasserts itself in all haste. However, during this short period, the work of Fraser, Billig and Zaleska has broadened our horizons. The prospects that have been opened up have received valuable support from it, even if today they need to be renovated and given new vigour.

Polarization and convergence

1

It is true that a fertile theory renders superfluous a host of *ad hoc* explanations and gives new meaning to facts hitherto neglected. We have just seen that the exceptions to the alleged tendency to take more risks in a group are in fact normal effects foreseen in the theory. In every case, it has been verified that the opinions and judgements of individuals when they meet converge towards the dominant pole of their scale of values, whether these be moderate or extremist. But the hypothesis also raises questions that had not been put but which it can answer. In the event, we want to know whether the distribution of initial choices in a group affects the process that takes place, and, if so, how? Now, the answer to such a question should come from discovering a precise quantitative relationship. This can be none other than to establish, on the one hand, the existence of a positive correlation between the average of individual positions and the shift towards the mean of positions around which a consensus is formed, and, on the other hand, the reduction in variance between the different positions after discussion in groups. These two relationships may express the convergence around a common value. Curiously, these relationships were known, but it was only once the hypothesis had been enunciated that their importance and significance were realized.

In the study by Moscovici and Zavalloni (1969) this relationship can be seen emerging, inasmuch as discussion of the person of de Gaulle led the participants to make a more favourable judgement on questions where the tendency is also favourable, and conversely. Nevertheless, no shift towards the extreme was observed with ambiguous questions. The experiment confirmed the relationship that Teger and Pruitt (1967) had already calculated between the level of risk chosen by individuals and the one they agreed on in the group. They obtained a very high correlation of between .70 and .90. As if to establish more firmly its specific character, they confirmed, with supporting statistics, that this polarization depended not upon the inclination of individuals to take risks or to remain prudent, but indeed on the form in which dilemmas are couched and debated, which causes the balance to swing one way or another. This is to state that judgements on imaginary situations which before the discussion gave rise to bold choices became even bolder afterwards.

What follows is a particularly clear-cut example, discovered among a church congregation. Myers (1982) carried out a three-stage survey of attitudes among 269 members of a church. In the first stage, 100 people had the opportunity to voice agreement or disagreement with sixteen propositions relating to their church, such as: 'The ministers should be free to adopt a position on a political question, after having distanced themselves from the function they fulfil.' Three weeks later, the rest were divided into three sub-groups. In the first they were asked to pronounce upon the propositions, and nothing else; the second sub-group did the same, after having learnt what was the average of the answers given by the hundred that were questioned first. In the third sub-group the frequency distribution of the answers from the hundred people was revealed, and then the same questionnaire was answered. Participants in these two last sub-groups exhibited attitudes more extreme than those of the first sub-group, who had no information given them. If it is true that this comes about through a shift in direction of values, the propositions in which a dominant tendency in the group could be discerned should theoretically have led to greater polarization during the discussion than those propositions which related to neutral questions. This was verified from the correlations obtained.

Other experiments assisted in throwing light on various additional points that are of importance. Thus they showed (Bishop and Myers, 1974; Myers and Bishop, 1970) that the mean of the decisions taken originally by the participants enabled one to predict the direction in which they would move towards the extreme, and by how much. In general, the statistical correlations were high. One cannot help feeling downright admiration for the persistent efforts made by these researchers to bring out the precise facts. Moreover, these experiments showed that the variety of individual positions was reduced and ended in a certain uniformity. This meant that they converged towards the dominant common pole. This convergence effect was observed a number of times in tests of decision-making dealing with risk-taking or in problems relating to social attitudes.[1] Hesitation may subsist; nevertheless the correlations arrived at strongly support the idea that the diversity of viewpoints among the participants is significantly reduced during discussion; in addition, these viewpoints shift in the direction of the values shared by all. No example was encountered that cast any coherent doubt on this observation.

Nevertheless we have to state that the observation was indirect and retrospective. For this reason we shall refer also to a remarkable study by Cvetkovitch and Baumgardner. They sought to show that

> group interaction will increase the participants' involvement with the discussed topic and eventuate in individual opinion and group consensus that is more extreme than pre-discussion attitude. Additionally, the direction of polarization will be towards the naturally occurring majority opinion of the salient reference group and not toward the average attitude within the discussion groups. (1973: 161)

With this purpose in mind they administered a 62-point questionnaire relating to problems of civil disobedience by Washington high-school students. They then selected six questions that represented the two extremes of a single-dimensional attitude relating to these problems. Three positive questions postulated a permissive attitude towards civil disobedience (for example, 'The police often treat demonstrators with too much brutality'), whereas the three negative questions expressed a more repressive attitude (for example, 'Men who go abroad to escape military service should undergo severe punishment when they return home').

The participants were selected according to their initial responses to the six questions and were classified according to whether they had a repressive, permissive or moderate attitude towards civil disobedience. Then they were assembled in groups of three, so that one of the attitudes described was in the majority (two out of three repressive in their attitudes) or in the minority (one out of three repressive in his attitude). They discussed together the various propositions until group consensus was reached. Then each one was invited to give his personal agreement on each item. The participants were told that this assessment after discussion was intended to allow them to state whether or not they were in agreement with the assessment made by the group consensus. The authors of the study found generally that the subjects polarized in the direction of the position held by the majority in the reference group. This occurred whatever the position of this group, whether repressive or not. For example, it meant that for groups comprising two 'permissive' and one 'repressive' participant, there was no significant difference in the polarization, on the average, as compared with groups where the proportion was reversed, with two participants repressive and one permissive. Thus it seems that, in a condition where the perception of norms was precise, group discussion led to a significant change in this direction.

Having taken into account the range of ingenious researches in this field,[2] we are particularly conscious of the fact that, save for rare exceptions, these lead to the same result. However, we have to say that most of their authors interpret their results in a way that destroys our original hypothesis. It seemed plain to them that the convergence observed was due to the fact that the majority shared the same values, and obliged the other participants in the decision to conform to them. In other words, it is not the moral and intellectual authority of the values that imposes on the process a direction leading to consensus; it is rather the pressure of the large number that subscribe to it and to whom the smaller number submit.

It can hardly be by chance that this explanation appears more natural than our own. It is even less an accident if, in social psychology – but is it the sole human science where this is the case? – we always fall back on conformity to account even for phenomena that at first sight appear to contradict it, whereas – and the fact has often been established (Baron et al., 1973) – majority pressure only has an effect if it is exerted in the direction of the values prevailing in the population. If this is not so, they have a lesser impact, and this gives the minority a greater opportunity to see its opinions triumph.[3] But we shall return several times to this apple of discord, which is of such capital importance in social psychology.

2

It can never be repeated sufficiently often that it is appropriate to take all hypotheses with a certain reserve. Are they not destined to be invalidated sooner or later? Meanwhile, since the bulk of research is favourable to them, we can rely upon our own conjectures as if they were true. They demonstrate a solidity somewhat rare in the human sciences, which have assumed the task of finding a meaning to the unforeseeable and complicated matters that are the stuff of human affairs. Racial prejudices occupy a prominent place among them. It rarely happens that we display these or acquire them by ourselves. Now, the worst that could happen is for them to become the subject of public debate because, if they exist, this debate, according to our hypothesis, would consequently polarize them. This was the motive behind the experiment of Myers and Bishop (1971) which was designed to see if matters proceeded in this way. They gave a sample population of a hundred high-school students a questionnaire whose responses could be divided into two categories, depending upon how many prejudices were expressed. Thus the mean of the responses lay on one side or other of the zero point of the scale of racism that was drawn up.

What will happen if small groups of people are constituted that think in the same way and are then subjected to questions relating to racial prejudices? It is clear that they polarize towards the pole of opinions to which they were originally closest. Consequently the two positions will become further removed from one another: the racists will become more racist, and the anti-racists will oppose racism even more, as can be observed at the present time in France, where the immigrant question has split opinion in twain. Our American colleagues therefore gave their groups eight propositions to be discussed. For example, 'It has been said recently that "white racism" bears responsibility for the condition of Blacks in American cities. Do you agree or disagree?' Of course each student was first invited to express his personal opinion, which he gave again separately after discussion in a small group. As was expected, the two samples shifted towards their respective poles, racist or anti-racist. Each one exhibited a kind of boldness in shifting towards the extreme, as if this came from a deliberate choice. The shift was not only significant but widened the distance between the two positions.

The experiment reminds one of the meetings that are a prelude to elections, when the defenders of opposing positions and the supporters of opposing parties come together. These gatherings bring together persons who think the same and exchange their ideas. The intention of the organizers is for this type of debate to bring them all closer together. It may well have the reverse consequence and widen still further the gap between the groups. We can see this every day: left- and right-wingers, when they meet in their respective groups, make what separates them stand out even more, and play down what draws them closer. The nation seems cut in half, made up of two peoples, those of the left and right. We can now understand the mechanism whereby this opposition is maintained and accentuated.

This at least is what the theory induces us to predict regarding everything that calls for a decision. On a jury, for example, values are reflected in a verdict of 'guilty' or 'not guilty'. The problem is that the verdict should be based exclusively on material proofs, the evidence of witnesses, the reports of experts, the system of indictment and the legal pleadings – in short, on facts from which an equitable judgement is made. This is not what happens in reality: a jury is something other than a dozen jurors. It is true that during the trial each juror forms his or her own opinion, a personal conviction regarding the culpability of the accused. When they retire to the jury-room, their judgement has already been made, and is often revealed in an initial vote. Then discussion starts in order to arrive at a consensus on the verdict, and sometimes a unanimous one. If our hypothesis is correct, the path towards a common decision may have the effect of polarizing the previous judgements made by a majority, and nothing else. This conclusion has been highlighted and confirmed in numerous studies, such as that of Myers and Kaplan (1976), who simulated in the laboratory the deliberations of a jury. Thus they constituted groups of six and put before them legal cases based on trials that had really taken place. These concerned breaches of the highway code, presented either as serious or non-serious offences. For example, they described the case of a driver of a bakery van who recklessly caused the death of a child of two. The circumstances of the accident, the personality of the driver and the details of the case were given, first presenting them in a grave light, and then toning down the items and merely incriminating the driver for not respecting the highway code.

The hypothetical jurors were invited to read one of two versions of the trial and to estimate the degree of guilt of the driver on a scale ranging from 'absolutely not guilty' to 'absolutely guilty'. They were also asked to work on the hypothesis that the accused was found guilty and to suggest the sentence that should be passed, choosing from a range of penalties the minimum punishment prescribed by law for the crime in question up to the maximum punishment. The first opinions canvassed for the two versions of the four cases under discussion represented the initial judgements of the participants. The hypothetical jurors then started to discuss, and afterwards each one assessed separately for a second time the cases, indicating once more the degree of guilt and the punishment proposed. In spite of the complexity of the cases put forward, and the unreal character of the situation, the participants put themselves in the place of the person whose role they had to act out. The results showed that where the initial judgements tended towards the 'absolutely guilty' end of the scale, after the discussion they shifted towards the extreme, and the jurors found the driver even more guilty. Likewise, in the cases where the initial judgements were on the side of 'absolutely not guilty', after discussion the degree of guilt was considered to be still less. The same held good for the level of punishment prescribed. All in all, it can be observed that the fictitious juries polarized substantially, with the initial votes turning into group verdicts even more extreme than the direction taken originally.

This outcome of deliberations in simulated juries has been found to occur on several occasions, and gives some idea of how general it is.[4] The observations agree inasmuch as the values intervene overwhelmingly in influencing the way in which the information presented is used and in the way in which agreement on the verdict is arrived at. Thus, even if the information is convincing, we can nevertheless be sure that the decisions taken leading towards consensus strengthen above all the norms to which each individual adheres. They represent 'a verdict before the verdict' which, at the end of the trial, emerges reinforced and more extreme. This is what a study by Kalven and Zeisel (1966) showed concerning the deliberations of real juries in 225 trials. They assembled the data regarding the initial vote of the twelve jurors, and the final verdict rendered. Now, in nine cases out of ten, the juries that had to reach a unanimous verdict did so in the direction that accentuated the initial tendency to condemn or acquit the accused. A mere 5 per cent of them modified their first opinion regarding innocence or guilt. One finds again that deliberations could have the same effect, so to speak, as developing an exposed film: the operation brings out the picture, but the result is fixed beforehand in the snapshot of the attitudes and values of the majority.

Walker and Main (1973) brought more direct evidence of how these deliberations emerge within the judicial framework by comparing the decisions taken by judges in cases dealing with civil liberties (affecting the rights of Blacks, women, etc.). In the USA these lie within the jurisdiction of federal judges, but in two different sets of circumstances. Most often the case is brought before a single judge who listens to the litigants and alone decides, after investigating the matter, what should be the outcome. But, if one of the parties so requests, three judges sit together to go into the case. After having studied it together and discussed what should be the outcome, they formulate collectively a verdict that closes the discussion. The group then breaks up and each judge reverts to his own individual duties. This situation is reminiscent of those mounted in the laboratory and provides material for a fine experimental study. It turns out that the judges when they meet collectively make twice as many (65 per cent) liberal decisions as do judges when they decide alone.

Part of their decisions relate to whether laws ('statutes') are in accordance with the Constitution. Main and Walker (1973) noted that in this respect the decisions were more liberal when the judges decided as a body (55 per cent as against 45 per cent). Knowing that only a minority of decisions taken by a judge presiding alone were of a liberal kind, the authors hypothesized that judges nevertheless had a liberal code of values. When they decided alone, the pressure of anti-liberal public opinion led them to a compromise. On the other hand, when they judged collegially their personal values came out and became more radical during discussion with their colleagues, who were of the same persuasion. In the final analysis, whether jurors or judges are involved, we observe that norms determine the direction towards which consensus will be polarized, even if they are represented, on the one hand, by a majority and, on the other, so one must believe, by a minority. This means that the ideology, whatever it might be, must emerge strengthened.

One cannot accept such an assertion unreservedly, since it is not based on a sufficient range of facts. But it complements all the facts we have just set out. The rare studies available to us give some verisimilitude to the assertion. One may take, for example, that of Bray and Noble (1978) who tested the hypothesis by setting up fictitious juries, some of which included very authoritarian characters, while the others included less authoritarian characters. Numerous arguments and observations give grounds for surmising that the former are more conservative and bring in a verdict of guilty more frequently, with the appropriate penalty being more severe, than do the latter. It is then reasonable to hypothesize that 'following the polarization hypothesis . . . the group interaction tends to enhance choice tendencies initially favoured in the subjects' population' (Bray and Noble, 1978: 1425). Thus juries made up of authoritarians will more often find the accused guilty and mete out heavier punishments than do juries made up of less authoritarian people. These decisions are polarized according to the direction taken by individual decisions formulated before deliberations begin.

The participants in the study – students – were first of all ranked according to a classic test relating to their degree of support for an authoritarian ideology. Next they were brought together and divided into forty-four juries of six each. For half an hour, they listened to a recording of a murder trial that took place in Illinois. The two accused, both drunk, killed with malice aforethought a woman in her Chicago apartment, probably because she had rejected their advances in a night club earlier in the evening. At the end of the trial the judge invited the jurors to bring in a verdict of guilty or not guilty, according to the law. After listening to the recording, participants in the study had to make up their minds separately and propose a sentence. Then they discussed in randomly composed groups for some forty-five minutes and reached agreement on a verdict. As was anticipated, the authoritarian characters most often brought in a verdict of guilty, and matched it with longer sentences than did the less authoritarian characters. These observations were statistically significant, both for the individual jurors, and, more importantly, for the juries. As regards the jurors, all the guilty verdicts came from the 'authoritarians'.

Other results may arise later, yet these fit in with a view of the situation that is even more coherent when one delves deeper, seeking to disprove them, because this is the only way in which we can be sure of their validity. Not only is this confirmed in the laboratory for a wide range of questions, but it also extends to one of the most important institutions in our society, the judiciary, which devotes meticulous attention to how it makes its decisions and affects the fate of the majority. In many respects this provides information on the way other institutions function, for which it provides a model. The theory, verified in this way, might be significant for committees and other bodies charged with arriving at important decisions for society. Thus it may help us to understand them.

Decisions leading to consensus considered as an innovatory factor

1

Let us summarize the above. The evidence that our conjecture predicts may be summed up in three propositions. First, there exists a positive correlation between the positions originally adopted by members of the group and those on which this group reaches agreement. Next, the direction in which these positions are polarized is determined by the dominant values in the population to which the group belongs. In no way could one see the consensus as the outcome purely and simply of the alternatives available. Nor is it the result of a whim, a fluctuation in attitudes arising from bringing together a number of individuals with no precise tendency, although such a fluctuation has often been described, but is probably imaginary. Finally, during the discussion the group members become involved collectively and change the way in which they judge, perceive and choose, depending on whether they are close to the dominant or the subordinate pole on the scale of values. This is tantamount to stating that the social universe resembles the organic universe of Aristotle, in which there can be distinguished a centre and a periphery, a top and a bottom, and a high and a low, rather than the mechanical universe of Newton, homogeneous and lacking any one favoured direction. Without wasting words, we may state that in decision-making there is no *tabula rasa*, any more than there are many decisions that are disputed once they have been taken.

Nevertheless one may have the impression that this evidence is only valid for the choices and attitudes debated on the basis of pre-existing norms and positions fixed beforehand, so that consensus is already foreshadowed and almost acknowledged without any fuss or major conflict among the members of the group. If our conjecture is generally true, it should additionally be applicable to the very frequent case when values are still fluid and, so to speak, in a state of virtuality. It can be said that they are awaiting the process of crystallization, as can be observed at the present time for matters relating to euthanasia, organ transplants or the environment. Each decision is a step along the road whose route is only known when it has been trod the full length. But what represents a real innovation is a series of decisions of such a kind that former relationships and norms are blotted out by new ones. However this may be, the expansion of a social trend that has been totally unforeseen can provide an opportunity to assure oneself how far daily controversies and public debates have the effect of making it more extreme. At the same time they prepare for a consensus whose values as they burgeon overturn the hierarchical values existing in a static condition.

At a certain time, the feminist movement afforded a possibility of putting the theory to the test, insofar as the movement was innovatory. The problems argued over by the participants during a laboratory experiment contained the same unknown elements as did those debated by the feminists outside, on which they were subjected to daily questioning. Each individual was asked about them, particularly because they cropped up in conversation, and on the radio or television. All this may be taken for granted, and one hardly need comment on it; that is, save for the fact that the experiment reproduced and gave a cross-section of part of the continual ebb and flow of the discussions taking place in society at large, which itself has become a source of new solutions. What does this mean except that, in the situations in which we study them – in the narrow confines of the laboratory –, the creations of the great laboratory of society seem less artificial and strange?

Taking this view into account, a series of studies were carried out in the Laboratory of Social Psychology in Paris, when the feminist wave was at its height in the 1970s and numerous movements arose in which the question of the rights of women came to the fore. In several studies it was shown – as if there were any need to – that the subjects most involved, for whom this question had maximum importance, that is, those of the female sex, had also a greater tendency to polarization. Let us investigate in greater detail the studies by Paicheler (1976, 1977, 1978, 1979). She began by formulating eight questions whose propositions were derived from discussions on the feminist theme. These questions – such as, 'Women are particularly suited for secretarial jobs' – were calibrated on a seven-point scale ranging from 'total disagreement' (-3) to 'total agreement' ($+3$), with one neutral point. Thus the favourable and unfavourable positions were clearly demarcated. As in all experiments of this kind, the participants first answered separately the whole series of key questions. Then they were brought together in groups and invited to discuss them until they had arrived at a unanimous consensus. Finally, each one of them replied once more separately to the questionnaire. For those groups that did not arrive at a clear consensus, the average of the individual responses after discussion was calculated and compared with the average of their initial responses.

The main interest in these studies is to show just how far consensus is polarized in the direction of an emerging norm, and how this acts upon the group. Let us first consider what happened in the 'pure' groups, made up individually either of girls or of boys. In both cases attitudes that already had a tendency to be pro-feminist became even more marked. This is in accordance with expectations with which we are already familiar. Those who care about a problem and discuss it polarize in the direction of the norms in process of formation and make them even more apparent. Doubtless when they returned home, like those students who discussed and arrived at a consensus, they regressed somewhat to their original positions. But in any case they remained more extreme than before and nearer to the position adopted by the group. The observations made in mixed groups highlighted a remarkable phenomenon. Here in fact the individual responses, even before a word had been exchanged, were already much more pro-feminist than those of the 'pure' groups. It was as if, foreseeing that they would have to discuss together problems relating to the status of women, each individual anticipated this and drew nearer to consensus, divining in what direction this would go. From the moment when the emerging tendency became apparent, it was adopted in advance, so the individual began by changing herself or himself.

Observing these groups, Paicheler noted that the participants faced with other participants, aptly named as of the *opposite* sex, perceived on both sides what their differences were. The female students prepared themselves for the possibility that their male counterparts might be more anti-feminist. In the event that they (the females) might have to make concessions, they hardened their positions. On the other hand, the male students tried to show themselves in a favourable light, that is, as liberals, and, fearing to enter into a conflict with their female discussants, also adopted more feminist positions. Thus, along opposing paths, the females prepared themselves for a confrontation, and the males for abandoning ground by drawing closer to a more extreme position, in the direction of the evolving norms. Thus the 'pure' groups polarized during the discussion, which led to a consensus, while the mixed groups began to do so before the discussion and continued to do so afterwards.

When a problem arouses great interest and stirs up great movements of opinion, militants are always to be found, volunteer confederates who come together to defend that interest, as well as opponents of the attitude that is emerging. They speak out as and when they can, justifying or attacking the new attitude, seeking to make converts. Starting from a certain number of assumptions concerning the influence of minorities (Moscovici, 1976 and 1979) which may be capable of changing the opinions of the majority, Paicheler introduced into the discussion groups a single-minded confederate who adopted a coherent, extreme position and never yielded when the other members of the group – the 'simple' participants – tried to draw him closer to their own position. His intransigence testified to his total involvement and his position was of overwhelming importance to him. This gave a special quality to the interactions within the group. Since by the end of the discussion a consensus was required, the participants were in fact obliged to arrive at an agreement with him – or, if this proved impossible, to acknowledge their failure. Moreover, in certain other groups the confederate defended positions that tended in the direction to which the norms were changing, thus feminist positions, and in other groups positions going against the emerging tendency, thus anti-feminist ones. It was exactly as a confederate or a stout opponent might act outside the laboratory, ready to defend his ideas to the bitter end.

What therefore emerged? The groups where a confederate of feminism was active polarized significantly their consensus ($F = 12.15$; $p < .01$), as well as the individual attitudes of the participants, once the discussion was over ($F = 9.9$; $p < .01$). All in all, the confederate of feminism succeeded in changing collective and individual judgements to an important extent in both the mixed and the 'pure' groups. We should add that this influence was stronger when the confederate recommending feminism was a woman rather than a man. In spite of a slight fall-off (see Table 5.1) the position on which agreement was reached publicly became that of each individual

Table 5.1 *Mean differential evolution of attitudes in groups with a feminist confederate*

	Pre-consensus	Consensus	Post-consensus
Least feminist	0.54	2.69	2.39
Most feminist	1.71	2.50	2.00

privately. We see in this one of the symptoms of involvement. All this seems to lead to one conclusion: a minority triumphs over a more reticent majority, one nevertheless tempted, but obliged to go further than it wished.

Let us now examine the reactions to an anti-feminist confederate who attempted to turn the attitudes of group members in a direction opposed to the emerging norm. He went, so to speak, against the spirit of the times, by adopting positions and putting forward arguments that the majority rejected. As was to be expected, a bipolarization could be perceived: those participants inclined to feminism before the discussion resisted him and those who were more moderate or anti-feminist followed him (see Table 5.2). Doubtless the former gave way during the group discussion, and even rallied round a consensus. But they did so only ephemerally and later returned to their originally generally feminist position. The latter, by contrast, rallied to the view of the extremist 'minority' during the course of the discussion, and stuck to it afterwards. In short, it might be said that they became definitively anti-feminists.

For a more refined analysis, let us look separately at the 'pure' groups and the mixed groups. We first note a surprising tendency, but one that is of marginal significance: that of male groups resisting the influence of the confederate. In the mixed groups, in spite of weak variations, interesting effects were to be found. The resistance of the group grew strongly if the confederate was a female. Paicheler writes, 'There is neither moderation nor polarization of attitude, but on the contrary, a counter-polarization begins to appear' (1979: 94). In other words the opinions of the confederate were vigorously rejected. If he was a male, in this group his influence was weak, but was not rejected so vigorously. His presence led the participants to temporize and moderate their attitude somewhat. Curiously, it was the female participants who made the largest number of concessions, as if they were not sure of themselves, nor of their adherence to the emerging norm.

Table 5.2 *Mean differential evolution of attitudes in groups with an anti-feminist confederate*

	Pre-consensus	Consensus	Post-consensus
Least feminist	0.02	−0.89	−0.44
Most feminist	1.46	1.03	1.55

As a whole, however, when the discussion was over and each one expressed his or her individual opinion, the subjects reverted to their original position. A male confederate defending an anti-feminist position encountered less resistance and had greater effect than a woman, probably because he was following a traditional attitude.

On the whole here we are looking at, broadly sketched out, the picture of what must occur when a problem evokes a large-scale movement of opinion. People participate in the debate frequently and with intensity. The series of decisions leading to consensus polarizes towards the norm that is emerging and, by this very fact, emphasizes it. Thus these decisions cause the norm to crystallize and facilitate its being embraced fully by each individual, who feels himself a little its creator. Therefore no coercion or forced consensus should enter into it. Paicheler and Bouchet (1973) discovered this to be the case in an experiment that was as simple as it was clear-cut. Young people who participated in it were asked to take up a position on the different problems raised by the student movement of May 1968. The study was carried out in Paris during the academic year following the events. Each individual still felt the pressure of the norms that had then prevailed in the high schools and universities, in effect, leftist norms. Thus it was not surprising to see that the standpoints to which the participants rallied in a consensus tended in a radical, extreme direction. Moreover, it is true that this consensus subsisted after the discussion, when these young people responded separately. The evidence was plain that there was a genuine change. However, a considerable proportion among them – 23 per cent – reverted to their previous individual position and swung back over the threshold to a more conservative stance. It may be assumed that these participants had followed unwillingly the group decisions, judging them to be too left-wing. They then redressed the balance in their own way, asserting their freedom by dissociating themselves from the forced consensus. In these groups the most extremist minorities succeeded in imposing their point of view because their rhetoric coincided with the rhetoric and values widespread among students at the time. Their intransigence, which brooked no contradiction, produced the opposite effect to the one desired, since they exercised a pressure that was not lightly tolerated. Such an experiment is perhaps of limited importance and interest, but it illustrates an important fact. To impose an agreement and require others to adhere to it brings with it undesirable consequences. Examples of this are not lacking.

2

All such studies show us that values as they emerge shape choices and attitudes in a direction that is favourable to these values. Nothing is more significant than the way in which the arguments that are exchanged about the values are received. On the one hand, those who defend them are generally welcomed; on the other, those who dispute them encounter resistance. Some have the effect of crystallizing and polarizing attitudes towards feminism, others bring about a bi-polarization or, at best, a compromise on these attitudes. To express it more concretely, these arguments most certainly play a part, but one that nevertheless has been very little studied. On the rare occasions when it has been, it was observed that the discussions were animated, the participants deemed themselves more involved than normally and judged the debates to be open and fair (Zuber, 1988). Clearly argument about subject content occupies the greatest part of the discussion, but that part of the discussion about the decision which leads to consensus is not restricted. One may doubt, however, that it is the cause of the polarized consensus within the group.

It was precisely in this field that Paicheler sought to understand more exactly the groups that were the subjects of her research. To begin with, she classified the arguments that were raised into six categories, according to their purpose: (a) information from each individual regarding his views; (b) interpretation of the questions to draw out their feminist or anti-feminist character; (c) feminist or anti-feminist arguments; (d) organization, denoting those contributions that sought to facilitate development of the discussion; (e) negotiation, those contributions the aim of which was to seek after a consensus; (f) relaxation of the debate or aggressiveness (laughter, silence, uproar, etc.).

Contributions that served to give information regarding respective positions were few, as were those concerning organization, particularly in groups with a feminist confederate in which a good atmosphere of understanding prevailed (see Table 5.3). More frequent interpretations were noted in groups where there was no confederate to distinguish more clearly between questions that were feminist or anti-feminist. Arguments for and against were to be found in practically all groups, but were more numerous, as was to be expected, in groups where the opposition was the strongest, that is, where a confederate was present. On closer examination, in spite of the bias towards feminism, it could not be stated that the arguments in its favour were expressed in an overwhelming proportion. On the contrary, the pros and cons roughly balanced out, particularly where an anti-feminist confederate was present. This indicates that the various aspects of each question had been gone into in depth. Negotiations in order to arrive at a consensus were much more numerous in groups without a confederate than in those where one of these caused the balance to be tipped in one or the other direction. To be sure, one supposed this would be the case, but it is gratifying to find it was so. We can regard this as an indication of the mutual influence that is exercised in a normal discussion where no one occupies a privileged position.

A score of years have scarcely passed since the feminist movement arose, and some fifteen since the study took place. It is closer to the truth to say that from an 'acute' state feminism has become a chronic one, since the ideas that a while ago were frowned upon figure nowadays among those accepted. Passions for women's rights have cooled, either because the rights have become legalized, or because opinion has tilted entirely in their favour – at

Table 5.3 *Frequencies of different categories of contributions expressed as percentages*

Experimental conditions	Total no. of speech units	Interpretation	Feminist arguments	Anti-feminist arguments	Information	Negotiation	Organization	Aggressiveness or détente
Groups with no confederate	2,511	22	28	19	5	17	5	2
Feminist confederate	2,622	15	38	29	6	5	3	2
Anti-feminist confederate	2,552	12	37	39	2	3	5	3

least as regards principles and conscience. To find out how things stood today Paicheler and Flath (1986) partially repeated these studies. They proposed to students similar to those previously involved that they should discuss as a group, and then arrive at a unanimous consensus on questions resembling those that had been put to their predecessors. This allowed the researchers to verify that the feminist movement had won the battle, since the initial attitudes were generally much more favourable to the propositions of the feminists. In the discussion among groups without a confederate, where no preference for one particular tendency was represented, there was greater polarization ($F = 10.77$; $p < .01$), as was to be expected.

What happened where a feminist or anti-feminist confederate was present? Of course both were confronting an attitude that had crystallized, had become solidly fixed, and was almost a cultural cliché. The feminist confederate was no longer proposing anything new, but was defending what had become a norm and his or her influence was reinforcing conformity, whereas the anti-feminist confederate seemed to be utterly conservative, a reactionary deviant. Upon examining the data, it was found that their influence had little room in which to be exerted, and that it was weak. Thus the feminist confederates succeeded in polarizing somewhat during the discussion, but to a significant degree ($F = 6.56$; $p < .01$), the consensus. On the other hand, the confederate defending an anti-feminist position brought about no reaction, as if this was already ruled out (see Table 5.4). This is why one can no longer observe the former bi-polarization, when the discussions on the status of women set pro-feminists against their adversaries. At any rate the heated atmosphere had cooled down. The researchers noted that there were fewer arguments, and that the discussions were flat and unenthusiastic. An air of nostalgia hung over the groups, who seemed to be asking themselves, 'But where are the debates of yesteryear?', just as the poet Villon had once asked, 'Where are the snows of yesteryear?' They knew they were waging a fight that had been won by others quite a time ago.

3

If we now cast an overall glance at the array of effects that explain and predict the hypothesis which, rightly or wrongly, we term normative, we realize that it allows us to comprehend a large segment of social reality. We thought it necessary to emphasize certain aspects of it. We were ready to leave out other aspects in order not to lose out in understanding what we would have gained by extending the number of examples and proofs. Thus we have kept silent on some very effective experiments that would have supported our proposition. Moreover, here and there authors maintain that a theory emphasizing the function of values is not a rational one, because it differs from a theory emphasizing information, which is rational. The problem raised by the relationship between these two ideas is by no means novel. Many thinkers have for a long time devoted themselves to it, even to

Table 5.4 *Means* of attitudes in the three phases of the experiment and at two periods of time*

Conditions	1974			1986		
	Pre-consensus	Consensus	Post-consensus	Pre-consensus	Consensus	Post-consensus
Groups with no confederate	1.02	1.61	1.38	1.89	2.43	2.24
With feminist confederate	0.93	2.58	2.02	2.21	2.53	2.44
With anti-feminist confederate	0.48	0.18	0.45	2.30	2.31	2.32

* Attitude scale of six items.

the point of obsession. There may be some advantage in reconsidering it, in the light of the experience that has been gained and the understanding of it that has developed over the score of years that have passed since. Inevitably we will end up by acknowledging the place of values in a world of information. Indeed the problem is to know which items of information to use and which to discard, in order to arrive at a particular agreement. The convention of the unimpeachable character, a scientific animal down to the tips of his fingernails, the repository of all the information required, is indispensable in order to ensure the success of the respectable part of a theory. But we are examining collective decisions, and one cannot exploit reality to the full or account for its specific characteristics if one does not include the qualities of the space within which these decisions are shaped.

We may say that values are their vertical and horizontal coordinates. Even if they are not rational, they make reason possible, reason which for us has – and we must not forget it – the meaning of a value or norm, the highest norm to which our society pays homage. Hence the requirement that is emphasized by two specialists in decision-making; it is 'a theory of rational consensus and commitment when, in fact there is a dissensus' (Lehrer and Wagner, 1982: 4). To fulfil this need, such a theory, as we have demonstrated, must establish a relationship between these ideas.

Doubtless few of us take this kind of hypothesis seriously enough to question what are its practical applications. We would discover that these are many, and one is particularly noteworthy. It stems from the fact that in the field of decision-making modest causes have great consequences. Let us suppose that one were capable of making up groups such as a jury, a committee of 'wise men' or a round table of experts, and so on, whose members originally inclined to one pole of values, guilt or innocence, harshness or clemency, etc. Externally they appear to be moderate and objective persons, whereas in reality they have a tendency in a certain direction. The discussion, and then the consensus, will doubtless exaggerate this tendency and bring about a clear change in attitudes and collective judgements – just as occasionally a difference of 0.5 per cent of votes produces the fall of one government and the rise of another. In short, very little is needed to transform these fairly moderate people into extremists.

When this happens and the exorbitant consequences are assessed, one cries scandal. The whims of public opinion or the fancies of collectivities in general are indicted. Yet in this we can see the perfectly accomplished result of a method that is being applied unconsciously, yet whose effectiveness can be understood using the hypothesis. This method, rediscovered in the laboratory, underlies our experiments.

Notes

1 See especially the studies by McCauley (1972), Marquis (1962), Singleton (1979), Wallach and Kogan (1965).

2 We refer particularly to the studies by Baron et al. (1970), Clark and Crockett (1971), Vinokur (1969) and Wallach and Mabli (1970).

3 See on this subject the studies by Laughlin and Earley (1982) and Baron, Roper and Baron (1974).

4 Among the most remarkable studies we may mention those of Davis et al. (1975) and Kerr and MacCoun (1985).

6

'Warm' and 'Cold' Communications

The climate of groups

1

Maupassant made a few excellent remarks on how one can become original, if one is not so already. The recipe is to be seated in front of a blazing fire, or a flower in the garden, or any object we encounter, and remain in that position until the flower, the fire or the object takes on life and appears different from all the other specimens of its kind. This hint on the method to be followed in order to become an original writer is certainly subject to caution. But it seems suggestive for us, and up to now we have stayed for a very long time contemplating our object, decision leading to consensus, in order to see it in a different light and to exploit its novel aspects. In any case we are ready to answer the main question: why do groups form a consensus sometimes by becoming more extreme, and sometimes by becoming more moderate? Or again, under what conditions do they shift away from or draw near to a consensus?

Hitherto we have established as a preliminary finding that the extent to which groups are collectively involved through the exchange of argument and public debate determines the extent to which they polarize. It is undoubtedly difficult to verify such a relationship directly, but the results of a number of studies give a rough indication. Moreover, we hypothesized and verified that the direction in which consensus is arrived at causes it to shift towards one of the dominant poles on the scale of values. It is as if, mutually stimulating one another, the members of a group were seeking to arrive at the position that expresses most strongly those values. Each individual then feels more sure of himself, more confident because he has made a change insofar as he has personalized, and made the common choice, attitude, and preference, etc. his own.

But, in order to complete the theory behind these phenomena we have to go beyond these preliminary conclusions and take into account the properties of groups. They comprise a flow of communications and influences that come together to settle disagreements. Now, conflicts obey rules, are subject to a hierarchy and to power relationships. Clearly this is a tautology, but it is one that is nevertheless worthwhile examining, to the extent that in this way one can come nearer to a concrete view regarding the reality of decisions in a social environment. We may add, because it is self-evident, that an exploration of this field is all the more needed because it has curiously been neglected. At the end of a searching analysis of research on the phenomenon with which we are dealing, American colleagues have written: 'Yet interestingly, few of the actual characteristics of the decision-making group that exist in organizations are paralleled in those studied in the laboratory. For instance, real groups typically contain status differentiations. Few of the laboratory experiments on group risk-taking experimentally introduce status differences between group members' (Dion et al., 1970: 371).

If that were only all! Very few researchers seek to set out side by side power relationships and forms of communication, whose capital role is however well known. This deficiency has arisen because of a lack of interest in anything that goes beyond the capacities and motivations of individuals, as if those prevailing in groups were secondary and of no effect. In decision phenomena, particularly, according to Turner, the British social psychologist, one treats 'group discussions as a mental environment responsible at most for some "noise" or random effect. The crucial causal variables are seen as having their office elsewhere, either in the information-processing strategies of the individuals or in their desire to enhance and maintain self-esteem' (1987: 151).

Whatever the judgement brought to bear on this question, we should certainly note that the nature of the consensus depends on how the groups are organized and their members communicate with one another. This determines the manner in which they take part in the defence and promotion of the interests and convictions they share. These represent the conditions in which individuals have an opportunity to participate in the resolution of conflicts and in decisions that affect them and their collectivity. Plainly this is what allows a community to become aware of itself, to surmount the obstacles which cause confusion over its goals; it even gives it importance in the eyes of its members, and consequently allows it to take charge of its own evolution. As Caldeira, the Brazilian thinker, wrote, after lengthy experience,[1] 'to participate is a method for the collective construction of a new beginning' (1988: 45).

This is a fact whose advantages and disadvantages have been emphasized so many times that one hesitates to repeat them, even by merely alluding to them. Nevertheless, it is a fact, one determined by communication rules and hierarchical relationships no less than by the mental and affective forces brought into play. Members of a group are not carbon copies of one another, 'nor are they like regimented followers: their commitment to the organization and its leader is not rooted exclusively in obedience . . . but rather is based on participation' (Bailey, 1988: 25). We may add that in whatever field, whether religious or political, there is always some institution or ritual to regulate participation. Therefore its organization is a matter of great significance. It includes a mixture of constraint and involvement, a very logical blending of voluntary and involuntary movements, which is nevertheless very difficult to bring about. As the purpose is to satisfy the need to make a choice, the operation, which consists in bringing together and mobilizing individuals, has to obey one imperative: to maximize the possibility of everybody being able to be a party to the discussion and the public choices made. The need for this is as essential as that of maximizing every useful means of assistance and every item of information available, for these serve to underpin the possibility and should therefore be prerequisites.

Thus, according to the third hypothesis, the 'participating impulse'[2] increases the possibility of participation by members of the group and determines the extreme or moderate nature of the consensus reached. In plain language, depending on whether the rules allow individuals to participate more or less intensively, to have a more or less direct presence at the decision by the group, this consensus will shift towards either extremism or compromise. We should not lose sight of the fact that it is a question not so much of a difference in the level of participation as of the different forms it takes, the one consensual, the other normalized, as a function of the power relationships and the rules of communication within the group. We have already anticipated the outcomes of this hypothesis – in fact, they are a synthesis of the previous hypotheses – and will return to them in the course of this chapter. In this way, through the particular characteristics of the group we can discern its specific function in fixing the kind of consensus that the group members are moved to adopt. In other words, it is they who determine the 'kind of sociability' that is allowed.

2

There is no need whatsoever for lengthy research in order to find out in which circumstances the chances of participating are greatest. The right way consists in distinguishing with the greatest clarity between the observations made when studying the solving of problems, the verbal or non-verbal communications, and the networks of exchange in a social environment. In this way one finds a coherent overall relationship rather than a sparse collection of facts. The relationship was described in precise terms by Burnstein, the American social psychologist, in an outstanding piece of work:

> A shift is more likely to occur when initial differences in choice emerge in unrestricted discussion and must be reconciled; such shifts are less likely to occur when members are restricted in their interactions so that either each has equal influence, confidence not being evidenced in behaviour, or unanimity is not required and deviant choices are perfectly required. (1969: 383)

He discovered a link between the direct character of the communication and a shift towards the extreme, even if this did not appear to be the logical consequence of this direct character. Doubtless this link has exceptions, but these are not ones that hitherto have prevented anyone from perceiving it clearly. He asked whether it is not by avoiding the communication claimed to be immediate that there resides the possibility of arriving at a compromise. To avoid it really means to force individuals to participate in a restricted fashion, without their being aware of it and realizing the limitations imposed on it.

Let us imagine a situation consisting of consensual participation of individuals free from all constraint: no one is excluded from the discussion of the various solutions to a problem and each individual is involved in the decision, on which all are unanimously agreed. This is an original situation that may last a fairly long time, until rules of procedure and a hierarchy are introduced. Take the example of a committee: it starts by electing a chairman and a secretary, fixes an agenda and chooses its manner of working. The belief is that a framework has been laid down to make the committee more effective. Yet imperceptibly, not realized by anybody, it changes and edges towards a normalized form of participation. It channels the exchange of arguments, regulates the relationships between members of the group, stresses the distance that separates them from one another and clarifies what is expected of each individual in order to attain the common goal. The appearance of spontaneity, of direct and frequent contact, may be preserved, at the very moment when, so to speak, reality turns away and detaches itself from the view that one has of it.

In one sense it is true, as we have maintained, that group discussion is the moulder of an extreme consensus. 'In 1969', we read in a book that proposed to rehabilitate the concept of the group in social psychology,

> Moscovici and Zavalloni demonstrated that group-induced shifts to more extreme positions occurred for more general attitudes as well. The term 'group polarization' became widely accepted as it became apparent that group discussion would enhance tendencies in a large range of situations, and was not restricted to choice dilemmas and the risky shift. (Turner, 1987: 143)

But, in another sense, this is not true. Everything depends not only on what is being discussed, but also on how it is being discussed, and on how people participate in the discussion. We have tried to bring out this hypothesis in the light of a number of experiments.

Where can one find a better place for observation than in the discreet modifications of the space in which the group meets to discuss? One may well surmise that these alter attitudes among participants and foreshadow the outcome towards which they are being attracted. In an enclosed space the tables and chairs are malleable elements that can be used to signify all manner of things, among them the various styles of discussion. Strictly fixed rules may lay down the way in which we are seated in the room where we meet, a lecture theatre, a consultant's surgery or a court of law. They indicate on a material plane the line of conduct or discourse to follow. The different positions that each individual occupies, at the end of a table or on one of its sides, determine the sphere of action within which he may influence others, and the weight that others' opinions may assume in his own mind. Thus it is in no way surprising to observe how heated the arguments are on how the space should be used when a meeting is being prepared, or an international conference, or even a formal meal.

To place people at a round table, a square one, or a rectangular one does not have an anodyne effect. The first two kinds do away with any hierarchy, the very expression 'round table' in fact denoting an intention to bring together the various participants without, at least in principle, any one of them dominating the rest. A rectangular table suggests an order of precedence and institutionalizes distances. It is clear, moreover, that the size of the room, the decor, the appearance – solemn or otherwise – of places creates an atmosphere. Thus in the law court the accused is separated from the jury by a more or less large space. Judicial procedures, impersonal in France, relatively personal in the United States, are also significant. Thus one has to investigate the relationship between the space chosen by a group and the relationships of exchange and communication that take shape within it. The words warm and cold are commonly used to describe environments or materials. It is said that wood is warm, whereas glass or plastic are termed cold. These words can also be applied to spaces, depending on the social atmosphere that is created, which has nothing to do with the temperature. It exerts its effect upon the persons meeting together, imparting either an impression of intimacy and closeness, or one of formality and distance. But it also has an effect between the persons and the problem that brings them together, influencing the degree of detachment and objectivity in relation to that problem. We note also that the same language is not employed in the two different circumstances: in the one it is more simple and concrete, in the other more elaborate and abstract (Moscovici, 1967). In a 'warm' space, frequent exchanges are observed, and more active direct discussion. In a 'cold' space, exchanges are less frequent, discussions less direct and less animated, as if what was in question was a more abstract and more distant object.[3]

In a very simple way Moscovici and Lécuyer (1972) set up a 'warm' space and a 'cold' space, inviting participants either to sit opposite one another or side by side in discussion leading to a consensus. In a classroom, the group found two ordinary tables. But in the 'alignment' position the two tables were placed end to end, with all the subjects sitting on the same side facing the place where usually the teacher is stationed. In the 'square' position, the participants were ranged two by two on each side of the tables. Each individual chose freely his own seat, and only the overall arrangement had been predetermined. Thus the two conditions differed as to the distance that separated the participants, the angle at which they perceived one another, and the space that was facing them, which was larger in the 'alignment' condition. The difference was also symbolic inasmuch as the first position was comparable to the regular, disciplined relationships that appertain in a French secondary school, whereas the latter, which was freer, conjures up more a seminar room or a progressive classroom.

In order to compare the results of the experiment to other ones, the authors used Fraser et al.'s (1971) modified version of the questionnaire on choice dilemmas giving rise to risk. It will be recalled that in this type of study, the procedure consists of three phases. The subjects give first their individual response (pre-test), expressing their personal opinion on the

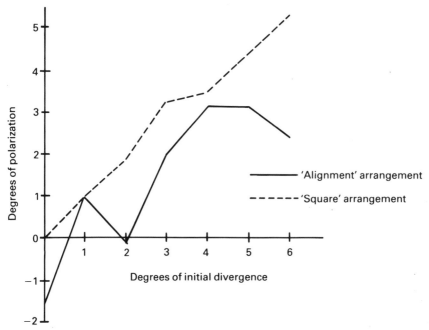

Figure 6.1   *Relationships between polarization, field of interaction and initial divergences between group members*

problem; in the second phase the consensus recorded is the one which the group arrives at after discussion; in the third phase, the post-test, or post-consensus, the subjects once more give their judgement in isolation. In all three cases the same scale for the responses is used, that is, a seven-point scale, in which 7 represents 'total agreement' and 1 'total disagreement'. It is reckoned there is polarization if a significant difference is noted between the mean of the pre-test responses and the mean of post-test responses for a group consensus shifting in the direction of the nearest pole on the scale, that of risk. The participants in the experiment were teachers and pupils of both sexes, in equal numbers. On the basis of our remarks above concerning the communication model, we hypothesized that the interaction would be more active and the involvement stronger in the 'square' tables arrangement than in the 'alignment' arrangement. The consensus would therefore be more extreme in the direction of the greatest risk under the first arrangement than under the second. On the whole (see Figure 6.1) polarization was indeed stronger when the subjects were arranged in a square formation, and thus face to face, than when they were aligned side by side. We had assumed beforehand that a greater divergence, by provoking greater interaction and greater effort to arrive at a consensus, would cause a more pronounced shift towards the dominant pole.

What does this experiment teach us? Merely that the polarization varies directly with the diversity of positions in the 'square' arrangement, where the discussion is more lively and direct, and the object of discussion is more concrete. On the contrary, in the 'alignment' arrangement the group members take a less active part in the discussions, which are less spontaneous, on a problem that seems to them to be more abstract. If, for all groups, in the first case ('square') the participation is spontaneous, it seems more or less normalized in the second case ('alignment'): thus, those in the first case polarize and in the second make more compromises, as if they were applying more or less rigorously implicit rules.

It may be supposed that in a 'warm' environment favouring exchanges, in which individuals participated more intensely, group pressure would be exercised more strongly than in a 'cold' environment. Individuals would be able to involve themselves, throwing themselves into discussion more wholeheartedly; afterwards, as in a mass meeting, they would try to reassert their independence by reverting to their original position or private opinion. In order to assess this difference in group pressure Moscovici and Lécuyer asked the subjects to record their private response after the discussion of *each item*, and not, as was normally done, after all had been discussed. They wanted in this way to reinforce the individuality of each participant. If the hypothesis was true, in the 'square' arrangement, where the pressure was clearly stronger, the subjects would tend to shift away from the group consensus. It would not be the same for the 'alignment' arrangement. And this is indeed what happened. The result confirms what can be observed in people who ask to participate in a discussion. After a certain time, they feel exhausted and oppressed, they wish to withdraw; it is as if they cannot breathe in the heated atmosphere. We may compare this fact with the cyclical character of social relationships, in which one passes from one state of participation to another one. Thus in the laboratory one can observe on a small scale what happens on many occasions in the real dimension, and on the streets.

The results produced through this experiment hold our attention for yet another reason. They reveal that certain aspects of a situation that bear no relationship to one another, such as the dimensions of a room and the decisions taken in it, that is, aspects deemed to be ancillary and which apparently should not be significant, may in reality be determining factors.[4] In other words, what one considers to be a factor of the world external to social relationships has indeed an action within them. Lemaine very adroitly noticed this in another context:

> What is remarkable is that social relations that have no connexion with the task performed have an effect on the dependent variable, that is to say the judgements of perception by the subjects. This influence of relations in or between groups on activities of a quasi-cognitive nature (judgements of stimuli) seems to us to be of great theoretical importance. . . . In any case this is a phenomenon which takes us right to the heart of social psychology: in what way do changes in relation to someone affect the subjects' relations to the external world? (1975: 94)

This could not be put more clearly.

3

However, these relationships may not be due to the warm or cold nature of the spatial arrangement, but quite simply to the difficulty participants experience in easily seeing one another. When we learn of the privileged position that certain psychologists ascribe to the face-to-face situation, a reasonable doubt might subsist about the role of space in the creation of an atmosphere influencing the manner of participation and the consensus flowing from it. Lécuyer (1974) dispelled this doubt by installing his subjects face to face on two sides of a rectangular table. But in one situation the table was placed in a large lecture theatre with 250 seats, and in the other in a small room holding thirty people. As often occurs, the mode of communication remained the same, and only the space gave rise to a warm or cold atmosphere. Reasoning by analogy, it can be predicted that consensus will tend to be less extreme in the large room than in the smaller one. This is effectively what was observed, including the fact that, following on from what we noted in the preceding study, a greater number of participants returned to their initial individual position in a 'warm' atmosphere than in a 'cold' one, although the difference was not so marked. What can one say about this save that, feeling himself carried along too far by the favourable atmosphere of the discussion, each individual seemed to want to recoil and recover a certain degree of autonomy?

From this series of observations it is tempting to conclude that the forms of communication affect the consensus obtained. It is as if, unbeknown to individuals, the social and physical space, apparently a matter of pure utility, predisposed them to polarize or arrive at a compromise. It is likewise interesting to note that by opting for one or other arrangement of the chairs, table shape or size of room, a group chooses the outcome of its deliberations. The tendency for consensus to emerge can already be discerned in the way the areas are laid out, just as from body posture one can occasionally divine whether the words coming out of a person's mouth will be friendly or hostile.

Given the close correspondence that exists between, on the one hand, a warm or cold atmosphere and, on the other, formal or informal relationships, it is not surprising to find that a researcher was tempted to forecast identical, or almost identical, results in an experiment contrasting the results of formal and informal discussion. Forgas (1981), the British social psychologist, asked groups to find solutions to various problems of everyday life. He drew his scenarios from the well-known questionnaires on risk-taking, but had the ingenious idea of appending to them a final paragraph indicating what solution the protagonist adopted and what the outcome was. For example, A, an electrical engineer, had the choice between a better paid job with a 'risky' firm and the secure employment that he already enjoyed. Four outcomes were possible. A decides to accept (reject) the offer of new employment. Six months later he realizes that he has made the good (bad) choice. The new firm prospers (goes bankrupt), and A becomes a partner with a much higher salary (loses his job). The different variants of the story were brought together in random order in a questionnaire booklet which included a solution for each variant: A took the risk and it came off; he took the risk and it failed to come off; he took the prudent option and it paid off; he took the prudent option, with disastrous results. Each participant, of course, judged each story, suggesting one single solution.

As usual, the subjects had to give their opinion and their interpretation of the scenario on a fifteen-point scale. They indicated whether the protagonist was responsible for the outcome, what view they took of it, and whether they would have made the same choice, or, again, had to evaluate the situation in which he took his decision; the level of risk, its unforeseen nature, etc. Moreover, the experiment proceeded roughly along the usual lines. After the participants had been informed that it was a study in decision-making, they were asked to respond separately to the various scaled questions after they had read the version of the scenario that was put forward. Then, meeting in groups of three or four, they discussed the same version and had to arrive at unanimous agreement at a decision in each case, using the scales described. For some, the discussion proceeded on an informal basis: they were encouraged to argue as openly as possible, taking all the time they needed to arrive at a consensus, while ensuring that each participant had the possibility of making a contribution. For the rest, the discussion proceeded on a formal basis: the group members were instructed to observe carefully the procedure adopted, not to exceed the time allowed (five minutes per scenario), and so far as possible to stick to a formal style of discussion.

Forgas predicted, as might be expected, that the groups would polarize more after an informal discussion than after a formal one. The tendency was still more marked in those scenarios where the protagonist made risky choices in which he was successful. The results certainly confirmed this. Groups were more extreme than individuals when it was a question of attributing responsibility to the protagonist, but only in the case where they were invited to interact openly and not formally. Where they had to argue in a formal, more disciplined way a tendency to compromise and moderation was detected. This short summary of the observations shows, moreover, that groups who participated fully in arriving at a consensus had a much better opinion of the protagonist who 'chose' a bold solution and attributed more merit to him. The reasons for this are not clearly apparent. By contrast, groups constrained to adopt procedural forms and time limitations also concluded their deliberations in this respect by a compromise.

Although the experiment carries conviction, a further word seems necessary. If we visualize its practical aspect, we can understand even better why committees, conferences and business meetings where decisions are taken as a group choose beforehand the decor, the rules of debate, time limits and style of relationships that will exercise an influence on the outcome of the discussion. One acts as if this framework designed for the decision were merely a means, a material and external aspect, carrying little weight as regards the conclusion adopted. Since for the majority the essential condition is not the manner of participating but the interests of the participants and the information they have available, what is important may not be to know their relationship with one another, but only that this exists. Now, this is clearly incorrect. The manner of participating and the style of relationship lead to polarization or to greater moderation by the group members. The significance of this conclusion must, however, be qualified: not everything depends upon it. For example, the fractions of groups when divided do not behave as united groups. The very size of the group plays a part. A study by the British social psychologists Stephenson and Brotherton has brought this out. They followed minutely the way in which supervisory groups of the National Coal Board arrived at their decisions and summed up their results as follows:

> Group involvement varies consistently with the size of the groups. Two-person groups had difficulty lasting out the full thirty minutes of discussion time allowed. Our recordings show that in terms of the acts exchanged, the rate of interaction was higher in the four-person groups, and that more diverse statements were made. In particular, the four-person groups evoked more statements about the other persons in the group, and these were more likely to be of an evaluative kind. Two-person groups were superficially more businesslike, seeing their job as one of seeking agreement in the shortest possible time. These groups concentrated their energies on procedural matters, and the business of proposing 'outcomes' for acceptance by the other. Given agreement, two persons will as solemnly unite, by *compromise*, and thereby come to hold less extreme attitudes at the end. Maybe the principal concern in two-person groups is to avoid the embarrassment of open conflict. Conflict challenges the intimacy engendered in the two-person groups. (1975: 250, emphasis in original)

Thus is depicted in vivid colours the reality that our theory attempts to encompass. We can clearly see the way in which people are involved in the decisions they have to take, how conflicts between them arise and how they settle them. Even so, the groups must be large enough for there to be a space in which differences can be expressed and the exchange of arguments about them can take place. It is true that the shift towards an extreme position is determined by the extent of these divergences, but on condition that the relationships between group members allow them to be debated and then reduced. What is most astonishing may well be the remark by our British colleagues that, in many cases, two people behave more formally than does a group of four or five. Is this the method which pairs of individuals employ to avoid conflicts that might get out of all control, and, lacking any outside witness or mediator, run the risk of being transformed into a duelling contest? Or does the true group only exist when there are three persons or more, so that the opposition between formal and informal relationships has a meaning producing the required effect? Whatever the answer to this, one is always struck by the riddles that lie concealed beneath the most ordinary human relationships as soon as they are minutely observed. This is why, in this field more than in any other, it is preferable to avoid snap conclusions.

4

Can one neglect the style of communication, when one seeks to explain decisions leading to consensus by starting from the psychology of the individuals that take them? According to a theory that had its moment of fame before the theory of polarization was discovered (Brown, 1965; Clark, 1971), to take risks in our Western culture, and above all in its North American variant, constitutes a higher value. Each individual is aware of it when he is asked to choose or to make up his mind alone. This is why he opts for extreme and risky alternatives. Coming together in a group, some are surprised to learn that the alternatives chosen by others are even more extreme, that is, even more rash. The former have therefore been in error, inasmuch as they have not gone far enough. They are like philanthropists who, having each decided separately to give a sum of money they considered generous, when they come together perceive that the sum by no means comes up to that offered by others. They will therefore revise their judgement and adopt a more extreme alternative or a more audacious position in order to fall in line with everybody else. It is of no importance whether they are intent on saving their face or feel good by showing themselves equal to the circumstances; or whether they fear to deviate and be despised by the others by being too prudent and timorous. Either of these motives has the same effect: by seeking to be like the others, each individual finds himself at one again with the rest, in a position that bears greater risk.

According to this theory, one can discern that the main point is the comparison between individuals, and not the confrontation of their opinions, arguments or convictions. Just as in a society that values everything in monetary terms, to ask 'what an object is worth?' does not mean assessing it according to some intrinsic quality it possesses, such as its solidity or beauty, but to evaluate it in relation to other objects of the same kind on the market and to assign a price to it. The question 'What is it worth?' is to be understood as 'How much does it cost?', 'Is it cheap or dear?' One does not think of the intrinsic value of what one is wanting, of the article of clothing that one desires, or the friend whom one admires, but of the garment or friend that or who has more or less value than others. Following this line of thought, Brown established at the outset that 'The content of discussion, arguments pro and con are of no importance by this theory. It is the information about people's answers that makes individuals move towards risk after the discussion' (1965: 702).

In other words the discussion does not revolve round the intrinsic nature of the value; there is no agreement on the choice of boldness or prudence, severity or clemency. The discussion hinges on the values of individuals and one reaches agreement on the specific point of learning whether they are more or less audacious, more or less merciful. It is on this basis that a common position is adopted. We can be really grateful to Brown for having discriminated so precisely between value as an ideal shared by human society, and value as a measure of people, which places them according to their relationship to others.

On the other hand, we are not sure that we can appreciate with any exactness the consequences of this distinction. Does it not involve imitation rather than comparison? Imitation of the leader, if you like, since group members line up in accordance with the position of the person ranked first among them. Moreover, the group has little importance and its norms hardly count. It is, up to a certain point, the mirror through which individuals see themselves, and, depending on the image it sends back to them, they adjust themselves to the others. The enduring nature of this point of view remains a mystery, or, at the very least, a curiosity.

On the other hand, this distinction between exchanges on the actual content of opinions and exchanges on the positions of each individual presupposes that some form of communication has been laid down. It is even an exemplar of certain codes of politeness and rituals of lifestyles. In the end, it exists wherever one wishes to avoid argument in depth, or controversies on the real problems, in order either not to poison relationships or not to commit oneself more than is appropriate. In this case, which according to Brown is typical, we should expect an emphasis on extremism and risk-taking; our own hypotheses, on the contrary, rather predict a compromise, since those participating do so with reservations and avoid becoming embroiled when votes are counted without first demanding everyone's opinion.

Putting such partial communication to the test, groups were invited to engage in a discussion for or against a subject, but without their initial positions being revealed. What was the result of this discussion? There was a shift as considerable as that noted in a typical situation of total communication (Clark et al., 1971; Myers et al., 1971). By contrast, no shift was noted in relation to items that had not been discussed. According to the authors of the experiment, the shift towards risk took place because 'individuals are culturally disposed to generate and favour risk argument when considering risky dilemmas in detail' (Madaras and Bem, 1968: 360).

None of these researchers, however, considered the rules that define these two kinds of exchange. We therefore set up an experiment (Moscovici, Doise and Dulong, 1972) the findings of which could reproduce both kinds at the same time. Students were brought together in groups of four and we proposed that they discuss dilemmas of choice on subjects by now familiar to the reader, and then arrive at an agreement on one of the solutions. Under one condition, we warmly encouraged them to discuss as fully as they wished until they agreed on a common position. Under the other condition, we asked them to pay heed to the procedure whereby they arrived at a consensus, and their respective positions. At the end of each discussion of a dilemma, one member of the group, taking it in turns, recorded the minutes of the discussion as would a rapporteur of any working session of a body. These minutes threw light on the way in which the group arrived at its decision. In all groups the time for discussion was limited to seven minutes per question, without this being given as a formal instruction. The exchanges related, on the one hand, to the positions adopted by each individual and, on the other, to the opinions and arguments that justified them. The exchanges concerning positions were most frequently included in the exchanges concerning opinions, and both likewise contributed to the common decision. Depending on the circumstances, one or the other carried more weight. We assume that methods of procedure have the effect of giving more importance to exchanges referring to positions. By contrast, 'spontaneous' decisions facilitate the exchange of opinions and arguments.

In the case where different opinions can be freely expressed, discussion allows each individual better to defend his own viewpoint and to become more involved in the activity of the group. Thus we expected that the consensus would stress the dominant tendency among its members – in short, be polarized. On the other hand, when the participants placed a distance between one another and paid attention to the manner in which they arrived at a decision, their attention was concentrated upon positional differences. The discussion of the latter could not involve them greatly. Moreover, they had no means of justifying or forcibly making their position prevail, and thus were thrown back on resolving their differences by a compromise. This is indeed what we observed. Consequently attention to rules of procedure, which direct discussion towards information regarding the responses, leads towards a decision of 'the just mean'. Discussion directed towards content produces the opposite effect.

Such a result may be said to have a bearing only on a special case and a procedural rule whose meaning remains tenuous. Let us then take a second rule, no less frequent in society, but more precise, that of duration of time. In the second experiment the participants, likewise meeting in groups of four, were split up according to two conditions. In the first, no instruction was given beforehand limiting the amount of time prescribed to discuss a dilemma. However, when the discussion had lasted six minutes, the experimenter intervened to suggest they arrive at a decision within the next minute. Under the other condition, he informed the participants at the outset that they had only seven minutes to arrive at an agreement. He checked the time with a stop-watch so that all could see, and intervened when six minutes of the time for discussion had elapsed. So that the participants bore in mind the time allocated for discussion, they were invited to remind the experimenter, at the beginning of the discussion of each topic, to set his stop-watch back to zero. In fact most of the groups did not take seven minutes to arrive at their decision. Thus it was a question not so much of a physical constraint as of a socio-psychological one. It is one that functions as a principle of order in all juries, committees, meetings, negotiations and parliaments where such a time limit is imposed. We naturally expected that, under the first condition, the groups would tend to polarize, and, under the second, to make compromises. And in fact this is what happened.

Before leaving this subject we may point out that to limit the time is

Table 6.1   *Average time used by the groups to arrive at consensus*

	No time limitation	With time limitation
Divided groups	5 mins 1 sec.	2 mins 44 sec.
Unified groups	1 min. 59 sec.	2 mins 0 sec.

equivalent to enunciating a rule that in reality limits the possibilities of bringing out the differences in viewpoints, and the conflicts. We were able to verify this as follows. In this experiment the scale was conceived in such a way that it allowed us to separate out the divided groups so that their members were distributed on one side or the other of the neutral point, whereas the unified groups had a majority of members situated on one side, either positive or negative, of the neutral point. Let us suppose, as is naturally the case, that the clash of opinions is sharper, the differences more accentuated, in the divided groups than in the unified groups. Next, we compared the amount of time actually used to resolve the conflicts and to take a common decision, first in the groups who had been instructed not to exceed a certain period of time, and then in those who had received no such instruction. Table 6.1 shows the difference. It is as if the former had abstained from a discussion, which of necessity is longer, on the content of the option, and limited themselves to choosing one outcome among the positions adopted among them. In this way, whether divided into opposing factions or having a majority, they took practically the same amount of time to overcome their divisions and arrive at a compromise. This was not the case for groups that decided with no time limitation. It is striking to see that, in this situation, the divided groups took twice as long to resolve their differences than those where a majority appertained. One can well believe that they probed deeply into the opposing alternatives and expounded their opinions in some detail before reaching agreement.

Re-reading these experiments some fifteen years after they were carried out, they seem to us still to illustrate the dual dynamic process inherent in collective decisions. They show to what extent divergence in the positions expressed provides the energy to effect changes. But these changes are regulated by the relationships between the individuals who are confronting one another, inclining them towards agreement, either one of compromise, or one of extremism. Meanwhile on several occasions the underlying hypothesis has received additional support. Let us consider the series of experiments carried out in Germany by Trommsdorff (1982) which centred on the theme of judgements relating to the future, and the waves of optimism or pessimism that sweep through our culture. More precisely, from a standpoint close to our own, the German social psychologist posed the question of finding out how individuals utilize, either individually or in the group, the information they receive. The question is knotty, but the experimental method followed was the usual one. It consisted of a discussion revolving round the degree of probability of a certain number of events occurring in the relatively near future, for example whether the Arabs and Israelis will live in peace with one another, whether the participant will make a journey round the world, etc. In accordance with the usual procedure the experimenter sounded out the attitudes of the participants at the beginning and the end of the meeting. In the meantime, they discussed the probability that the events mentioned would happen, or enunciated separately the arguments backing the likelihood that each event would take place.

Nor was this all. In order to vary the manner in which they had to treat the information, the researcher distinguished between two conditions. Under the first condition, she let the groups discuss how they liked, or let individuals write down the arguments justifying the chances that these events would occur before the year 2000. Under the second condition, she asked them, as individuals and as groups, to note down systematically in advance the circumstances of these events, the obstacles to their realization, etc. It was exactly like the way in which we prepare an agenda and the priorities for any committee on which we may be serving.

Among the very numerous results that agreed with one another it may be noted that, under the first condition, agreement was reached on the more extreme judgements, while under the second condition, the latter were close to the individual judgements. In two out of three experiments those groups that had to deal with information according to a set method, following directions, took compromise decisions. By contrast, with groups who could deal with the information without being subject to any constraints, the decisions were more extreme than the individual decisions. In principle we have here a confirmation of what we had always supposed to be the case: a normalized form of participation, which involves individuals less, leads to a moderate decision.

That the observations are not always as consistent as one might wish will surprise nobody, given the vulnerability of the methods and the complexity of social facts. The sole course to follow consists in tackling them from a different angle. We have already mentioned the outstanding experiments of Forgas in Australia. He tried to test our hypothesis in a different way. With great care he prepared new experimental material and asked nine actors to indulge in a conversation and to represent different characters, giving very varied answers about their family, religious and social origins, on their conception of life and the preferences of the character they had adopted. This conversation, filmed on video, was assessed by some thirty subjects using the characteristics they deemed most appropriate. From an analysis of these spontaneous descriptions, twelve bipolar scales (sincere/hypocritical, happy/unhappy, intelligent/stupid, rational/emotional, etc.) were formed and verified with some sixty other subjects. At the end of these operations, Forgas retained for his study four conversations and seven scales. He added to these four expressions of attitudes: 'I like this character (I detest him) – I would ask (I would not ask) his opinion on an important matter – I would (I would not) hire him as an employee – I think that he would be capable

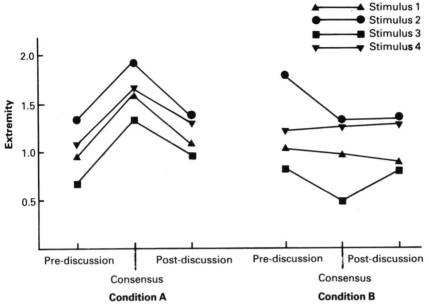

Figure 6.2   *Mean opinion shifts in conditions (a) and (b)*

(incapable) of committing a crime.' All these responses were given on a nine-point scale.

The way the experiment was carried out followed the well-known procedure. First the participants looked at the four recorded conversations and afterwards each filled in individually the questionnaire. Meeting in groups of three, they then viewed again the four conversations and replied as a group to the questionnaire appended to each one. This occurred under two experimental conditions. A. *Free discussion* – the experimenter insisted on the spontaneous nature of the discussion: 'You are completely free to discuss any subject of the conversation.' B. *Procedure* – the two constraints of our own experiments were made more rigorous: 'Try to observe carefully the processes of decision-taking within your group. You have only ten minutes available to complete your task.'

The results showed that, under both conditions, the groups used a comparable period of time. The hypothesis was confirmed insofar as the consensus, for each conversation, tended to be more extreme when the participants discussed with no constraints (see Figure 6.2). By contrast, where they followed a procedure they tended to be less extreme after they had discussed together. The fact that our own results were confirmed when different and richer material was used is worthy of note. This is particularly because the situation studied by Forgas was, because of its complexity, closer to real life. We commonly have to judge people, for example in juries, round table discussions, class meetings, therapeutic groups, etc. The judgements we formulate are often more extreme than those that individuals would make separately. Forgas, like us, bears this out:

> Group polarization is more likely to occur in situations where open opinion exchange is encouraged, procedural rules are at a minimum, and group members are not influenced by implicit or explicit restraints. Such a mode of interaction, bearing practical situations in mind, is more likely to prevail when (a) group members are of equal status, (b) previously acquainted with others, (c) mutually dependent, (d) sharing a common frame of reference, and (e) having a positive attitude toward each other. It is perhaps reassuring to find that such conditions are unlikely to be characteristic of formal decision-making groups in organizations. (1977: 184)

One can only concur with these remarks. They formulate the goal we have pursued throughout these studies: to identify two or three elements in any organization and demonstrate their impact on decision-making. In this respect what at first sight appears to be a neutral factor, or even a purely extraneous one, seems essential. Further confirmation is found in a study that appears at first sight to be very remote from our own. It is that of Kelly and McGrath (1985), who were interested in the relationship between actual performance and the interactive style within the group. Starting from a similar hypothesis, the researchers considered that if the group were working under a stringent time constraint, it would choose a less than adequate procedure to carry out its task. Moreover, the researchers assumed that a group which had first carried out its task without a strict time constraint would continue to apply a method more appropriate for carrying out subsequent tasks when this time constraint was tightened. On the contrary, a group that had begun under what, after all, was a rather unfavourable constraint would retain its less appropriate method, even if this constraint was relaxed and conditions became more favourable.

To verify these hypotheses Kelly and McGrath set students of the University of Illinois to work in groups of four. They had to carry out two successive tasks, the first in ten minutes, the second in twenty minutes, for half the groups. For the other half, the times were reversed: first twenty, and then ten minutes. The tasks were very varied: production (for example, to string together in a coherent story extracts from children's tales); discussion (for example, what is necessary to succeed in our culture?); planning (for example, plan an anti-tobacco campaign for the government). The study provided an abundance of rich data; those which interest us are singled out here. For the first working sessions the impact of the time constraint was very clear. Groups that had ten minutes to carry out their task provided 'products' that were shorter ($p < .001$) and less original ($p < .0001$) than those allocated twenty minutes of working time. Constraint also had qualitative consequences. These differences proved weaker at the second session, but continued to subsist for length ($p < .001$) and creativity ($p < .01$) for the products of the second groups, even with more time available. It seems in fact that to have begun to work under favourable conditions as regards time maintained the quality of the performance, even in conditions that had grown less favourable, and vice versa.

These differences can be explained by the interactions that were observed. In the first task, carried out in ten minutes, relatively fewer interventions among the members of the group were made relating to points of agreement and disagreement, few positive or negative judgements were passed on one another, and there were more frequent silences. On the contrary, in those groups which had twenty minutes available for the first task, interventions relating to agreement or disagreement, and positive or negative judgements on participants, were both more numerous, and the silences less frequent. It was noted that once a style of interaction had been adopted, it was carried over to the second session, although the time limits had changed. It is true that the authors of the study were not concerned with the decision phenomenon. But their data illustrate the fact that in cases where the time constraint was strong, it was as if people avoided confronting one another or taking notice of disagreements. Consequently participation was less intense. Thus one arrived at cognitive activity that was less fruitful in relation to a situation where this confrontation and these mutual influences exerted between individuals were not impeded.

Whatever the circumstances, the difference between the two modes of participating explains and anticipates the decisions that lead either to an 'extreme' consensus or to a moderate one. In the former, the debate dealt with the content of the views expressed, stimulated the exchange of arguments between group members and involved them all. In the latter, the normalized discussion followed rules that toned down the exchanges and directed them towards an awareness of the position of each single member, who consequently was involved to a limited extent. In both there were observed conflicts sparked off by procedures and time limitations that forced participants to exercise greater restraint and maintain a greater distance between one another. It is true that what astonishes one person causes another to retort 'So what?' But one cannot fail to be astonished at the regular character of these observations and their underlying meaning. Why should one fix rules of procedure and duration if it is not apparently to guarantee greater rationality in the discussions? Rules diminish conflicts, carry with them a method and ensure a settled distance in relation to the object of discussion; in short, they have everything that allows one to judge after mature reflection and without bad temper. Yet these rules direct the participants' attention to their respective positions and divert attention from the object of the discussion. The rules make them more sensitive to how they observe the procedure than to the significance of the information imparted and the alternatives available, which have to be examined in every light. Thus we note a paradoxical effect. Spontaneity allows group members to turn away from their own concerns, to go to the very limit of an argument and in the end to focus on the object of discussion. Rules divert them from the object, since this is a cause of conflict, restrict the examination of the arguments and finally turn each individual's attention towards his fellows in order to learn their positions and to make comparisons. Practically everything inclines us to believe that the decisions leading to consensus are all the more subjective when the rules are more strictly obeyed. On the contrary, the more the decisions are free a priori from rules, the more chance these decisions have of becoming objective. One would hesitate to say that this truth was borne out experimentally, but it is not far removed from it.

Hierarchy and behavioural style

Thus the psychological law on which we can rely with every confidence is that people are all the more disposed to compromise when their attention is diverted from the problem to be solved, turning it away from the ends to the means. Moreover, it is on this that a hierarchy relies, which limits differences, imposes rules and forces people to agree for its own benefit. At its lowest level, the group's members are equal and communicate with one another without any restrictions, as can be seen when for an 'anthropomorphic' group is substituted an 'electronic' group linked up by a computer network that each member can use as he thinks fit. Although physically at a distance from one another, the group members feel close, and have a precise image of one another without being able to see one another; although isolated, they are participants belonging to the same entity.

Within a few seconds a message reaches the one for whom it was intended, without having to take into account time zones, geography and local customs. Exchanges are facilitated, as they are occasionally over the telephone, because the speakers are encouraged to express matters that they do not like to say face to face, and do not feel held back by a gesture, by mimicry or a mood reaction. Failures are attributed to background noise, misunderstandings to the question of distance. Thus an intimate communication, conducted at a distance, abolishes all the signs that indicate a hierarchy – clothes, social attitudes, authoritarian postures, etc. This brings about consequences that were recorded in the work of Kiesler (1987), an American social psychologist from the University of Pittsburgh. Persons communicating through a network feel less the differences in rank and organizational pressures, and express themselves more freely. They participate very intensively – as demonstrated by the number of contacts and sources of information used – and more easily, without having to take into account any limitations other than physical ones. For all these reasons, one can understand why electronic groups tend to take decisions that are more extreme than those of anthropomorphic groups. The short cut provided by technology, it is no exaggeration to say, gives us the satisfaction of seeing that science and science fiction follow the same hypothesis.

By introducing a hierarchy the reverse consequences are naturally to be expected. From the very first studies on decision-making, social psychologists established that decisions depended on the ideas and arguments of a leader. Convinced himself, and persuasive, he is able to incite others to follow him, no matter what stance he has chosen. More precisely, this theory of leadership maintains that persons taking high risks and who are sure about their choices exert more influence during the discussion, causing their extreme, rash options to be accepted. In the end polarization is therefore explained by the presence in the group of one of those dominant personalities who flaunt their radical opinions and values. They persuade the majority to settle for an agreement on a solution from which they would otherwise shrink. This theory has undergone a series of vicissitudes, without, however, provoking really interesting research studies.[5] It could hardly be otherwise, if leadership is defined as a personal character trait, and not as a mode of social relationship. The statement has been made: 'Thus, a unique feature of leadership interpretation is to lay stress upon the personality factors as determinant of the risky shift effect' (Dion et al., 1971: 327). That is to say, certain individuals take risks and are capable of winning over their more prudent colleagues, so that they become their leaders.

Let us now change the perspective and envision leadership as a relationship of dependency and authority in a collective organization. Undeniably it rests on the behavioural style of superiors towards their subordinates, a style that encourages or discourages their being able to take part in decisions. Simplifying matters, it should be expected that where the conduct of leaders increases the level of participation, the polarization phenomenon is observed. Where the behaviour discourages participation, the tendency will be towards compromise. Whatever our reservations on the value of these predictions, we must acknowledge that the small number of experiments that have been carried out yield positive signs that this is the case.

We may begin with a study showing that the presence of a leader makes group members more prudent in their decisions and curbs their boldness. After the Second World War, since public curiosity on the subject was great, Ziller (1957) undertook a series of studies relating to the effect of the organization of groups on their capacity to solve problems. In all the situations participants had to imagine that they were members of a wartime bomber crew who had to make choices. Either they had to try to save themselves by landing on an uninviting stretch of ice six kilometres long, and whose thickness was unknown; or they might try to reach a village situated on the coast, at double the distance, running the risk of being captured by the enemy.

The experimenter compared the decisions under four conditions: (a) the bomber's captain took the decision without any group discussion; (b) he announced openly his position after having thought over the problem and then launched into a discussion with the group; (c) the crew discussed the problem straight away, with the captain chairing the discussion but only giving his opinion afterwards; (d) as in (c), save that the captain did not voice his opinion at all or adopt any position. We therefore observe a progressive disappearance of any hierarchy and an increasing possibility for the crew to participate and choose entirely freely the solution it judges to be best.

Correspondingly, it can be noted that in an organization revolving round the leader, the choice is less decisive (the two alternatives were chosen equally) than in organizations revolving round the group, in which 80 per cent of its members opted for landing on the ice. This was the more risky solution, one leading to certain death if the ice was too thin. Moreover, the members of those groups who took their decision entirely freely were more satisfied with their worrying choice than those of the groups covered by an officer's authority.

A prime example that comes to mind is, once more, linked to the celebrated research studies by Lewin, Lippitt and White (1938). They showed that the social environment and performance in groups of children varied according to the behavioural style of the leader who was directing them. When it was authoritarian, the group worked harder, but its members showed themselves to be more aggressive and their attitude towards the task in hand reflected a latent resistance. When the leader was democratic, the groups were more creative, their originality was revealed, and they were more inclined to work spontaneously. When the leader was of the 'laissez-faire' type, the group worked less and its work was of uneven quality. We know, moreover, that leaders who take part in the activity of the group are more effective than those who content themselves with supervising it (Preston and Heinz, 1949).

More recently exploration has begun of the relationship between behavioural style and the nature of decisions. Flowers (1977), for instance, instructed certain groups to work under an open type of leader, who allowed them to express the most diverse opinions in order to arrive at a reasoned decision. Others, on the contrary, were invited to arrive at a unanimous decision at all costs, which comes down to adopting the leader's own imposed solution. It would appear that the former sought information more diligently and put forward a greater variety of solutions than did the latter groups. This did not mean that the first groups felt themselves freer to do so than did the other ones, for neither felt they were undergoing pressure exercised by their leader.

It is true that one has long wondered why, if the feeling that one is free plays no part, the style of the leader who does not impose his opinion, invoke arguments based on his authority, or come down on one side, that is, is 'open', has a positive effect on the quality of the solutions chosen. The sole answer one can give is that he enhances the level of participation of group members. Hence he adds value to the discussion, in the course of which the various viewpoints have an opportunity of being expressed. In particular, he protects the minority from the pressure of a majority wishing to silence it and impose a solution, a verdict, etc. which all will acknowledge. By his action the leader sparks off arguments[6] and confrontations that force the alternatives proposed on all sides to be considered with roughly equal attention. Observations show that such an 'open' leader in fact checks the group from sliding down the natural slope to conformity, in what is called 'groupthink', acting like sheep. Moreover, he encourages the consideration of dissentient or innovatory ideas. In short, the leader attempts to obtain a consensus to which both the minority and the majority contribute. Since this contribution by a dissenting minority depends 'upon the function of a leader, this aspect of the leader becomes an important leadership function and it constitutes a positive contribution that a leader can make to improve the quality of a group's thinking' (Maier and Solem, 1952: 286). Or, we should add, it completes a common agreement that is at the same time more extreme.

This is indeed the case, as it turns out, in a remarkable study by Wehman and his colleagues (1977), comparing the effects of three styles of behaviour by leaders, ranging from the most authoritarian to the most laissez-faire, relating to the degree to which a group's decisions polarize. Employing the usual material on risk-taking, they put forward dilemmas for discussion by groups made up of four 'simple' participants and a confederate put in by the experimenter. The latter acted as leader but received very strict instructions not to try to influence the others either towards risk-taking or towards prudence. His role was therefore limited to creating a social climate and organizing relationships between group members. There were four conditions. The 'laissez-faire' leader acted as if he were not there. Sometimes his presence proved disconcerting, sometimes it was disregarded. Thus the choices and reactions within the group took place under no constraint. The 'democratic' leader respected the rules and was like a secretary who reminded members that there was a procedure for discussion. According to Lippitt and White (1960), a characteristic of a democratic climate seems indeed to be the choice of and respect for a certain procedure, by common agreement. The 'authoritarian' leader impeded the discussion and the confrontations arising from the viewpoints put forward by members of the group. The fourth condition was that of groups with no leader.

The following hypothesis may be postulated, leading on from this comparison: groups with an authoritarian or democratic leader tend more towards a compromise. Those who have a laissez-faire leader or no leader at all tend to make 'bolder' decisions. The results obtained seem to confirm this conjecture. We note first that the laissez-faire style of behaviour allowed a greater number of risky decisions. The authoritarian or democratic style encouraged decisions that were relatively prudent ($F = 46.69$; $p < .01$). Simplifying, we may state that the authoritarian style is more fitted to circumstances where it is a matter of innovating, and the democratic style to preserving the attitudes or judgements of the group.

The two poles of hierarchy and leadership produce, so it would appear, the same status quo effect. Is this one of the reasons why, like established and permanent groups (Semin and Glendon, 1973), they favour compromises between the various points of view? For the moment we have no means of giving a general reply to this question of a practical order. However, we may note that the idea that leadership is associated with the choice of an extreme, bold decision, because of personal qualities, lacks all foundation. What alone counts is its social aspect, the leader's way of participating and communicating, in brief, of organizing relationships between group members. The example given above is interesting in this respect, affording an opportunity to compare very precisely the characteristics of the relationships brought about by the behavioural style of the respective leaders.

This topic was one to which Jesuino (1986), the Portuguese social psychologist, devoted himself: developing our hypothesis, he sought to set out its consequences in detail. In order to do so, he detailed the conditions and the style that leaders should adopt by giving formal instructions to the members of the different groups. In the first situation, which was plainly a directive one, their task was to arrive at a rapid decision. The leaders had therefore to control the discussion and determine the agenda in the group for which they were responsible. Each member spoke in turn, then a short discussion followed, but again with members taking it in turns to speak. As soon as a majority emerged from a decision, the leader summed up the discussion and requested the group members to come to a definitive decision.

In the consensual situation, the leader and the other participants were invited to intervene as often as possible so that all the arguments put forward could be scrutinized. However, they were not forced to achieve unanimity. With this aim in mind, they were given special instructions. The leader played a role reminiscent of the democratic behaviour described in the classic study by Lewin et al. (1938). Finally, in the 'laissez-faire' situation, a document was given out stipulating that one of the group should serve as coordinator. But he had to restrict himself to contacting the experimenter if any difficulty arose, and not exercise the slightest influence on the members of his group. Our Portuguese colleague publicly designated the leaders who had been chosen in the three situations, selected from those participants judged to be the most suitable to carry out punctiliously the task of leader. Thus, there was no confederate as there had been in the preceding experiment. The material used was nevertheless the same, which therefore allows a comparison to be made. To it were added a certain number of tests on the atmosphere within the group and the interaction among its members.

As was to be expected, under the directive condition, where the participants had rapidly to arrive at a decision, the time taken was comparatively short, at forty-two minutes. By contrast, under the consensual condition, where it was recommended that interactions should be maximized, the time averaged seventy-three minutes. In the groups with no leader, this time came down to thirty-seven minutes, contrary to forecasts that it would increase. Moreover, regarding the decisions, Jesuino obtained results fairly close to those of Wehman and his colleagues in the United States. Generally they were more extreme in groups with no leader than with groups with one (see Figure 6.3), with the exception of those who were led by a laissez-faire leader, where the opposite tendency was observed: the Portuguese groups polarized less than did the American ones. According to Jesuino, this inverse tendency was due to the fact that the leader was perceived by all as having no power and, not being able to rely on him, each

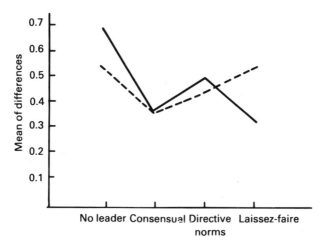

Figure 6.3   *Pre- to post-test difference scores (the broken lines show the results of the Wehman et al. [1977] study)*

individual stood by his own position. The proof is that under this condition roughly one group out of two did not arrive at a consensus, while more than nine out of ten did in the other situations.

The conclusions from this study help us to focus the ideas more clearly. Naturally the main task a leader is called upon to fulfil in ordinary circumstances is to organize the conditions for arriving at a consensus. To do so, he must first have the ability to arbitrate and to decide, and next, the ability to lead a sufficient number of persons dependent on him to approve the decision. Moreover, he must be aware of the style of behaviour adopted when fixing what are called the rules of the game and determining the direction of the consensus, whether towards compromise or polarization. Essentially this relates to the degree of insistence on the prerogatives of a hierarchy and the extent to which conflicts and compromises are permitted. More especially, when routine procedures are set aside and a bare minimum of organization is shown, whether there is a leader or not, the decision that leads towards consensus tends towards the extreme and changes are accentuated. Beyond this, vacillation can be observed, with a clear propensity of groups to become moderate.

It is here that the difference appears between the two forms of participation, the one illustrated by the exchanges and ties between individuals within an organized framework, the other characterized by the direct and fluid nature of the relationships between them. Each form of participation appears to involve them to an unequal extent;[7] less for the former, more for the latter, thus leading them to take decisions of a specific nature. This is certainly not surprising. The various cultures have devised the institutions that have allowed them to direct the pattern of conflict and influence, depending on the action undertaken. Without being aware of it, those who share in these institutions as members of an assembly, a committee or a jury are induced to come to an agreement, either on a moderate or on an extreme position. They have conceived a rhetoric in relation to the spaces where they meet, the procedures of choice, the time limits prescribed and the behaviour of the leader, a rhetoric that is as clear as the rhetoric of thought and words, all of which combine to determine the outcome even before the problem has been tackled, the information reviewed and the first arguments set out for discussion. Those who take part cannot afford not to pay attention to the laws and limits of this rhetoric. We have tried to highlight some of these. There can be no doubt that even large administrative bodies, firms and unions in the society in which we live respect them, in spite of profound upheavals in technology and the economy.

However this may be, this overall conspectus of the known studies gives an impression that the underlying hypothesis explains the facts. One after another, they show that the nature of the consensus depends on the warmth or coldness of the environment, the hierarchical relationships and the way in which the group organizes the participation of its members.[8] It also depends on what often pass for secondary aspects: the room in which a group meets, the role of the chairman, the choice of the agenda, the turn to speak, etc. appear to fashion the outcome of the decision. For the time being, we have only laid down markers in an extensive field. At this stage the conclusions still remain open. But they could or should be integrated into a more general conspectus.

Notes

1 Researchers in Latin America who devote themselves to literacy, to community psychology, and to social movements have stored up a rich experience relating to the phenomena of participation. They have also published very important studies that rightly deserve to be summarized, instead of occasionally being the object of a covert allusion.

2 The study of political movements and public controversies about nuclear energy, organ transplants, etc. has highlighted the decisive role played by what British sociologists call the 'participating impulse' (Nelkin, 1979).

3 It might also be thought that in a warm space decisions take on a more public character and commit one more than in a cold space. Several remarkable studies with simulated juries demonstrate that there are more changes of opinion in public deliberations than in private ones. What is more, the participants are more confident and more assured. This subjective reaction is perhaps due to a greater 'investment in the interaction of the individual' (Davis et al., 1976), a public situation and a change in preferences (Stasser and Davis, 1977). Then again, it may be due to the fact that members are inspired with greater confidence in the collective decision when they are induced to commit themselves (Castore and Murningham, 1978). All these interpretations are very close to one another and emphasize particular facets of the process as a whole.

4 One of the least well-known aspects, yet one very important in teaching, is that of pedagogical 'space'. Communication between students and teachers depends upon it, as the studies by Guyot (1970) have shown.

5 Since the time that Marquis (1962) put forward the theory it has been alternately confirmed (Rabow et al., 1966) and denied (Hoyt and Stoner, 1968). A discussion of the question in depth is to be found in Clark (1971), Petrullo and Bass (1961) and Vroom and Yetton (1973).

6 Uli Windisch (1987) has written an excellent little book on the sociological value of the polemic and its cognitive consequences.

7 On the importance of involvement in agreements within organizations, very closely related considerations are to be found in Arrow (1974).

8 The studies we have reviewed arrive at parallel results to those concerning simulated juries and the creativity of groups (Steiner, 1972; Strodtbeck et al., 1957; Vinokur et al., 1985).

7

Consensus in Closed and Open Groups

Decisions taken with rival groups

1

Clearly no group is ever alone. All that it does is done under the gaze of other groups, some friendly, the majority hostile. They form a closely-knit environment similar to that of a family surrounded by other families in an apartment block located in one town which is one among many, in one nation among other nations, on a continent. It follows that the manner in which each group judges, chooses and conducts itself is determined in relation to this environment. At the beginning of this book we paid tribute to the 'accuracy' of the decisions taken at the highest level by the American President's advisers, and to the measures that were recommended to him by these committees at the time of the attack on Pearl Harbor, the invasion of Cuba and in other crisis situations. They were certainly biased by a combination of career considerations and esprit de corps. But it would be wrong to underestimate, as has been done, the role played by patriotism, the hostility towards the Japanese enemy during the 'hot' war and towards Communist ideology during the years of the Cold War. One may conclude that this conviction of the superiority of the United States as compared with other countries in the world must have weighed heavily in the balance, stifling to silence any dissident views that might have been deemed anti-American, as well as any differences among those who shared in the decisions in general. We instinctively know that, faced with a common adversary, one stands shoulder to shoulder, soft-pedalling quarrels about ideas and persons, and one unites solidly behind shared values in order to assert one's just rights. And the maxim 'My country right or wrong' halts any discussion, seals lips in advance and bans any criticism as being treason.

Merely to set out these facts suffices to express what are the preconditions required for decision-making in the midst of other groups. Norms need to become more apparent, and the common traits whereby group members recognize one another need to become more distinct. A Frenchman feels himself more French among foreigners, closer to his compatriots when he meets them outside his own country, and never finds France more beautiful than when he is far away from it. Naturally any attack directed against his own community, its beliefs and practices arouses a powerful emotional reaction and binds him more to it. We exaggerate our resemblance to those who form part of our community and each one of us conducts himself as if he were its stereotype representative, without being asked to do so. This extreme reaction, aiming to stress cohesion and unity, is inevitable. In it there can be observed a well-known trait, that of mutual identification between individuals and with their social class, city, church or party. It accentuates everything that makes them similar to one another and makes them even more different from those who form part of another class, city, church or party.[1]

Under these conditions there is nothing more striking than to see how the faintest resemblance draws people together, whereas the slightest difference draws them apart. On the other hand, the slightest difference between similar persons is heartbreaking to their nearest and dearest. It is, as it were, as if people were seeking to make themselves distinctive the more identical they are (Moscovici, 1986) by fighting their partners more fiercely than their opponents – for example, the communists attacking more violently the socialists than the right, Catholics attacking more unmercifully Protestants and Jews than atheists, etc. One might say that under love of one's neighbour there broods a hatred of great similarities, which is openly a variety of self-hatred. In this sense the impossibility of agreeing arises from the mute silence and dissimulation which we feel when the characteristics we attribute to others are precisely those we detest in ourselves. This is how one might explain the paradox of the French National Front, a xenophobic movement which recruits the largest number of its battalions in regions where there is the greatest concentration of immigrants. This could just about be understandable were it not for the fact that other, older generations of immigrants have been settled in the area for a century. The population may indeed be very heterogeneous and have had experience of foreigners, but it is precisely this population that in peremptory fashion suffers them less gladly. This is a reaction to be compared to that of the newly converted, who wish to be more French than the French, more royalist than the king. From where does such excessiveness spring if not from a hostility towards these new immigrants who resemble them and present a mirror-image of the way they themselves once were, how they might still be and of what they detest in themselves? It is precisely this balance of contradictory appearances between long-settled immigrants and one hundred per cent Frenchmen which is threatened by the presence of the newcomer, whose strangeness obtrudes. The fear then is that the general population will lump together both the old and the new immigrants, and say to itself that it may have been mistaken about them, that the old ones have not been assimilated and not become true Frenchmen. Herein lies the secret of all xenophobia: identity is not acquired once and for all.

The least that can be said – and this justifies these remarks – is that the socio-cognitive conflict that explains numerous decisions within a group becomes even more marked in relationships with other groups. For, in a group envisioned in isolation, conflict and influence are associated together; they occur between the same individuals and have as their goal the same collective action. But for a group in relation to other groups conflict and influence are dissociated. This is manifest insofar as conflict is directed outside the group, stirring up antagonism and debate with others who are not like we are. Meanwhile influence continues to be exercised mutually between members of a group, and is intensified, with the aim of securing greater uniformity. Room for expansion of both these factors is created by transferring quarrels to outside the group and by seeking to underline identities within it. Conformity is reserved for themselves and conflict is kept for others. The reasoning is not flawed, but is a logical consequence, so that one ends up by thinking in categories, with everything in black or white. The result is that one sees in each individual not himself, but the category to which he belongs: the worker, the Black, the woman, etc. This allows free rein to be given to differences and rivalries, since one is assured that nothing can halt them save the limitations imposed by reality.

Although not systematic, this brief overview showing how a group locates itself among other groups, and how the socio-cognitive conflict becomes dissociated, allows us to formulate the previous hypothesis in slightly different terms. In a situation that intensifies the participation of members in their group and distinguishes it from other groups, decisions leading to consensus tend still more to the dominant pole of its scale of values, to the exclusion of all others. Prudence in this matter is nevertheless justified, for the relationships between groups are very complex and, at the moment, not sufficiently known. In this field, more than in any other, one risks arriving prematurely at a conclusion from case studies, basing oneself more on common sense than on real science.

2

The first studies based upon this hypothesis were carried out in Montparnasse, a quarter of Paris where there are numerous art schools. In one such study Doise (1969b) tried out the following scenario. Let us assume the imaginary presence of another group. This will lead each individual to define his own group in a simplified, distinctive manner – by way of contrast – in the same way as we define Frenchmen by thinking about Germans, and vice versa. Clearly such a contrast leads one very often to employ judgemental categories and extreme attitudes. It may be asserted that the differences between the two groups are in this manner made to stand out and are emphasized. At the same time the identity of the one who is judging becomes clearer. This occurs in two ways. On the one hand, it is normal that, on points where members consider their group superior, after examining the other group's opinions they rank their own group even higher in comparison with it. The converse likewise applies for points on which they judge their group to be inferior. After such a comparison it can be expected that on these points consensus will shift in the direction of the dominant image, sometimes positive, sometimes negative, that students will have of their school.

Moreover, the extremists, those close to the dominant pole, will better express representative opinions and serve as the model when the contrast between the two groups is highlighted. They then exercise a preponderant influence, one which the majority acquiesces in and acknowledges. In short, the extremists are accepted more readily and change the opinions of the majority more when the rival group is evoked. Thus it is hardly surprising that judgements and attitudes are polarized, and that participants adhere to them all the more strongly when at the same time they think of the group to which they are linked in terms of a difference or an opposition that serves as a model or an example not to follow.

This reasoning provided the guideline for an experiment the background for which was X, a school of architecture which, in the minds of its students, rivalled the state École des Beaux-Arts. X, a private school, founded by progressive architects as a reaction against the official tradition, provided its students with a valuable training. However, they did not benefit from the advantages reserved for diploma-holders of the state school, and undoubtedly enjoyed less prestige. Those participating in the study were brought together in groups of four, according to the now familiar procedure. They were first asked to answer individually a questionnaire comprising ten statements, such as 'The private school constitutes an open-minded group', or 'Aesthetic education is neglected at school X.' They gave their replies on a seven-point scale ranging from total agreement to total disagreement.

The experimenter then announced to the participants that he was interested in the opinions that might arise within a group. He therefore invited the members of each group to arrive at a consensus for each item of the questionnaire. They therefore filled in a second questionnaire, identical to the first, in which each one recorded the judgement of the group, and not his own. Finally each individual was invited to note down again, alongside the judgement of the group, his own judgement. These were the conditions under which half the groups worked. The other half received additional instructions. When they filled in the second questionnaire participants were requested to enter also the judgement they assumed would be that of students from the École des Beaux-Arts. More exactly, they were requested to indicate the reaction they presumed would be that of its students to statements relating to the private school X.

All the data collected showed that, after discussion, those groups who had been instructed to keep in mind their rival school arrived at a more polarized consensus ($p < .005$, Wilcoxon test) than the groups who had not been given this instruction. In which direction did the consensus shift? It might have been expected that it would shift in a negative direction if one takes into account the fact that the French education system imparts a positive image to state schools. Indeed, the students of school X depicted a more negative image of their own institution, when compared with the École des Beaux-Arts, on every characteristic save two. One of these, for example, was: 'On completion of their course, the students of the private school of architecture have undergone a sound initiation into functional architecture,' which involved their professional future. On both items the groups concerned judged their school to be superior to the École des Beaux-Arts. Thus one also noted a significant shift towards the extreme of the scale for group judgements as opposed to individual judgements, particularly when the rival school was mentioned. Moreover, this shift persisted after the discussion was over and once the decision had been taken. This signifies that the participants had internalized the consensus at which they had arrived as a group. Clearly the imaginary comparison with the rival school stressed a twofold difference: inferiority as regards most characteristics, but superiority on two points concerning the school to which they belonged.

Let us now ask if the extremists possessed greater influence and how they were looked upon. To assess this each participant was asked to classify the three other members of his group according to: (a) the extent to which the others shared his opinions; (b) the extent to which they would like to pursue the discussion with them on the same subject. In the student groups who compared themselves with those of the École des Beaux-Arts, the extremists were judged more favourably on both these questions than were the groups who did not make this comparison ($t = 2.37$; $p < .025$, and $t = 1.76$; $p < .05$). The extremists therefore exerted more influence and participants felt themselves more drawn to them when the presumed opinion of the rival group had to be taken into account. Moreover, in this comparative situation, the extremists changed their opinion less frequently than did the moderates, who modified theirs during the discussion in order to arrive at a consensus ($t = 2.16$; $p < .025$). In other words the majority position was more often nearer to that of the extremists than the reverse was observed when the existence of the École des Beaux-Arts was evoked. The participants were aware of this, since, to the direct question 'Who among you has most influence in the discussion?', it was the extremist who most often came out on top. He was judged to be more definite in his opinion, if not more objective or closer to the attitude of most of the participants in the study (see Table 7.1). This is hardly astonishing.

Something similar took place to what was previously observed by Charters and Newcomb (1952), when individuals were reminded of their membership of religious groups. They gave replies closer to the norms of these groups, as did the students of the private school of architecture. Consensus is facilitated in this way and crystallizes round the most representative positions that normally everyone shares. To remind participants of a group that they are constantly using as a reference point and with which they compete revitalize an interior dialogue. Those private, inner conversations are revived in which each individual in fact becomes embroiled with his closest opponents even more than he does in public discussion. This occasionally becomes an obsession with 'inferior' groups and those who are being discriminated against (Blacks, Jews, etc.), who have continually in their mind the model of the groups that discriminate against them, classing them as inferior (Whites, Gentiles, etc.). They argue with these latter who, for their part, do not respond or do not bother about

Table 7.1   *Averages of the classification of extremists in replies to the post-experiment questionnaire*

	Groups	
Statement of the question	Experimental	Control
Definiteness of opinion	6.98	8.25
Perceived influence	7.42	9.20
Objectivity	10.40	10.60
Extremism	7.48	8.65
Closeness to the opinion of the subject	5.48	6.70
Prolongation of the discussion	5.45	6.40

them. The same probably holds good for the students of school X in Paris, in relation to those of the École des Beaux-Arts, at least at the time when the study took place.

In this we have a clear view of the polarization phenomenon that occurs in a group whose opinion and identity are dependent on those of a rival group, which is superior. Occasionally the result is an ideological effect of extreme contrast: the inferior groups judge themselves to be even more inferior, and the superior groups even more superior than they would judge themselves in isolation. This often shocks, but does not surprise. The explanations provided in this study have been supplemented by many others, following the same line of argument. That by Skinner and Stephenson (1981), in particular, confirmed in detailed fashion how greatly, from the mere fact of passing from a judgement made in terms of 'me' and 'you' (singular) to one in terms of 'we' and 'you' (plural), or 'we' and 'they', not only is the subject changed, but also the forms of thought, which become more stereotyped and more extreme. This is because the values and the common norms loom larger and predominate over individual diversity. In these situations no one judges without assessing, or assesses without judging.

But does this still hold good when the groups are supposed to negotiate in order to arrive at an agreement, instead of contenting themselves with expressing an opinion about one another? It would seem to be so, if one refers to a fine study by the Dutch social psychologists Rabbie and Visser (1972), who asked whether the polarization of consensus is indeed, as we maintain, a general phenomenon, even in the relationships between groups. The following is a brief account of their experiment, which simulated the relationship between workers and employers.

The participants played the part of a 'team of union representatives' who were preparing for negotiations between the two groups. First of all they indicated their individual position about what was at stake during the discussions. These varied in importance: salaries, holiday time and travelling expenses. More precisely, the experimenters asked them to write down what would be the minimum position they would be prepared to accept, how much ideally they would like to receive, and what they hoped realistically to obtain by negotiations with the employers. Having replied separately to the questionnaire, the subjects, meeting in groups of three, discussed these points and attempted to arrive at a common position.

Within this general framework Rabbie and Visser introduced variations. First, half the groups were requested to adopt a cooperative stance during the negotiations, the outcome of which had to satisfy both sides. The other half, on the contrary, were requested to adopt a combative stance, so that the gains obtained would be made at the expense of the other side. Under both conditions, moreover, half of the groups were informed that their position in the negotiations was a strong one; the other half were informed that it was weak. This comes down to committing firmly the former to their position and inspiring confidence in the outcome of the negotiations. The latter, on the other hand, were on the defensive, since their commitment and their confidence were undermined.

If these suppositions were true, it was to be expected that the former groups would shift towards a higher level of demands, while the latter would make more moderate demands and be more ready to compromise. Let us, however, allow the authors to enunciate the overall hypothesis they wished to test out:

> If the polarization hypothesis is as general as Moscovici and Zavalloni (1969) assume, it would be expected that the group consensus on the negotiation demands would be more extreme than the average level of prior individual judgements. Moreover, in view of the key importance of the involvement variable in their theory, it would be predicted that the shifts toward the more extreme ends of the scale would be stronger the more important the issue. (Rabbie and Visser, 1972: 402)

No matter what the conditions, results clearly indicated that the groups, at the prospect of negotiation, pitched the level of their claims clearly much higher than did individuals. For the most important question, salary demands, a significant polarization effect was observed. As regards travelling expenses, a question deemed moderately important, the shift noted was, on the other hand, towards prudence. For the least important question, there was no one overall effect. Rabbie and Visser also observed that the power relationships between 'union representatives' and 'employers' had marked consequences. Under both conditions, it will be recalled, they informed one half of the groups that their position in the negotiations was a strong one, while telling the other half that it was weak. It was predicted that the former, more sure of themselves, would agree on a somewhat extreme position, and the latter on a more moderate one. This was indeed the case.

Up to now we have assumed that relationships between groups have as their function the reinforcing of their social identity, or even their mental one. This function would, in its turn, explain a tendency to exacerbate differences and the degree of extremism (Meindl and Lerner, 1984). But power relationships intervene to check this tendency and even to lead to compromise if they are unfavourable, thus proving the truth of the well-known saying 'Might is right'. This is particularly so when might really does take the form of a reason, and is not an act of violence. In the end the principle of reality has often the last word. It is this which charts the limits within which the phenomenon we are considering operates.

Closed and open groups

1

In his famous work *The Two Sources of Morality and Religion*, Bergson propounded a distinction, which enjoyed immense success, between closed and open societies. The former rally individuals round obligations and special rules, prescribing a form of thinking and behaviour that suffers no deviation. The latter arise because of the attraction individuals feel for one another and an ability to throw up ideals to be pursued. The former inculcate a devotion to certain beliefs and a distinctive type of personality, causing certain individuals to associate together, on condition that others, declared to be strangers or enemies, are excluded. The latter put forward an exemplar of universal validity, such as the saint or the citizen, in which each individual can see himself mirrored. In the one case a man is for another man a compatriot, and, in the other case, a fellow human being – a fellow tribesman or one of the human species.

You have already grasped that for Bergson closed societies are families, clans, churches and, in the end, nations. Large or small, they incline towards the same authoritarian hierarchy, the same mental stereotype, the same religious faith. Likewise they tend towards the same ethnocentricity, according to which the values of their own society are superior to all others, or even unique. They direct their disdain, or even hostility, against those neighbours, families and clans, etc. who differ from them. We know that most of the peoples we call primitive deem their members alone to be 'true', 'good' or 'excellent'; they alone have the right to term themselves 'men'. The members of other clans, conversely, are excluded from the human race: 'earth monkeys', 'lice eggs', are some of the names given them. In short, praise is poured out and preference is reserved for one's own, and insults and abhorrence are heaped only on others. Bergson sums up the relationships between these two hyperboles in one sentence: 'Let us merely say that the two contrary maxims *homo homini deus* and *homo homini lupus* are easily reconciled. When one voices the former, one is thinking of some fellow-countryman, the other relates to foreigners' (1976: 232).

A different impulsion animates open societies marked by the American Revolution and the French Revolution, which recognize that individuals should enjoy autonomy and assume for them universal values. These values, embodied from time to time by exceptional men such as Socrates or Christ, break with a mere tribal representation in order to affirm we belong to a human community. We may recall Montesquieu's maxim in the *Lettres persanes*, 'Justice is eternal and does not depend on human conventions' – an image that has the same value for everybody and does not invoke any distinction that makes some superior to others. For a while it was believed that closed societies would retreat in the face of open societies, whereas, on the contrary, they survive and are even gaining ground. As Isaiah Berlin observed in a famous essay on nationalism, which rekindles the desire to belong to a homogeneous group with which it is easy to identify,

> This kind of homogeneity emphasized the differences between one group and its neighbours, the existence of tribal, cultural or national solidarity, and with it, a sense of difference from, often accompanied by active dislike and contempt for, groups with different customs and different real or mythical origins; and so was accounting for and justifying national statehood. (1981: 338)

Thus, depicted in a few lines, is the portrait of closed human groupings, from the family to the nation or the party. They are their own reference group and have as members all those who identify with it and resemble one another. It may be assumed that relationships with one another differ from those in open groupings. Without emphasizing it, it may be said that in closed groupings relationships are those of exclusion and discrimination, whereas in open groupings they are ones of contract and recognition. Behind the closed groupings is to be found, in some form or another, the idea of the 'chosen people', which, transposed to nations, families, etc., is the counterpart of social identity. The idea draws its popularity precisely from the fact that any member of these groups, which believe themselves to be superior, can, on the same grounds, proclaim that superiority subjectively for himself. Open groupings, by contrast, rest upon a balance of interests and rights depending upon the power of each individual, the compatibility between how they represent these interests and rights, and upon society in general. One last remark – the most important one: what we have just perceived explains why closed groupings live in different worlds, and open groupings in the one, same world.

2

How does all this relate to our subject, you may well ask? There is a clear relationship to the extent that up to now we have spoken of the group in general, and nothing else. Now, it is plain that several kinds of groups exist which sanction different modes of participation. From the viewpoint of relationships between them, the distinction between closed and open is the most significant. It is all the more so since most research on relationships between groups concerns ethnic groups and racial prejudice. All in all, following Bergson, the research envisages the existence of closed groupings and discriminatory relationships that value all that is peculiar to each one of them, and decry all that seems foreign. Hence in all circumstances an inclination exists to favour one's own and disfavour all others, no matter what injustice this may entail. Cooperation within and competition without, this is the formula of the closed system. It is as if to stay among one's own was the very condition for life in society.

In his theory of social identity, the most recent and the most fertile of the theories in this field, Henri Tajfel (1981) explains this ineluctable fact. His theory supposes that individuals are motivated to improve the image they have of themselves, by attempting either to acquire a personal identity, or to acquire a positive social identity. How far does the preference for one's own tribe or nation, or ethnocentricity in general, contribute to attaining this goal? These value social identity highly and build up the favourable image that the members of the group have of themselves. By comparing themselves, on a scale peculiar to themselves, to members of other groups, such as Frenchmen to Englishmen, Americans to Europeans, women to men, the advantage of belonging to their own group stands out more vividly (Tajfel, 1981). It is as if they were placing themselves in a category apart, whose qualities would shine forth not only in their own eyes but would be conceded by other categories or peoples. Their position is an entirely reasonable one, but goes one stage further: it is perfectly compatible with disdain for and denigration of the majority of these categories or peoples. It is not the superior character of their own identity that establishes their distinction or difference, but the inferior character of the other identities which, by comparison, serve to improve their own image. Turner (1987) has extended this idea in a way that possesses special interest for our purpose. According to him, cognitive identification with the group is of greater importance than affective motives. The identification is expressed in the fact that at first every individual is defined, and then perceived as belonging to one or other of two distinct groups, such as the supporters of two rival football teams, the protagonists of two opposing schools of thought who flaunt their own prejudices. The scenario he proposes is as follows: the categorization of qualities or modes of behaviour peculiar to a team or a school of thought underscores the prototype of each that individuals must resemble. It characterizes one to the exclusion of the other. Consequently the attributes and values that define the group appear more homogeneous and more extreme than they are in reality. So we speak about the Germans or the British according to a uniform model and as a collective individual, almost forgetting differences of class, region or education, believing that they are all fair-haired or phlegmatic. We also speak of ourselves, moreover, although we simplify less, but still seeing ourselves as more homogeneous and more distinct – these are signs of closure round a common identity – than we really are. This reinforces cohesion between the members of a group, who see themselves according to a prototype and conform to one another. Turner writes, 'Ethnocentrism and group cohesiveness are different sides of the same coin. One refers to the value of the in-group perceived by members in comparison with out-groups and the other to in-group members' mutual attraction on the basis of the value of shared in-group membership' (1987: 62).

The stage that follows adherence to the social prototype consists in internalizing it, in attributing to oneself the characteristics of the category to which one belongs, even almost submerging oneself in it. One becomes an individual worthy to serve as an example, such as student or cricket player or 'typical Frenchman', acknowledged as such. By dint of shedding one's own personal identity, of depersonalizing oneself, one assumes the social identity and its positive image. Hence the assimilation that leads one no longer to distinguish between individuals (in the plural) from their prototype (in the singular), the French from 'the Frenchman', the students from 'the student', etc. Our British colleague writes, 'It follows from the nature of depersonalization that the salience of an in-group–out-group categorization increases the mutually perceived proto-typicality of in-group members on the stereotypical dimensions defining the in-group category' (1987: 59).

One cannot do justice to the subtleties of the theory without exceeding the limits of our subject. Whereas Tajfel conceived it to explain relationships between groups, his pupil Turner reformulated it in such a way as to extend it to almost all psychological and social phenomena. And the effects of polarization are among these. To arrive at this he substituted for our normative hypothesis a categorical hypothesis which sought to explain them as follows. Participants in a discussion on a controversial problem expose themselves to the opinions of others and perceive that they belong to the same group. This discovery reinforces their identification with one another, just as strangers who in talking together might discover that they attended the same school, have common ancestors or share the same religious faith. This increases their tendency to emphasize their similarities, displaying and accentuating the characteristics of the category that binds them to one another. But, in drawing closer to one another in this way, participants intensify what distinguishes them most markedly from any different category. This is the only way in which they can clearly express their identity, what they are in relation to what they are not or do not wish to be. There can be no doubt that in this way all that is personal and heterogeneous becomes blunted; the judgements, attitudes and qualities of the group are perceived by its members as being more typical, and thus more extreme, than they are in reality. The group's positions on a problem are likewise perceived to be more extreme or more categorical. Hence participants in a decision, as soon as they identify with the group, adopt these positions and come to an agreement on those that are closer to the extreme.

We shall confine ourselves here to following the main threads of the argument that maintains groups become more extreme, first by reinforcing the identity that exists between their members, then by distinguishing themselves from other groups, and finally – it is presumed – by marking themselves off from all others. One may well think that it is not discussion, the exchange of information or opinions that influence decisions in one direction or in another. These merely allow individuals to recognize that they belong to the same school, social class or party, as well as to acknowledge the nature of the prototype they share in common. Once categorized in this way they come to share the illusion that their choices and understandings are uniform and close to one of the dominant positions. Logically, all the rest follows: that is, the polarization of attitudes and judgements arises from the need to conform to the category or prototype of one's own group. By acting in this way, each individual feels himself identical to the others.[2]

Here a consequence manifests itself that must be stressed. We had deemed the phenomenon of polarization to be significant, since it lays emphasis on an effect that goes against conformity, with the group shifting away from the mean attitude instead of moving towards it. Moreover, it consolidates a possibility of changing of its own accord. Since then, it is true, many and frequent attempts have been made to prove that this phenomenon reflects

> conformity to a norm that is provided by a shared and relatively extreme value rather than by the central tendency in the group. Then the presence or absence of such a value may be a key to predicting when group discussion of a topic will result in extremity shifts or simple conformity (i.e., a reduction in variance with no change in mean position). (Sanders and Baron, 1977: 311)

One may well ask why so much value is placed upon conformity. It is as if social psychology had some vague interest in proving that change is of little interest, since most of the effects which it studies are due to pressures to uniformity and to the search for a balance. This is carried to the point of blurring the distinction between the class of phenomena resulting from this pressure and the class of phenomena, such as collective decisions, that suppose innovation and consensus, conflict and a search for harmony. A long time ago Asch remarked,

> These highlight another aspect of social determination. They refer to conditions that create a conflict between tendencies in the person and the forces extending from the social field. They differ from the instances mentioned previously in that they present an issue and involve a choice among alternatives. As soon as this is the case, the happenings are a function of the conflicting alternatives. The problems in this region concern the operation of conformity *and* independence, not of conformity alone. (1959: 381, emphasis in original)

Now, it is about the operation of conformity alone, a consequence of the hypothesis, that Turner and his colleagues enlighten us through their analyses and empirical predictions. Thus Wetherell (1987) examined how far polarization depended on the way in which members of the group perceived an alternative, either as typical of a common category or as characteristic of an individual. On the basis of a preliminary imaginary survey, the participants were informed that they possessed consistency in their propensity to decide: some would choose the risky solutions, others the prudent ones. The division naturally took place by chance. In the *stereotyped group* condition, this information was conveyed to them by highlighting the difference that this propensity created among the groups. After having indicated to them what was to be their own propensity concerning decision, they were asked to join Group X – 'risky decision-taking' – ranged on one side of the room, or Group Y – 'prudent decision-taking' – on the other side. In this way the identity of those belonging to a group was highlighted and contrasted with that of another group. Under the second condition the participants learnt that they had a propensity to risk or prudence, by means of a similar method. But they were led to understand that this was due to a difference in personality.

Then, split up into groups of four, they were asked to discuss a series of dilemmas and to reach a consensus concerning the preferred solution in each case. Thus, on the one hand, the tendency to risk was presented as typical of the group, on the other, as a personality trait. It was predicted that with stress being laid upon the propensity of the group the effect would be to polarize it towards increased risk or increased prudence, regardless of the initial standpoint of the individuals, whereas, without this emphasis, a compromise would be reached. In short, it was postulated that the pressure to conformity would have the effect on each individual of shifting him towards what he perceived to be the common shared attribute of the group. This is indeed what happened. Those groups qualified as rash tended to shift towards more risky decisions, and those qualified as prudent made moderate choices. Nothing similar could be observed when the same attributes were applied to individuals.

Following the same line of thinking, Mackie and Cooper (1984) invited students to participate in a research study designed to highlight those aspects of group discussion that shape a decision taken in common. They began by informing them that, divided into two blocks of groups, they would be participating in a competition relating to the degree of animation in the discussion and decision-making process. Among the topics to be debated figured that of discovering whether standardized tests for admission to institutions of higher education should be abolished, and problems related to this. In order to make the competition more entertaining, they were informed that the decisions recorded would be assessed by an impartial judge, and the best ones would receive a money prize. The evaluation criteria communicated to the participants were of a technical nature. For example, each individual had to express his opinion and do so in a precise and relevant way. These are in fact the criteria recommended for any committee or meeting that is called, in order to ensure effectiveness in its deliberations.

Once these instructions had been given, the participants listened to a recording of a series of recent discussions. Under one of the conditions, they were informed that the recorded discussions were those of the group of which they would form part during the experiment. Under the other condition, the recordings were assumed to originate in the rival group and were to allow them to become familiar with the discussion. But the tape, they were informed, would stop before the taking of a decision, so that they should not be influenced. Before the beginning of the listening session, the experimenter remarked – but without dwelling upon it – that the group were not always in agreement. Then the students listened to the discussion on the subjects that concerned them. Finally, before they were to meet the other members of the group and participate in the discussion (which in reality would not take place) they were made to fill in a questionnaire to express their definitive position on the problems. In this way could be observed the influence exerted by the group on a person who imagined that he would be joining it in the immediate future.

In accordance with what had been predicted, attitudes shifted considerably ($F = 26$; $p < .001$) in the direction of the position postulated by the recording, for the case where the discussion was thought to have originated in the group to which the students believed they were to belong. Their attitudes most certainly tended to become more extreme, confirming that a polarization had taken place. In a second experiment, it was noted that the position of the imaginary group itself was perceived to be more extreme. According to the researchers, these experiments showed that the members of the group considered that the group's attitudes were generally more extreme than they would appear to be to impartial judges. Why, therefore, is this so? It would seem that this tendency to perceive the information concerning one's own group as more extreme may be the result of a cognitive prejudice and of a desire to be distinguished from other groups.

This is a plausible explanation, particularly in an environment where to adopt an extreme position has positive value. This is because we know how much, in other environments, an effort, on the contrary, is made to be distinctive by adopting a moderate position. Indeed, often politicians and experts make themselves prominent by expressing 'centrist' opinions and stigmatize their opponents, labelled fanatics, as extremists who 'are going too far'. In another study Mackie (1986) tackled precisely the question of finding out what is the causal role of the fact that the group is perceived as extreme. At the beginning of the experiment the subjects, once again students, were instructed to discuss and to take decisions relating to a certain number of attitudes on ecology and nuclear energy. Under the 'group' condition, they had to express their opinions and decide as a group, with their exchanges nominally being recorded and analysed. Under the 'individual' condition, they were informed that they would have to set out their own personal opinion and take a decision that would be recorded and analysed. Each time, in order to familiarize them with the task that awaited them, they were first made to listen to recordings of others carrying out the same task. But the decisions taken by these were wiped from the tape and for each session new problems were posed.

In reality, the question was of how to influence them by attributing these recordings to three distinct sources. Under the 'individual' condition the subjects were led to believe that each speaker recorded his decision alone, but that afterwards their reasoning and arguments were mixed up in order to preserve anonymity. Under the 'group' condition part of the students were led to believe that they were listening to a recording originating in 'another group', whereas they themselves were part of a new group constituted for the occasion. The other part were informed that the recording came from a group of three and that they would be used to replace one of the three. This part listened to the debates of what would be their own group and had an opportunity of identifying themselves with it. In order to measure their degree of perception of the attitude of the so-called recorded groups, the experimenters asked the participants to indicate on a scale the position that seemed best to represent the opinions they had heard. They then gave their own choice as well as that of the three persons they had listened to on the tape.

It is not easy to sum up so complex an experiment, but the results are nevertheless clear. As was expected, the representative position was judged more extreme by the subjects under the group condition ($F = 2.39; p < .025$) than under the individual condition. Thus it was inevitable that their own opinions would be more extreme. But this was especially true for those who listened to the recording of the group which they assumed would later be their own group ($t = 4.56; p < .003$), and not for any other group at all. One might believe they already saw themselves as forming part of it and defending its viewpoint.

Matters can be carried a little further, and one can say that group members should perceive themselves to be alike and in a state of cohesion. A fresh experiment by the American researcher, similar to the earlier one (Mackie, 1986), centred on the moratorium on the production of nuclear weapons, showed this to be the case. Following a proven procedure, the experimenter, laying down several conditions, announced to the participants that they would be engaging in a group discussion. But he introduced an element of competition. The members of certain groups were informed that they would be competing with one another to produce the best arguments. The remaining groups were informed that they would be in competition with another group. Once more they all listened to a recording and had to judge the arguments expounded. Afterwards they expressed their personal attitude and were asked to describe the members of the imaginary groups, as well as themselves, according to a list of personality traits. Let us fasten on one observation that is of interest to us here. Clearly, in a situation of collective competition, it was discovered that opinions were perceived as being more extreme. One might say that rivalry with another group reinforces internal cohesion, contrasting with everything that remains external to the group. On the other hand, in the situation where the emphasis is put on competition between individuals, these both judged the representative position to be more moderate and moderated their own judgements accordingly. One might say that they wanted to forestall any future disagreement and prepare for a compromise. Thus, faced with the prospect of a future conflict, groups prepared to confront it, whereas individuals prepared themselves to avoid it. The groups affirmed what distinguished them from a future adversary, and individuals what drew them closer to their eventual partner.

The studies yield more complete data about the tendencies brought to light by the studies of Doise and Rabbie referred to above; that is, when it is among rival groups, the group shifts its consensus towards the extreme. But, to return to the theory, it is salutary to note what it explains. It informs us that, in the collective situation, which occurs fairly frequently, where individuals identify with a social category, they always view it through what is typical or stereotypical about it. They conform to it, giving their assent to what represents their type and stereotype. In this way they draw closer to those characteristics that allow them to resemble the category as a whole, as well as one another. However, when one adds that individuals come together on an extreme position, whatever their initial positions may have been, this does not show, as is thought, the general nature of the explanation, but its limitations. It deals with the phenomenon of extremism, and not that of polarization, which is better defined. The phenomenon of polarization corresponds to a shift in the attitudes and opinions in a predetermined direction by the population, and not in any direction whatsoever, independent of the individuals that constitute that population, if one may express it in this way.

Here there arises some hesitation, and maybe even an objection, regarding the general purport of this hypothesis. It attributes a crucial role to conformity in this field, and thus to majority pressure. Yet we must remember the meaning that many institutions attribute to consensus. It is valid if it is obtained under appropriate conditions. In particular, sufficient diversity must be ensured so as to mitigate any open or covert pressure, and to guarantee freedom of expression to everybody, so as to obtain agreement *within* the group and not *by* the group. In very many cases, the unanimity rule has in fact as its purpose to restrain the tendency to conformity and to allow two opposing influences, those of the majority and of the minority, to be exerted at the same time. This is because one should take into account deviant opinions and discuss them with those who uphold them (Nemeth, 1977). Where this rule is not applied, however, the majority can deliberately ignore the minority – the extreme individuals – since it has no motive for wishing to convince them or to concede to them anything at all in order to arrive at a decision. Now, in spite of this limitation on the pressures to conformity, groups that arrive at a unanimous consensus polarize just as much and even more than groups that make their decisions according to a majority, and on which no such limitation is imposed. This has been found in very many of the studies that have been described up to now, and still more recently in that by Kaplan and Miller (1983), who asked groups to take a series of decisions on factual and value judgements.

One point that interests us especially here is that part of the groups had to take their decisions according to the unanimity rule, and the others on a mere majority. Now, the only significant shift noted between the opinions before and after discussion was found among the former groups – and that was concerning value judgements. This was therefore in groups that were not subjected solely to conformity but, on the contrary, could take into account the views of extreme individuals during the discussion. It is often stated that it is more difficult to obtain a unanimous rather than a majority decision, if one takes into account the time spent in discussion. The experiment did not reveal that any difference of this kind existed. Moreover, the members of the groups who applied the majority rule had a tendency to be less satisfied with the development of the discussion and with the decision taken than were those who took unanimous decisions. Comparing the ways in which they underwent the experiment, it would appear that, in the first case, more participants felt the pressure to arrive at an agreement and felt more tension within the group than in the second case, where both majority and minority were able to express themselves freely and to come to full agreement.

All in all, it could be said that, having shared equally in the consensus and shaped it to the same extent, each individual, in the case of unanimity, felt he had achieved greater recognition. He then felt less the pressure and the tension, which were compensated for by the common outcome. Here also one must be prudent, for experiments such as those of Van Knippenberg and Wilke (1968) show how the values of a particular social category, such as those of men or women, operate in subtle ways. We know too little about this segment of reality, which is still shrouded in obscurity.

3

Since this is so, we must accept that the relationships between groups are in no way fixed. As in all relationships, a struggle is carried on in every society as to whether they should be closed or open. Is this a matter of economics, or politics, or morality? Here it interests us from the viewpoint of social psychology. If one had to dig deep down to the roots of this struggle, one would encounter a hotchpotch of facts and values. For reasons of clarity, we have evoked the useful distinction between open and closed groups. Then, in the light of an innovatory research trend in Europe, we have elucidated the effect of relationships between groups on the decisions that each group might take. In reality, observations in and outside the laboratory confirm the idea that a strong social identity, just like a definite collective type, causes opting for extreme choices. This is the striking product of orthodoxy (Deconchy, 1980), whether within a nation, a party or a church. Nevertheless it is logical to think, following in the footsteps of Bergson and Popper, that relationships among closed groups differ from those among open groups. If closed groups – a fact of which no one is ignorant – cling to hostility and discrimination, open groups seek to make alliances and acknowledgement to others. That the former are more stable than the latter is not enough to confer upon them a more basic character, unless one takes the word 'group' to be synonymous with 'closed group', just as, for some, society is also the closed society of the nation.

In any case we have to enlarge the range of ideas in order to include a number of realities, among them that of a decision taken in an environment where there is a greater degree of freedom. For the moment, it is no more than a necessary support in order to make progress and put forward a few questions, such as: Could polarization cause groups to evolve towards greater openness? Although it is true that clues are scarce, there are some that provide us with an answer. Thus Hewstone and Jaspars (1982) carried out a study of racial prejudice. They brought together in pairs either Blacks mainly from the Caribbean, or White adolescents belonging to the working class, recruited in local clubs. The pairs then read four statements that highlighted examples of racial discrimination (for example, 'More Blacks than Whites are arrested and accused of suspicious behaviour'). Each discriminatory statement was attributed to a negative trait of Blacks' character or to the image of Blacks as they were seen by White authorities. As usual, after having read these statements participants assessed the reasons explaining these discriminatory measures. Certain pairs of young-sters read the statements without discussing them; others discussed them and had to come to an agreement on the causes of racial prejudice.

As was to be expected, a polarization of judgements was observed, but not in relation to the two possible causes. In general, the character of Blacks seems to have been questioned less often when the participants discussed than when they did not. The choice of Whites as the cause seems to have been less subject to the effects of polarization. Taken together, after discussion had taken place between them, these results signify that both Blacks and Whites saw the Blacks themselves less as a cause of discrimi-nation. We can therefore observe that 'egalitarian' ideology, notably on the part of the Whites, held them back from explaining racial discrimination by the negative traits of Blacks. This does not mean that they had no prejudices – far from it. However, this ideology morally obliged them to dissimulate or repress them, a fact whose significance must be taken into account. In any case the tendency described is indeed present and it should even less be underestimated, because it is one of the obligatory channels through which all change must pass.

This is not an isolated example. Other social psychologists have been able to show that discussions between members of the same group drew them close to another group. Ng, of the University of Dunedin in New Zealand, was one of these. In several studies he verified that decisions concerning people belonging to external groups became less discriminatory if the decision-makers discussed them collectively (Ng, 1984; Ng and Cram, 1987). We are therefore reminded of an observation made by Billig (1973), which for a long while went unnoticed, doubtless because it did not fit in with the climate of the times. In fact, seeking to investigate the existence of possible discriminatory norms favouring the group to which people be-longed or that of equity between groups, Billig (who was Tajfel's pupil) had set up at that time an experimental situation. Before taking decisions concerning another group, each participant discussed them with a colleague who had already taken such decisions. Contrary to the experimenter's expectations, subjects initiated in this way did not take more discriminatory decisions. On the contrary, in the author's words, communication between individuals 'seems to have weakened the norms of the situation' (1973: 342).

Let us compare these results with those obtained by Rabbie (1982) in the

Netherlands. In various ways he induced a cooperative attitude towards the other group, particularly by bringing forward a meeting with it. Under such conditions – and this is hardly surprising – discussion between members of the same group far from always increases their animosity towards the other group; on the contrary, it may also reduce it. Visser (1975), for example, one of Rabbie's assistants, studied the effect of the active presence of the members of a group on the conduct of their representatives in negotiations with the other group. When they were present, the group's members could intervene in the negotiations; when they were not, they were reduced to following them on closed-circuit television. Rabbie summed up the results of this experiment as follows:

> As expected, cooperative groups found it easier to reach an agreement with the other group and also had more positive attitudes toward own and other group when they could influence the intergroup negotiations than when they could not. Competitive groups found it more difficult to reach agreement with the other group and had more negative attitudes about themselves and others in the influence condition than in the no influence condition. (1982: 140–1)

Rabbie's explanation does not chime with that of Billig. For us what is important is to note that one need not consider the group as more discriminating or more intolerant than the individual. In this research, discussion produced an effect, and caused to prevail over partisan motivations the desire to come to an agreement with others.

Communication plays an important role, both as anticipating, and as a consequence of, a specific procedure for relationships between groups. This is a viewpoint we cling to. We are also aware that it requires a great amount of organizational work within the group and between groups. How otherwise can one conceive the effectiveness of the negotiation process, when the representatives of conflicting groups meet to determine future procedures for the relationships between their groups? A quarter of a century ago Blake, Shepard and Mouton (1964) were already insisting on the role of discussion in such negotiations. They described three interventions made in relation to industrial disputes. Each time it was necessary to organize several meetings for discussion, alternately between the members of the same group and between the representatives of the two groups in dispute. Members of each group discussed the representations and attitudes they had, first, regarding their own group, and then regarding the other group. Afterwards the first meeting took place between the representatives of the two groups, who were accompanied by observers. The purpose of this meeting was to have participants describe precisely the representations they formed regarding their own group as well as those regarding the other group. Back in their own group and discussing with their partners, the representatives tried to understand the differences existing between the images presented by their group and those presented by the opposing group. Other discussion meetings between the groups had then to allow distortions to be corrected and to develop an awareness of the main differences between the positions of the two parties. Only at that stage could negotiations begin, based on positions that had been discussed and set out in common.

This application of discussions has similarities with that practised by Touraine (1978) in his sociological investigations designed to uncover the nature of a social movement. It has been found a priori that a group may appear to be somewhat more inclined to cooperate than to oppose, and vice versa (Deutsch, 1985). But this tendency is not inevitable, and the group can evolve in a different direction from the original one, from competition to cooperation, for example. The conflict is, so to speak, carried upstream, before relationships are formed, and consequently is weakened.

A late, very recent experiment (Rabbie et al., 1989) gives us an even more direct idea of this flexibility in relationships. The task was presented as one of decision-making. The participants – a dozen each session – both men and women, were categorized according to one criterion, that is, the preference they showed for a genre of paintings. In fact they were divided at random into two groups of three who were assumed to like Surrealist painting, whereas the two other groups of three were presented as lovers of the school of Magical Realism. The experimenters installed them in small rooms in such a way as to vary, on an almost physical plane, the permeability of the boundaries between the two groups.

The experiment took place in two stages. In the first stage, each participant had to allocate a monetary remuneration to an unnamed member of his own group and an unnamed member of the other group, using matrices thought up by Tajfel (the use of these matrices continues to spread). After the first distribution of cash decided by each individual separately in his own small room, the participants were requested to meet together to discuss the allocation of sums that they would suggest in the second stage. They arrived at a consensus and therefore decided to remunerate either a group that shared their own painting preferences or a group with different tastes. The comparison of the average sum allotted before the group discussion with that proposed after discussion should certainly provide an indication of the degree of polarization of the group on the choice made in accordance with the matrices. Now, it would indeed seem that, under certain conditions, the participants reinforced their initial tendency in favour of the group whose members it rewarded. This was all the more so because the need to cooperate with them was highlighted in an almost physical fashion. The greater the permeability of the boundaries between the groups, the more they felt closer on a psychological plane, and consequently the greater then was the equity and cooperation. At the same time, under these conditions there can be seen a decrease in the discrimination and favouritism shown by one group for the other.

However, it must be assumed that if individuals are less discriminatory, they feel themselves more linked to the two groups, or in any case in a state of dependency less exclusive of their own group. One may therefore expect that once they come together to make a decision their consensus is extreme, but less so than if they were shut away and depended exclusively on one group. This was found in this study, since the consensuses that were established concerning the allotments of money were more polarized in a situation of unilateral dependency than in one of bilateral dependency. This is an indication that the members of a group are less inclined to discriminate than to seek out a mutual advantage by favouring their own members without disfavouring the others to an exaggerated extent.

The authors of this research study would have gained more from it if they had recognized the difference, essential in our view, between closed groups, in the one case, and the open groups that they studied. Nothing that we learn about open groups can either confirm or invalidate what we know about closed groups, since the psychology of each is distinct and their reality is different. This is a distinction as fundamental for theory as for the importance it has in practice. We have undertaken to throw a little clarity upon this, and to widen the range of relationships that remain to be explored in order to have a precise view of the decisions between groups that lead to consensus. Clarity is of course a grand word, and there is not a single theory – as we are often reminded – which in many respects is not disarmed when faced with a variety of phenomena which are cloaked in an unfathomable obscurity. This element of variety is always present and we are faced with it; doubtless it helps us to keep within modest bounds.

Notes

1 In this chapter we shall draw upon the studies on relations between groups (Doise, 1979; Rabbie and Visser, 1972; Sherif, 1966; Tajfel, 1982; Turner, 1987).

2 By making polarization one effect of conformity it is doubtless transformed from being a general phenomenon to being one of its sub-categories. One even runs the risk of returning to a way of envisaging the question that dates from before the present research studies. At that time one could read, 'This brings us back to the centre of this discussion: under what conditions is degree of polarization more predictable from stereotypic and perhaps pathological response style, and under what conditions is degree of polarization more predictable from meaningfulness of the stimuli being rated and/or the rating scale being used?' (O'Donovan, 1965: 364).

8

Decision-making

From individual representations to the social representation

1

Essentially it is a theory of decision and consensus, and thus of the group, that we are in the process of elaborating. Up to now our attention has been concentrated on the role of collective involvement. Hypotheses on which we have dwelt explain its effects. However, one cannot assert that a simple relationship links this causal factor to the consensus to which it contributes. Nor can we say that a quantitative equation joins cause and effect. Some would wish this to be so: they judge the value of a theory according to whether or not it is capable of answering the criteria of physics. But social psychology is in the same category as biology and one has to consider oneself lucky if it succeeds in discovering some vast framework of thought in which new facts can be predicted. Crick, the great British biologist, has declared,

> The basic laws of physics can usually be expressed in exact mathematical form, and are probably the same throughout the universe. The 'laws' of biology, by contrast, are often only broad generalizations, since they describe rather elaborate mechanisms that natural selection has evolved over billions of years. . . . For this reason a theorist in biology has to receive much more guidance from the experimental evidence (however cloudy and confused) than is necessary in physics. (1990: 6)

It is evident that collective involvement – which is intensified by controversy, the burden of values, the possibility of participating and the identity of closed groups – is one of those broad generalizations, and we have set out an array of facts that support this. Reality imposes limitations on proofs that back up the theory expounded, and this we freely acknowledge.

The moment has come to spend a little more time on the second factor – one might call it the internal factor – of the theory: that is, the socio-cognitive conflict. Who has not discovered that the preparation of a decision – which, after all, is the definition of choice alternatives – is the opportunity for those who are participating to display their competence, to manifest, whether consciously or unconsciously, their value judgements, representations, interests and knowledge? For sure, before taking a decision, the data are collected; the lesson is drawn from past failures and the temperature of the body social is taken. But from the outset one finds oneself in a situation of conflict, without which one can indeed do nothing.

This is a very strange phenomenon: it reduces disagreements only on condition that new ones are produced, like the effect of a vaccine. This conflict is born when several alternative ideas relating to the same dilemma are proposed simultaneously. They are only alternatives if they match the same quest for a solution, and do so in almost similar terms. The conflict becomes a social one when each alternative is conceived, and then defended, in public by a different member of the team or group whose task it is to resolve this dilemma.

But when one devises a plan to confront these alternatives, and then to reconcile them and put an end to differences, serious tensions arise, the outcome of which cannot always be controlled. We are speaking of socio-cognitive conflicts that are measured by the relationships between agreements and disagreements that arise among individuals, whose task is to argue, to negotiate the passing on of information, to assess the chances of modifying the views of others in order to draw them closer to a common option. In reality, these conflicts are sparked off at various levels. Each time a person involves himself, even to a very slight extent, by participating in a committee or a meeting, he opts for an alternative. Thus the members of a jury express their opinion before discussing. The subjects of our experiments, whom we asked to choose an appropriate position regarding a particular topic (attitude towards de Gaulle, risk, etc.) had to meet afterwards to discuss the problem. This simple requirement, which bound them to their position, might well engender more conflict as each individual progressively takes note of the different opinions expressed around him. But, at the level of the group as a whole, conflict appears as a process that operates when the group strives to reach a consensus, at the expense of concessions from each individual.

To arrive at this goal the assertion of preferences and alternatives should coincide with the search for a mutual influence that is acceptable in principle. Now, the most economical way of arriving at this[1] is, as we know, to enlarge the common basis for the arguments. It is a matter of combining the elements of a conspectus of the problems and convictions that individuals have the opportunity to share, in a controversy or discussion. Even people who at first are completely unknown to one another will always find a germ of an idea or a meaning that leads to such a conspectus. Yet, as we also know, the conspectus is not the conclusion of a reasoned argument about the comparative advantages and disadvantages of the different alternatives that present themselves. It is rather the outcome of a series of influences, debates and choices, whose index of success is the consensus reached by those who participate in them. This is what distinguishes the decision from the reasoning: 'Making a choice implies a greater commitment and conflict than does making a judgement: it also tends to bring responsibility and regret into consideration' (Abelson and Levi, 1985: 235).

This is why one should not confuse an agreement between people with one regarding things. From one to the other, the register is completely changed. This is an additional reason to stress the effort accomplished during any such conflict, which pits individuals against one another. Every kind of intellectual and affective means comes into play as soon as the slightest hint of difference arises, so that arguments are invented, opposing views interpreted, to find the grounds for disagreement, but, above all, in order to find a way out of them. This is even more so because the need to be reconciled in public, to think and act towards this end, appears more urgent. As the debate progresses, the number of alternatives can be seen to diminish, but each one of them looms larger and the number of those supporting it increases. This is because their significance for the decision to be taken is clarified, and the relevant parameters, having become more prominent, appear more uniform in the participants' eyes. This denotes that their cognitive orientation has changed and become clearer, since people and things are no longer seen in the same light as before the meeting, during which the arguments take place. Communication has 'tuned them in', organizing the elements of information into a common conspectus which is all the more unified because it is shared in more actively. This at least is what studies show which lay down 'that transmitters activate cognitive structures which are more differentiated, complex, unified and organized than those activated by receivers' (Zajonc, 1960: 166).

Thus the outcome of the socio-cognitive process is not so much to reduce the differences between points of view in order to make them conform to a single one but rather to clarify them and integrate them on a higher level, after which the members of the group see the problem in a different light. They rank the alternatives on a different scale, that of the group in which they are participating and in which they feel involved. It is no mere play on words to assert that the decision has the effect of transforming the representations of each individual into a social representation, which is the common basis sought after. Asch already grasped the need for this:

> Social action requires that the individual participant be capable of representing to himself the situation that includes himself and others. These individual representations contain, in cases of fully-fledged interaction, a reference to the fact that the others also possess a corresponding view of the situation. These similar and mutually relevant representations in individuals provide the equivalent of what group mind theorists sought and individual psychologists denied. (1959: 371)

This means that each participant, after having reflected aloud on the same problem, exchanges publicly arguments relating to the various solutions, and normally comes to internalize this relevant representation on the intellectual plane, making it his own. It becomes the framework within which the rest of the attitudes and judgements are adjusted so that every individual is on the same wavelength as the group. If, after having taken a decision together, individuals remain loyal to it and feel themselves committed, it is most certainly in order not to disrupt the harmony once it has been reached. Consequently a social psychology is shaped and makes headway at the expense of individual psychologies, since, in this case, as Durkheim wrote, '*consensus* is therefore as perfect as possible; all consciousnesses beat as if in unison' (1978: 125).

The work of decision[2] is started in order to transform representations that appear distinct from one another into one shared representation that corresponds to them. It brings to the surface and explains the complete set of categories, judgements, value hierarchies and knowledge of which individuals were the repository of, and which each one thought he alone possessed. It is thus an effort of mutual recognition through that very consensus which henceforth is common to them all. It associates them, in some way, in a moral and intellectual compact. Now, *pacta sunt servanda*, they must be respected and bind all the participants. By causing the majority to converge towards a social representation, the multiplicity of decisions that lead to a consensus do more than draw viewpoints closer: they initiate or reinforce social ties. Beyond the specific dilemmas that each decision resolves, they correspond to this general aim. They produce a mass effect in the network of groups that choose and discuss, creating and re-creating the bonds in our society by a common action, just as at one time public opinion originated in the market-places and cafés, and from drawing-room conversations. It is the surplus value that we extract from this task of collective decision-making, the diversity and multiplicity of which have reached so high a level that it has become a profession – we speak of decision-makers – and a significant factor in our social and moral world.

2

The socio-cognitive conflict inherent in any decision taken in common combines together two permanent tendencies. The one aims at maintaining existing uniformity and agreement, the other at changing them by imparting an original form to things and ideas. The choices that are made usually express a balance of forces between the two because, without any element of novelty, they are mere stereotypes or ritual, and, without a dose of conformity, they become fancies and fluctuations that lead to disorder. It is of real theoretical interest to recognize at work in the socio-cognitive conflict a dual process of social thought. It can only be dual, in view of the opposing functions that it fulfils and of the simultaneous use it makes of divergent and convergent thinking, the one the badge of innovation and the other of uniformity.

Divergent thinking can be described as being open and spontaneous, loath to eliminate alternative solutions or to restrict a diversity of viewpoints. On the contrary, it is on the alert for dissensions, causing them to proliferate and encouraging debate. Like scientists, it attempts to falsify concepts and, by discovering new facts and ideas, engenders dissensions to serve the forthcoming consensus. Within the framework of knowledge and research, what other meaning than this can be given to it?

For its part, convergent thinking selects and classifies, combining the common elements in competing representations, until it encapsulates them in a single, acceptable one, to which everybody finally is converted. It 'freezes', to adopt one of Lewin's expressions, those representations that, on a social or moral plane, give commitment at various levels. Some are accepted, provided that there are no reasons to believe the opposite, while others must be retained at all costs. These are the limiting cases, but no one could adhere to them to the letter. Nevertheless it is certain that they are met with in science:

> Scientists constantly relate their decisions and selections to the expected response of specific members of this community of 'validators', or to the dictates of the journal in which they wish to publish. Decisions are based on what is 'hot' and what is 'out', on what one 'can' or 'cannot' do, on whom they will come up against and with whom they will have to associate by making a specific point. (Knorr-Cetina, 1981: 7)

This is a family scandal, and thus a well-kept secret, for the freedom to research to which one is so strongly attached in society is so restricted in the scientific community that most of the published work, even if it is revolutionary, bears this stamp of servitude.

Yet a set of assumptions does not constitute a proof, as we will readily agree. The important thing is that the two kinds of thinking should be set in motion in the course of every decision. Perhaps there can even be no real decision without these dual modes of social thought, which characterize it and make it possible. Hence the normal tension that exists, summed up by Kuhn, the philosopher of science, as follows:

> Some divergence characterizes all scientific work, and gigantic divergences lie at the core of the most significant episodes in scientific development. But both my own experience in scientific research and my reading of the history of sciences lead me to wonder whether flexibility and open-mindedness have not been too exclusively emphasized as the characteristic requisites for basic research. I shall therefore suggest below that something like 'convergent thinking' is as essential to scientific advance as is divergent. Since the two modes of thought are inevitably in conflict, it will follow that the ability to support a tension that can occasionally become almost unbearable is one of the prime requisites for the very best sort of scientific research. (1977: 226)

To resolve the conflict by eliminating convergent thinking would be to abandon discussion and any choice made in common. To resolve the conflict by censoring divergent thinking would condemn participants to routine, to stereotyping, to what is termed 'groupthink'. On the other hand, to negotiate this conflict, which is both social and cognitive, is an arduous task. We all know this, however humble the occupation one follows or the association to which one belongs. It is an elementary datum of our mental life. Naturally all the facets of that life are of interest. But to know how to direct tensions in this dual form of thought is of special concern, both for theory and for practice in general.

The tension between divergent and convergent thinking

1

Leaving aside many secondary aspects, the parallel, on the one hand, between discussion and consensus, and, on the other, between divergent and convergent thinking, is blatant. There can be no doubt – as we assume – that the latter continues to develop at the expense of the former. This occurs during the existence of the group, which, compelled to define itself and to discuss as it begins to take shape, once it is constituted, avoids contradictions and seeks agreement on ideas and values (Witte, 1979). It is not easy to distinguish between the two phases. When we seek to observe them, we have no sure indication available to allow us to decide when the second phase begins and when the first phase is over, so great is the overlap. Nevertheless we know the two ways in which divergent thinking is not only permitted but positively encouraged. On the one hand, it is by lessening the pressure to conform that spontaneously arises between individuals when a group is constituted. In this way the members discuss by exploring all alternatives and every piece of information, creating new ones and opposing one another without being too worried about others' reactions. Very fortunately an investigation carried out in the United States (Hall and Watson, 1970) has shown how this is possible.

The students who took part in it had the task of resolving a problem relating to survival in the cosmos. A space ship having crashed on the moon, a team of astronauts has to cover a distance of some 300 kilometres in order to reach the spot where they have a rendezvous with another team. Before embarking on this perilous undertaking, the members of the team have to decide which of the fifteen objects necessary for survival – oxygen reserves, concentrated food, signalling equipment, heating requisites, etc. – they will take with them. Those participating in the study were asked to draw up a list of priorities for these objects, first separately as individuals, and then in groups, by arriving at a consensus. Half of the groups received no special instructions for this common task of decision-taking. The other half were instructed to confront other members of the group and resolve the differences between them. They were informed that they had to set out their arguments lucidly and were not to change their opinion with the sole aim of avoiding conflict, nor to seek agreement using procedures such as a majority vote, the establishment of a mean position, bargaining, tossing a coin, or in other ways. Moreover, the instructions emphasized the need to look upon differences of opinion as both natural and useful, so that any precipitous agreement would be suspect, so long as the reasons for it had not been gone into thoroughly. The main thing was to resist group pressures that tempted one to yield to others without sound reasons, just in order to attain a consensus, which would lack any guarantee of success.

Hall and Watson were persuaded that by weakening such pressures they would encourage divergent thinking to be displayed. This would lead groups first to produce solutions of a superior quality, and then to make better use of the resources of each member, so that overall performance would exceed even that of the group's cleverest members, and finally to discover novel solutions. Most of these hypotheses were verified. By confronting opposing views, members of the group were more open to innovation, exhibited creativity and chose new solutions that had surfaced during the debate.

The other means of encouraging divergent thinking is by the presence of a minority participating actively in the group's discussions. This is a comparatively natural means for use in decisions leading to a consensus, since it arises solely from the obligation to respect one of the essential conditions. These assume in fact a state of equality between the members of the group. This means the majority recognizes the right of the minority to express itself, and will set very great store by its opinions; otherwise the agreement arrived at would be worthless. Let us remind ourselves at this point that among the institutions in society the peculiar characteristic of decisions is precisely to afford the minority one of the best possible opportunities to influence the majority. Notably it does this by stressing the conflict between opposing viewpoints, and this stimulates each member to consider a larger number of aspects of the question, to discover novel solutions, and to suggest different choices from those perceived initially.

This hypothesis was confirmed and broadened by several studies by Nemeth (1986) showing that individuals exposed to such minorities set about reflecting on data concerning the reality of the situation in a different way, perceiving solutions previously unthought of and taking decisions that are 'better' or 'fairer'. In one of the first studies illustrating our brief comments, experimenters (Nemeth and Kwan, 1985) brought individuals together in groups of four and then showed slides to them separately. Each slide consisted of a group of five letters, the three in the middle being in capitals, for example tDOGe. The task was to name the first three-letter word that appeared – here, obviously DOG. After each subject had performed this task for five slides, the participants were all informed of the choices made by the other members of the group. Under one condition, termed 'a majority' one, they were told that three other members saw each time the word formed by the three letters in reverse order – in our example, GOD, and only one had seen DOG. Under the other condition, termed the 'minority' one, the subjects were told that only one member of the group had seen GOD, and the three others had seen DOG. They were then again presented with ten slides and asked this time to make up as many words as possible from the letters. One result emerged: the subjects under the minority condition found the most words. They exploited all the possible combinations, reading from left to right and from right to left, shifting the letters around, etc. Under the 'majority' condition the participants primarily used the method that had been suggested to them, that is, reading from right to left. Sometimes this prevented them from seeing words whose letters could be read in the natural order. In short, their performance had been affected by the fact that they followed a single strategy in a conformist manner, to the detriment of other ways. By contrast the subjects under the 'minority' condition resorted to all possible strategies and drew benefit from them.

The observation was confirmed on several occasions, in various situations and with different tasks (Nemeth, 1984, 1985). Depending on whether the individuals were under a 'majority' or a 'minority' influence, their mode of thinking became convergent or divergent. Thus it is not difference or conflict between points of view that encourages the one mode and discourages the other; the determining factor is to know who is expressing the viewpoint, as if the majority was associated with one kind of thinking and the minority with another.

Under these conditions it is normal for the quality of the discussion and of the alternatives proposed on which agreement is reached to be affected. A committee, a meeting or a jury prejudges up to a certain point this quality, depending on whether it highlights the positions of the minority, ensuring for it – or refusing it – the chance to participate and to express itself fully. In this way it facilitates or hampers the familiar tension of the underlying social and cognitive conflict that is always at work. Every group has an interest in keeping it alive, in order to maximize its members' contribution and their desire to participate. It follows from this, as we have noted on several occasions, that the optimum agreements, those best internalized, will be those concluded between parties whose relationships normally assume a character of greatest conflict and the least quantum of spontaneous conformity. However, one must avoid endangering the cohesion of existing links – to which every individual reacts, either by withdrawing from public discussion and retiring into his shell, or, on the contrary, by intensifying opposition to the point where the participants no longer understand one another and give up trying to reach agreement.

The movement towards consensus spontaneously evokes convergent thinking. We shall consider this a little further.

2

Scheidel states:

> An isolated individual can alternatively follow both divergent and convergent lines of thought, but within an interacting decision-making group, the suggestion here is that divergent processes may emphasize and permit a greater individual focus, while convergent processes may often require talk, interaction, co-orientation and cooperation, assimilation and adaptation as the group moves toward a consensus. (1986: 122)

Taking these remarks into account, it may be said that the exchanges of information and arguments between the members of a group clarify and guide their opinions in the same direction. It is presumed that their representations of the problem and the alternatives shift closer and become uniform. To have some concrete idea of the process indicated, one need only think of the method used in most of the research investigations mentioned. It consists in employing a scale on which the subject must rank an opinion either higher or lower, and an alternative on a calibrated dimension. Thus, on the dimension of risk-taking, the alternative put forward to the imaginary person of leaving his job for a more attractive position from the financial viewpoint, but offering less guarantee of security, is placed higher than the one suggesting that he keep his less attractive employment, but one offering greater guarantees. The latter attitude is that of the public official, the former that of the 'young go-getter'.

However, the reasons that cause one to opt in favour of either the former or the latter may be numerous. The risky choice may be dictated by audacity, the love of money or the desire to advance rapidly in one's career. The prudent choice may spring from tradition, a sense of family responsibility or loyalty towards a firm. These reasons may in turn be assigned to a scale that measures what rank they occupy and how far they determine the level of acceptable risk. Finally, and this is not the least important, different individuals can arrive at an agreement at the same level, while ranking their reasons in a different order. When all these aspects are envisioned, one can see there is room for variations and heated disputes about the meaning of the positions adopted by each individual.

Now, by seeking together to come to a decision, at the same time they end up by agreeing on the reasons and the respective weighting of each. It can be said that their representations converge and become uniform, crystallizing round some of the reasons that henceforth they share in common. Consequently the range of judgements diminishes and their variability decreases. It is as if a fusion were being effected between them, in order to create a continuum along one single, common dimension, whether it be one of risk or prudence, innocence or guilt, and so on, all understood in the same way.

This is what emerged from an experiment by Doise (1973) undertaken in two schools in the canton of Geneva. The experimenters presented to the pupils eight placards of brown cardboard, measuring 35 cm wide by 33 cm high – thus, fairly big. On these placards were stuck geometrical figures established according to three criteria that were systematically varied: colour (orange or blue), form (triangular or square), size and number (two large or six small). The pupils stood around the eight placards laid out on a table and were told that they had been designed for a project to decorate their classroom. In order to learn what their tastes were, they were invited to choose individually the placard that pleased them most. Once the choice had been made, the placard was turned upside down and placed on a side table, and the pupil was invited to make a fresh choice among the remainder, until all eight placards had been ranked.

As can be surmised, the study took place under two conditions. Under the first, each pupil made his choice by himself; under the other, the subjects, in groups of three, had to reach an agreement on the placard that suited them best for decorating their classroom. Here we shall not go into the detail of the calculations made, but the fact is that the collective choices were more uniform and better structured than the individual choices (median test: $\chi^2 = 4.50; p < .025$). It turned out that the children structured their aesthetic choice better as a group than on their own. This was because they assessed more systematically the relative weighting of the criteria they employed.

It might be asked whether this presupposes a stereotyping, or, in other words, a systematic impoverishment of the elements used by the group in comparison with individuals. There is nothing to show this is the case. This at least can be demonstrated in another study by Doise (1973) in which school pupils, also from Geneva, were assigned the task of expressing their preferences for various occupations – baker, secretary, doctor, etc. – which were presented to them in pairs. They began by making their choice separately, and then made it again collectively, explaining the reasons for choosing one occupation rather than another. In this study Doise analysed the results by calculating the number of criteria according to which the pupil justified his choice and the number of items of intransivity. The latter index takes account of the frequency of such items, of the kind: the doctor is preferred to the baker, the baker to the secretary, but the secretary is preferred to the doctor. On an average the participants employed more criteria in the group than in the individual situation ($t = 2.94$; $p < .01$). Contrary to what one might have thought, their variety increased when one passed from the individual to the collective level. But it is interesting to note that this greater variety was accompanied by a cognitive structure that was more organized and clearer. The proof is shown in the number of 'intransitive' choices, which, for its part, decreased ($t = 2.94$; $p < .01$) when one shifted from the collective to the individual level.

3

Moreover, the existence of a common representation is marked by the emergence of a series of categories of opinions and judgements most frequently used, and, one might say, more general. Stripped of any singularity, and in a way simplified, they assume a prominence, and in so doing make explicit the alternatives that are at stake and orient the decision to be taken. In addition, and this must not be forgotten, they offer focal points around which the personal representations of group members can be organized and articulated more easily. In his theory of cognitive tuning Zajonc (1960) brought out the same argument; that is, by communicating actively one tends to think more coherently and systematically, and to transform, by unifying them, the categories one employs.

Moreover, these facts were exploited in our first experiment dealing with polarization (Moscovici and Zavalloni, 1969). We looked for indications of this cognitive transformation of individuals in a group. It is no exaggeration to state that the decisions, in the broadest sense, prepare the way for it and make it their prime target. The students who participated, it will be recalled, had to adopt a common attitude towards de Gaulle and the Americans. In order to arrive at this, particularly if the attitude were unfavourable, they had to acknowledge a common set of values and a common code. This most possibly assumed, among the categories available to each individual, the use solely of those that corresponded to that code. These were the ones that were retained, that were used frequently, and towards which individuals would converge. In order to verify this we calculated an entropy index (H) of the distribution of categories, borrowed from information theory. The

Table 8.1   *Individual versus group categories*

Scale	Dispersions		
	H$_i$	H$_g$	f
Opinion			
de Gaulle			
Individual categories	2.3		
			3.1*
Group categories		1.8	
Americans			
Individual categories	2.1		
			3.3*
Group categories		1.5	
Judgement			
de Gaulle			
Individual categories	2.1		
			6.6**
Group categories		1.5	

* $p < 0.1$
** $p < .001$

computation showed that the dispersion diminished significantly (see Table 8.1) when passing from individual to collective decisions. It is as if, when progressing towards an extreme consensus that everyone embraces, the subjects merely retained a range of general categories to which they resorted most frequently.

This is not an isolated observation. Indeed, in the study described in the preceding chapter, the groups of architecture students polarized if their rivalry with the École des Beaux-Arts was aroused. Doise (1969b) has calculated the same entropy index (H). He noted that individuals, particularly when they made their choices alone and without reference to any adversarial group, used a very wide range of categories. It was sufficient merely to get them together and invite them to discuss for this range to narrow. This was even more true when they were making comparisons with a rival group.

Yet more may be said. Up to now, we have above all considered what happens when, after having made their decisions separately, individuals discuss and make a fresh decision in the collective situation. The cognitive transformation might be attributed to the change of situation and not to the discussion and the interactions between group members from which there emerges a polarized consensus. This may be so. However, in another experiment (Moscovici, Doise and Dulong, 1972) we had the opportunity of regulating these interactions by asking the participants to arrive at an agreement, either freely and spontaneously, or by following a procedure. It was assumed already that the entropy that measured the distribution of categories before the groups came together to discuss would indicate a decrease in the number of such categories. It was a decrease that reflected a shift that tended to unify them, to make them converge in respect of categories, which thereby acquired a collective character.

The observations recorded allow us to go even further. A compromise consensus, as has been emphasized several times, preserves a certain autonomy as regards individual representations. In reality it only forces the surrender of divergent viewpoints to a limited extent. By contrast a polarized consensus around a dominant value tends to integrate points of view and to root them firmly in a group representation. This is indeed what was found, since groups discussing freely ended up by using less categories than did those which did so following a set procedure. The difference was marked. One might well think that the representation of the former groups became more social, if one may say so, than that of the latter.

Thus it is true that in a group in which individuals participate more intensively, they tend to stress what draws them closer, and to make explicit what they share in common. What in this manner they lose by way of information, since entropy decreases, they gain in comprehension and mental sociability. At this point the reader may wish to stop to ask a question: if the variety of choice categories and attitudes decreases, does this mean they become broader and at the same time more general? To answer this question we have to fall back on one of the rare experiments that appears to confirm this proposition. We owe the experiment to Vidmar (1974), who carried it out precisely for this reason. She employed a well-known scale, the Pettygrew Category Scale, invented to measure whether individuals use broader or narrower categories when they select information regarding some form of behaviour. The following is a sample of the items of which it consists. Between 1900 and 1940 there were on average forty-eight alleged lynchings a year in the United States. The person answering the questionnaire had to indicate what was the largest and the smallest number of lynchings he presumed took place each year. This questionnaire is often used to study racism. In this particular experiment the participants first filled in one of these separately. Then they were assembled in groups of four to discuss each item and take a unanimous decision. Once the meeting was over, each person was invited to indicate his final decision, it being made clear to him that there was no need for it to coincide with that of the group. So far as the decisions taken in common were concerned, the gap between the minimum and maximum estimates was much greater (80) after the discussion than before (69.7). We may add that the change was a lasting one. Indeed, the tendency to employ broader categories subsisted even when consensus had been reached, when each participant replied afresh and in isolation to the questionnaire.

There are reasons to think that the categories used by groups take on prominence. They give a special contour to one dimension of the problem, and to the angle from which one should look at and judge it, so that it can be discussed in optimum terms. This was seen in an experiment in which Doise (1970) compared the judgements of individuals to those of groups constituted for the purpose of ranking a series of descriptive terms along a principal dimension. The material used consisted of eleven stories that recounted the conduct of a schoolboy called John. In the first story, he seems completely introverted. However, as the stories proceed, he appears more and more extroverted. The participants in the experiment, pupils in a Paris secondary technical school, were invited to describe how they viewed John's behaviour by ringing one of three adjectives – introverted, extroverted, 'equiverted' (equipoised in disposition) – that were printed at the end of each story. The stimuli were presented to twelve groups in a random order, to six other groups in an order ranging from introversion to extroversion, and in the opposite order for the six last groups. Each group consisted of four pupils who gave judgements before consensus, at consensus and after consensus for each one of the eleven stories. If this principal dimension describing John's character became more marked, the extrovert and introvert answers should have increased in number during the process of consensus for the corresponding extreme stories, and have decreased for the story located on the opposite side to the given category. The 'equivert' answers, by contrast, should have increased for the story placed at the middle term and have decreased for the others.

Considering as extreme the stories for which at least half of the participants had individually ringed the introvert answer (stories 1 to 5), or the extrovert answers (stories 8 to 11), all the changes, almost without exception, shifted in the direction predicted. These changes persisted with individuals when they replied separately after the consensus. It is therefore appropriate to conclude that exchanges and interactions did really emphasize the position of the social stimuli on a principal dimension. One is persuaded of this when one observes that the variety of responses used to describe John's behaviour decreased. In fact the entropy of the distribution of these responses decreases in the same way at consensus as it did in previous studies. The groups therefore tackled the different stories on which they had to reach agreement according to a common code (see Table 8.2).

This study allows us to follow the shift that leads the groups to organize their representation of a person or a problem according to one salient

Table 8.2   *Average entropy by group for extreme and intermediate stimuli**

	Items 1–5	Items 6 and 7	Items 8–11
Pre-consensus	0.82	0.76	1.04
Consensus	0.49 (4.07)	0.25 (3.40)	0.76 (3.03)
Post-consensus	0.60 (3.53)	0.41 (3.50)	0.92 (2.76)

* In parentheses are the values of Wilcoxon's *z* relating to differences from the pre-consensus. They are all significant at a threshold of at least 0.01

dimension.[3] This dimension effects a cohesion that facilitates communication between the various viewpoints until the adoption of a single viewpoint. This is what individuals are least inclined to effect spontaneously.

Thus it appears from several sources that we have confirmation of the power of social and cognitive conflicts to transform the representation of individuals into an overall social representation during the process of decision-making. Not that the thinking and the discourse that converge towards it become as stereotyped and repetitive as one is inclined to believe. They are above all free from ambiguities on the mental plane as well as from doubts on the plane of values.

'It takes two to make a truth'

1

'Nobody', wrote Pascal,

> is ignorant of the truth that there are two approaches through which truths are received into the soul, and these, the understanding and the will, are the two principal powers. The most natural one is the understanding, for we should only assent to truths that have been demonstrated; but the most common one, although it goes against nature, is that of the will; for the majority of men are always inclined to believe not by proof, but by pleasurable approbation. (1985: 85)

Why is the most natural power not also the most common one? If it is truth by the understanding, expressed by an authority, why does it not carry conviction, as do other authorities? Does it lack that sensation which, in the event, signifies pleasure and agreement? Why, in short, when the proofs exist, is not success assured to the arguments put forward by the will?

These mysteries and many others in the process of decision-taking arise again just as much for the one who is observing as for the one who is participating. One realizes that during discussion the participants accumulate a host of items of information, of reasons for and against, of contrary signs on which each individual has necessarily his own opinion. And each individual is concerned with the quality of truth and of the proofs presented to him. Although it is not the main motive, this concern leads him to converge on a shared representation, which alone allows one to pass judgement with certainty. One may certainly say 'Each individual has his own truth'; but the truth of each individual arises from a decision taken by several. The guarantors of the worth of a piece of information or a proposition are one's partners and adversaries, and they alone. Austin, the British philosopher, suggests this in an admirable formula, 'It takes two to make a truth.' This cooperation plainly commits one to place value on the common elements and devalue the individual elements. May one say that such a prejudice has the effect of shifting ideas and sentiments in the same direction? It is a prejudice that consensus does not fail to emphasize, by retaining as true and credible what works in its favour, and dismissing what goes against it. In this is found the root cause of its importance and the hold it exerts. After all, what is the shared representation that it gives its blessing to if it is not the invigorated and enriched knowledge of the group, which, from the knowledge of individual members, seeks to grow?

One of the best conceived research programmes, that of Burnstein and his colleagues at the University of Michigan, shows us how items of information and arguments are bound to such a representation. This plainly deals with the process of persuasion, which underlies everything that is occurring when discussion and debate takes place among the participants. According to the hypothesis on which this programme is based, each group has available a stock of possible arguments in the defence of an attitude, the solution of a legal or political dilemma, etc. When the members of the group among whom this stock is distributed express their opinions and positions, they are exposed to the arguments of others, arguments that had previously not occurred to them. And discussion itself produces fresh motives for favouring the attitude or the solution that the majority had really preferred at the very beginning.

Burnstein and his colleagues attached very great importance to the difference in the amount of information among individuals, and to the number and novelty of the arguments whereby they sought to persuade one another. However, it was clear that this stock of information and arguments was the expression of a system of representations and beliefs common to the group, rather than the sum of ideas or propositions. Even clearer still is the fact that these arguments and items of knowledge were acknowledged to be similar, to have the same relationship to the dilemma, and presupposed a representation or belief defined by the culture. We know, for example, that those favouring free choice for women as regards motherhood are for abortion and share a political vision, whereas those who speak in favour of protecting the unborn child are against abortion and share the same religious vision of humanity. If this were not so, how could one disentangle the meaning of their arguments and the concordance that exists among them?

In any case, it appears reasonable to think that discussion and exchanges stress the social aspects of attitudes and dilemmas, making more explicit the public character of the representations that each individual entertains in private. In the light of previous studies, we cannot say, as is too often suggested, that the number of arguments is sufficient to persuade and to induce individuals to join the majority. Even less can we say that it causes the minority to adopt the positions of the majority, once consensus has been established and discussion is over, instead of reverting back to its original position. The discourse of persuasion, and we have numerous proofs of this, unfortunately does not have the power that is ascribed to it, that is, of changing attitudes and opinions in a lasting way or in proportion to the abundance of arguments put forward. (Eagly, 1974; Eagly and Himmelfarb, 1978). Something else is needed, a representation or belief shared in common (as the saying goes, 'one only preaches to the converted'), or indeed involvement in a common purpose. To arrive at a consensus, one has to reach wider convictions, as do religions and social movements. Just as it is preferable to have a hypothesis in order to observe facts, so the sketchy outlines of a representation must be shared in order to assimilate information and arguments and move in the direction towards which they point. Even more, one must be motivated to look for these in the common stock, and choose and present them in a convincing fashion. 'Thus members who are motivated to persuade others may concentrate on their stronger arguments. Members who have more extreme attitudes tend to dominate discussion' (Anderson and Graesser, 1976: 221). Probably they should also be more involved in the beliefs and values of the group, making them their personal concern, as we have seen recently among the dissidents of Eastern Europe.[4]

To have some idea of the process revealed by this research programme and to compare it with the viewpoint expounded here, we may refer to the study by Vinokur and Burnstein (1974). They first asked participants to reply separately to five dilemmas facing a person who had to make risky or prudent choices. They were then invited to draw up the list of arguments and reasons they might think up in favour of the alternatives for each dilemma. Moreover, the subjects had to indicate whether this or that argument or reason favoured risk-taking or prudence. When put together, these lists of arguments and reasons provided a complete picture of the individual representations relating to the five dilemmas. It was observed from the outset that the initial choice of the participants was determined by the balance of representations between risk and prudence. The participants were then assembled in groups to discuss the various options. For this part of the study the authors hypothesized that the decisions following upon a discussion would be polarized. But they would be so only if and to the extent that the individual representations, and thus the arguments and reasons, were shared by a certain number of individuals. The findings indicated that the hypothesis was verified. This leaves us to suppose that the seeds of a common representation only existed with certain members, but these sufficed to secure the adherence of the rest.

Merely to know the position of others could not have this effect. It is self-evident that only a systematic exchange of opinions and information, in the course of which the groups discovered familiar arguments and then produced new ones, allowed these phenomena to take root in a shared representation. As very often occurs, people seek after what is most consistent with this representation, and what brings them closer together, at the very moment when they learn what sets them against one another. 'Knowledge that others' choices are discrepant from his own induces the person to reconstruct a line of reasoning which he thinks could have produced such choice. That is to say, knowing others have chosen differently stimulates the persons to generate arguments which could explain (and thus support) their choices' (Burnstein et al., 1973: 244).

This is an admirable description of the social and cognitive conflict that sets minds working, provokes an effervescence of ideas and clarifies the alternatives between which a choice will have to be made. At that moment, moreover, in our terms, the task of decision-making openly begins, each individual being called upon to mobilize his moral and intellectual resources in order to overcome differences.

Provisionally, we shall stick to this description of the conflict in question in order to emphasize that, besides the intellectual aspect, it has a motivating and energizing one. This emerged from a study in which the participants had either to defend or attack their initial choices. By appropriate instructions, the experimenters created the impression that the positions on the scale of choice were assigned at random. This meant that it appeared impossible to discover whether a specific person presented arguments in favour of or against his initial choice, and thus whether he was prejudiced or not. As was to be expected, shifts took place in a group when the members defended their initial choices. But if – and this happens more frequently than is believed – they were asked to defend a position that at first they had rejected, for them this came down to defending what they deemed indefensible. Not only were they not motivated to generate many arguments, but, moreover, they did not care to express them in a convincing way. Furthermore, when no information on the choices of members of the group was passed on, the situation was resolved by a compromise. This was understandable since, in the event, they did not know what alternative they should opt for, nor what line of reasoning they should follow for their views to converge. 'This is to say,' Burnstein and Vinokur write,

> when choosing, the person weighs what he knows about the alternatives at hand (the relative importance of reasons or arguments for selecting one over the other, etc.); then, based on this knowledge, he makes some inference about their relative value, and eventually he chooses the alternative which appears most desirable, proper or correct. Analogously, when a group decides among (or merely discusses) these alternatives, in essence it infers relative desirability, propriety or correctness by possibly evaluating the arguments in its possession. (1975: 423)

Under these conditions, the decision is taken not to make a decision, and no shift occurs in any direction whatsoever, or there is only a minimum shift.

The acid test of the phenomena described and of their interpretation is of a quantitative type. We find it was used in a well-designed study (Ebbesen and Bowers, 1974), which used five dilemmas with which we are very familiar, selected according to a strong shift towards risk down to a strong shift towards prudence. For each dilemma the experimenters conceived of and drew up five different discussions in which they combined in varying proportions the arguments favouring risk and those that tended towards prudence. Each discussion was then tested and recorded and ten relevant arguments were selected. For each dilemma one of the discussions comprised nine arguments (90 per cent) favouring risk, and one argument favouring prudence. The other dilemmas combined arguments in varying proportions: 70/30 per cent, 50/50 per cent, 30/70 per cent and 10/90 per cent respectively for risk and for prudence. These proportions of the arguments were applied to the five dilemmas, although these latter led to different choices in one direction or the other.

Playing the role of passive listeners, the participants first replied to each question, then listened to a discussion on that question, and finally again replied separately. The purpose of the experiment, as can be seen, was to discover whether the proportion of arguments in favour of one of the alternatives influenced the direction and the degree of change in the choices that each individual made separately. It was indeed noted that, as the proportion of arguments in favour of risk increased, the shift towards risk was accentuated. The shift would be in the opposite direction if the arguments favouring prudence were increased. In reality, such a perfect correspondence between the frequency of the arguments and individual choices is so exceptional that there is something astonishing about it, and it can give rise to scepticism, or even jealousy.

We can allow that this shift towards the extreme is very gradual and very marked, in the absence of any discussion or relationship that modifies the decision of individuals when they take their collective decision. But everyone knows (and it is common sense) that relationships can just as well lead to a compromise in order to avoid conflicts. When we are attempting to make a question less contentious, to defuse a controversy and create a more relaxed atmosphere, it is better to agree to concessions in order to prevent people from taking up extreme positions, regardless of the number of arguments that may be exchanged afterwards. On several occasions we have seen that groups tend to polarize when they wish to distinguish themselves from other groups and oppose them. This has been proved. However, by modifying relationships so as to make them less hostile, and even more open, we would find a shift towards compromise. (This was observable at the time when relationships between the United States and the Soviet Union were becoming warmer and seemed to be passing from the Cold War to a really peaceful coexistence.)

This phenomenon has been demonstrated in a study by Vinokur and Burnstein (1978) conceived on the same principle as former studies. They assembled the participants in groups of six to discuss four standard dilemmas. Each group was made up of two factions or sub-groups of a homogeneous nature, one of which adopted an extreme position that differed markedly from the position adopted by the other group, and even opposed it. This might be indicated by some visible sign, or explained before the discussion and highlighted during the whole process of interaction by the seating arrangement and by the labelling of the participants being clearly visible. What then occurred? The most striking effect was a compromise and a shift towards the mean, as was very clearly shown.

Let us look at matters in greater detail. It will be recalled that a neutral dilemma is one in which the whole of the arguments put forward are in equal proportion in favour of risk or in favour of prudence. The risk items are those for which the stock of arguments favourable to risk that have been collected definitely exceeds those that recommend prudence; it is evidently the reverse for items relating to prudence. What do we find when these items come to be discussed by two opposing groups? The groups will certainly agree on a compromise, and the two extremes are drawn closer together. But we note also another outcome: for items bearing on risk the group nearest the extreme of risk shifts less towards prudence than the shift of the group located nearer the extreme of prudence, which, for its part, draws much closer to that of risk. The reverse occurs in the case of an item tending towards prudence. The compromise arrived at or the fresh position adopted is thus moderated as a whole, but is also closer to the dominant pole for this particular type of dilemma (Burnstein, 1982). The fact that one has or has not given prominence to the opposition between the groups has no repercussions on the phenomena observed.

If a counter-proof were required, it might be provided in the study by Wetherell (1987) and Turner (1987). This followed the format of the studies we have just described. The authors modified it, however, by separating distinctly the positions for and against, with a neutral point in the middle. Then they asked the participants to discuss without requesting them to reach a consensus. In short, if the cognitive data are roughly the same, the social conflict is accentuated, since any reconciliation is neither mandatory nor facilitated. Under these conditions – and this is normally the case – the participants do not reach a compromise, and this is even more so because their opposition is made apparent by symbols. Clearly this kind of relationship regulates the use that is made of information and intellectual faculties.

2

We are therefore prepared to envisage the role that is played by the content of the message, about which very little is known. The little that is known is not sufficient to satisfy our curiosity. The predominant impression is that a disagreement that arises and persists has some relationship to the content of the message and the degree to which it involves us. This is what impels us to seek for information, to enrich the stock of arguments and to discover new ones. All in all, we are impelled to nurture the relationship with others, then to dismantle obstacles in the process until we can arrive at an agreement on a common position, either one of compromise or an extreme choice. It has a particular quality, of paramount interest: that of fixing the contours of the reality in which the group is located.

This can be observed in another study by Vinokur and Burnstein (1978). It is no exaggeration to state that the way in which individuals occupy themselves with a problem, seek information about it and discuss it, gives a rough measure of the knowledge they possess of it and of the interest they take in it. When it fixes their attention, occupies their thoughts, leads them to read books or articles, and to talk about it among themselves, they become ever more involved and are better informed as to what one may think about it. Their knowledge more or less coincides. Moreover, being involved in the object and perhaps committed to a position, they will be motivated to recognize this knowledge in the form of arguments or reasons. Furthermore, individuals who rarely think about a problem, who do not inform themselves about it through their reading and do not discuss it with one another, will be somewhat indifferent to it and not know much about it. Their knowledge will have little chance of coinciding with that of others and their lack of involvement will hardly induce them to reconstitute their fragmentary knowledge or to defend a position. Thus, the more an object is significant, the more arguments will be shared, and the less chance a group discussion has to end up with a compromise.

In their study Vinokur and Burnstein brought the participants together and divided them into two sets in exactly the same way as outlined above. But, instead of suggesting they discuss dilemmas, they submitted a series of questions to them. Some were of a social kind (for example, 'Is the death penalty justifiable?'); others related to personal taste (for example, 'Do the warm colours [red, orange] seem more attractive to you than the cool colours [blue, green] in order to decorate a living room?'); finally, the rest alluded to facts that are fairly obscure (for example, 'How many metres below sea-level does Sodom, on the bank of the Dead Sea, lie?').

Presumably the participants will be more inclined to make concessions towards a compromise if their individual representation already coincides with the existing social representation, when the latter is more comprehensive, and thus the difference that separates them is one of a minor order. In short, interest, like the object at stake highlighted by the content, is not very much to the fore in this case. Leaving out the details, we observe that, in the divided groups, the strongest compromise took place concerning the obscure facts, and the weakest concerning the social problems, with those concerning taste in the middle. Numerically, the proportional reduction in the standard deviation is .81 for the first category of questions, .18 for the second category and .35 for the third. Although these indications are very few, they are nevertheless enough to show the intertwining of cognitive factors and social relationships in the phenomena that concern us here. Undoubtedly the indications we have are hardly surprising, but the fact of supporting a hypothesis that complements others gives this study very special value.

However, let us not stop at what has become to us already familiar. During our study, we have suggested a series of hypotheses that have in common the explanation of collective decisions. From the very beginning they were of a character that situated the phenomena described and predicted, among them that of polarization, at the level of the whole group. Undoubtedly, later, following a natural bent in contemporary social psychology, these same phenomena have been brought back to the level of the individual. In other words, people have thought that they signified that individuals, as members of a group, change their attitudes because they persuade one another and in consequence adopt a more extreme attitude. In this way individual change modifies in turn the reaction and consensus at group level.

Who will claim that we can clearly distinguish between the two levels? It is all the more difficult for us because the decision that leads to consensus associates them closely together. Since there is no abstract solution to the problem of individuals who have to take part in an agreement as members of their group, our hypotheses must start from a general, concrete factor; namely, from the social and cognitive conflict[5] due to a difference in positions and levels of knowledge, and to the opposition between viewpoints, all of which allows individuals better to express their various representations of the problem and the reality with which they are faced. Each individual thus becomes the ardent defender, against the rest, of his judgements and his own attitudes, and becomes involved almost without knowing it. Consequently he participates more intensely and feels himself more committed to his position than previously. The arguments that each individual brings forward for public discussion contribute to strengthening that involvement, but also the conviction that his judgements and attitudes have the same value for the other members of the groups as they have for himself.

Yet this group, in which they are participants, assigns to them the task of finding the best solution, one that suits them all. This inclines them to give more weight to the arguments that correspond to the values they share and foreshadows what will be the common tendency. Thus this is to give weight to what bound them already before the conflict and will bind them still more afterwards; namely, the dominant values in the environment to which they belong. Even without their being aware of it, they prepare a line of convergence for their minds and interests, the consensus of the majority and of the minority, in spite of everything that opposes them to each other. Once the decision has been taken, since everyone adheres to it, one feels one's own personal conviction strengthened; one is certain that one has judged reasonably and opted for the best solution. The situation is the same at a political congress: from the moment one of the candidates has been elected, he is looked upon with a different eye and everyone feels changed and converted; so, during the task of decision-taking, once one of the alternatives has received everybody's assent, each individual feels himself bound by it and through it to the other participants, as if their relationships have fused together. Superficially one can note a convergence of viewpoints, an enlargement of the categories of thought and the prominence of a common dimension. But deep down the subtle movement of individual representations is being transformed into a social representation of the members of the group. There is no longer any question of debatable alternatives. In their place there is an exact vision, the overall vision arising from several individuals, which is eventually shared as an unquestionable norm.

We recognize here the consequences of the task of decision-making, which go much further than those attributed to it: to deal with items of information, to harmonize values, and to reconcile divergent attitudes and interests. These are the outcomes of the links made between persons as soon as they begin to communicate and discuss together, and, above all, to commit themselves to a course leading to an agreement. Afterwards they feel themselves bound by it as if it were a moral duty or a religious oath – even in the absence of partners or adversaries – and this, in a permanent fashion. For the moment we have some theoretical glimpses of this, supported by a network of foreseen facts intended to illustrate it. It gives a glimpse, certainly inadequate, of this unknown territory in social psychology. But let us be comforted by the thought that an explanation exists, and that it is general enough to comprehend a significant portion of reality.

Notes

1 We are referring to the conceptions of Austin (1962) and Grice (1975), which have become common today.

2 We suggest the expression 'work of decision' by analogy with that of the 'dream work' used by Freud, to designate the transformation of the latent thoughts of dreams into manifest thoughts. The expression signifies that the formation of consensus has the aim not of aggregating individual opinions and preferences, of rectifying them by providing better information, etc., but of transforming them into social opinions and preferences. This is why it is appropriate to speak specifically of the work of decision in incorporating them into everyday social life.

3 Other research does indeed show that the salience of the categories entails extreme attitudes and judgements (Eiser and Stroebe, 1972; Upmeyer and Layer, 1974). This research reveals the effect of the controversies and discussions inherent in choices made in common, which is what concerns us here.

4 The theory of persuasive argument believes it possible to dispense with norms and values. It assumes that the arguments from the stock can vary in number, availability (that is, the probability that such and such an argument will come to mind), direction (for example, for and against drugs), and in the degree of persuasiveness. Knowing these things, one can forecast the distribution of opinions within the group before the discussion; when the preponderance of arguments in the stock favours a particular position, the initial opinions of the participants will reflect the direction and size of this preponderance. Next, they indicate the direction of polarization of opinion towards the alternative, which relies on the greatest number of arguments, and/or the best of them.

But the theory ascribes too much to itself and yet too little. It ascribes too much by placing things that are too disparate under the same heading of information, to a point where the latter becomes imprecise. In spite of everything, if to know the norm of a group is the same thing as knowing its opinions on this or that problem, the very notion of norm becomes unreal. Yet the theory does not say enough about how one learns of what this stock consists, or what makes one argument better than another in the eyes of the member of the group. This leads, moreover, to minimizing greatly the importance of the relationships between them (Burnstein et al., 1973; Lamm et al.; 1973; Vinokur and Burnstein, 1974). One thing appears to be certain: the theory relies too heavily on a dichotomy that we deem likely to lead to error, the dichotomy between the influence of information and normative influence, the scientific worth of which now belongs to the past. It is true that there should be no forcing of reality. Yet, when the authors of the theory insist upon the necessity for the arguments to be new for polarization to take place, on what are they insisting? It is upon the element of social and cognitive conflict between old and new representations, on what intensifies the participation of members of a group and involves them in the process of decision. Unless it is upon the complexity of the arguments, which always are assessed more extremely than their familiar components, and on condition that these components all have the same negative or positive sense (Anderson and Jacobson, 1965; Manis et al., 1966).

A large part of respectable cognitive psychology operates in this area, without, however, succeeding in eliminating what is embedded in the reality of individuals, insofar as they form part of an institution. It is always useful to recall that decisions leading to consensus, whether implicit or explicit, are established, legitimate psychological phenomena. This is not without having profound consequences on the relationship between causes and effects, which must needs be explained. One cannot profitably inquire into the 'black box' of the individual without at the same time looking into the social 'black box'. It is even impossible to distinguish the one from the other, as is demonstrated in the study by Burnstein and Vinokur (1975) where the common value is strongly correlated with the cognitive activity of individuals. To sum up, the theory and the studies that inspire it allow us to use one basis, among others, in order to assess the changes in attitudes in groups exposed to arguments of persuasion.

5 A few studies devoted to social conflict in other fields arrive at analogous conclusions (Ames and Murray, 1982; Campbell, 1969; Doise and Mugny, 1981; Mahoney, 1977; Mahoney et al., 1978).

Bibliography

Abelson, R.P. and Levi, A. (1985) 'Decision-making and decision theory', in G. Lindzey and E. Aronson (eds), *Handbook of Social Psychology*, Vol. I, New York: Random House, pp. 231–309.

Abric, J.C. (1971) 'Experimental study of group creativity: task representation, group structure and performance', *European Journal of Social Psychology*, 1: 311–26.

Adams, J. (1851) 'Discourse on Davila', *Works*, Vol. VI. Boston.

Alker, H.A. and Kogan, N. (1968) 'Effects of norm-oriented group discussion on individual verbal risk-taking and conservatism', *Human Relations*, 21: 393–405.

Allport, F.H. (1920) 'The influence of the group upon association of thought', *Journal of Experimental Psychology*, 3: 159–82.

Allport, F.H. (1924) *Social Psychology*. Boston: Houghton Mifflin.

Allport, F.H. and Hartmann, D.H. (1925) 'The measurement and motivation of atypical opinion in a certain group', *American Political Science Review*, 9: 735–60.

Ames, G.J. and Murray, F.B. (1982) 'When two wrongs make a right: promoting cognitive change by social conflict', *Developmental Psychology*, 10: 894–7.

Anderson, N.H. and Graesser, C.C. (1976) 'An information integration analysis of attitude change in group discussion', *Journal of Personality and Social Psychology*, 37:210–22.

Anderson, N.H. and Jacobson, A. (1965) 'Effects of stimulus inconsistency and discounting instructions in personality impression formation', *Journal of Personality and Social Psychology*, 2: 531–9.

Aragon, L. (1958) *La Semaine Sainte*. Paris: Gallimard.

Arendt, H. (1961) *Between Past and Future*. New York: Meridian.

Arendt, H. (1983) *The Human Condition*. Chicago/London: University of Chicago Press.

Arrow, K.J. (1963) *Social Choice and Individual Values*. New York: J. Wiley.

Arrow, K.J. (1974) *The Limits of Organization*. New York: W.W. Norton & Co.

Asch, S.E. (1959) 'A perspective on social psychology', in S. Koch (ed.), *Psychology: a Study of a Science*, Vol. 3. New York: McGraw-Hill. pp. 363–83.

Atkinson, J.M. and Heritage, J. (1984) *Structures of Social Action: Studies in Conversation Analysis*. Cambridge: Cambridge University Press.

Austin, J.L. (1962) *How to do Things with Words*. Oxford: Oxford University Press.

Bailey, F.G. (1988) *Humbuggery and Manipulation: the Art of Leadership*. Ithaca, NY: Cornell University Press.

Barnlund, D.C. (1959) 'A comparative study of individual, majority, and group judgment', *Journal of Abnormal and Social Psychology*, 58: 55–60.

Baron, P.H., Baron, R.S. and Roper, G. (1974) 'External validity and risky shift: empirical limits and the theoretical implications', *Journal of Personality and Social Psychology*, 30: 95–103.

Baron, R.S., Dion, K.L., Baron, P.H. and Miller, N. (1971) 'Group consensus and cultural values as determinants of risk-taking', *Journal of Personality and Social Psychology*, 20: 446–55.

Baron, R.S., Manson, T.C. and Baron, P.H. (1973) 'Conformity pressure as a determinant of risk-taking: replication and extension', *Journal of Personality and Social Psychology*, 28: 406–13.

Baron, R.S., Roper, G. and Baron, P.H. (1974) 'Group discussion and the stingy shift', *Journal of Personality and Social Psychology*, 30: 538–45.

Bartlett, F. (1932) *Remembering*. Cambridge: Cambridge University Press.

Bell, P.R. and Jamieson, B.D. (1970) 'Publicity on initial decisions in the risky shift phenomenon', *Journal of Experimental Social Psychology*, 6: 329–45.

Bem, D.J., Wallach, M.A. and Kogan, N. (1965) 'Group decision-making under risk of aversive consequences', *Journal of Personality and Social Psychology*, 1: 453–60.

Bennett, E.B. (1955) 'Discussion, decision, commitment and consensus in "group decision"', *Human Relations*, 8: 251–73.

Bergson, H. (1976) *Les Deux Sources de la morale et de la religion*. Paris: Presses Universitaires de France.

Berkowitz, L. (1953) 'Sharing leadership in small, decision-making groups', *Journal of Abnormal and Social Psychology*, 48: 231–8.

Berlin, I. (1981) *Against the Current*. Oxford: Oxford University Press.

Billig, M. (1973) 'Normative communication in a minimal intergroup situation', *European Journal of Social Psychology*, 3: 339–43.

Billig, M. (1987) *Arguing and Thinking*. Cambridge: Cambridge University Press.

Bishop, G.D. and Myers, D.G. (1974) 'Information influence in group discussion', *Organizational Behavior and Human Performance*, 12: 92–104.

Blake, R.R., Shepard, H.A. and Mouton, J.S. (1964) *Managing Intergroup Conflict in Industry*. Houston: Gulf Publishing Co.

Bogdanoff, N.O., Klein, R.F., Bock, K.W., Nichols, C.R., Troyer, W.G. and Hood, T.C. (1964) 'Effect of group relationship and the role of leadership upon lipid mobilization', *Psychosomatic Medicine*, 26: 710–19.

Borgatta, E.F. and Bates, R.F. (1953) 'Task and accumulation of experience as factors in the interaction of small groups', *Sociometry*, 16: 239–52.

Brandstätter, H., Davis, J.H. and Stocker-Kreichgauer, G. (eds) (1982) *Group Decision-making*. London: Academic Press.

Bray, R.M. and Noble, A.M. (1978) 'Authoritarianism and decisions of mock juries: evidence of jury bias and group polarization', *Journal of Personality and Social Psychology*, 36: 1424–30.

Brengelman, J.C. (1960) 'Extreme response set, drive level and abnormality in questionnaire rigidity', *Journal of Mental Science*, 106: 171–86.

Brim, O.G. (1955) 'Attitude content-intensity and probability expectations', *American Sociological Review*, 20: 68–76.

Brown, R. (1965) *Social Psychology*. New York: Free Press.

Brown, R. (1974) 'Further comment on the risky shift', *American Psychologist*, 29: 468–70.

Burnstein, E. (1969) 'An analysis of group decisions involving risk ("the risky shift")', *Human Relations*, 22: 381–95.

Burnstein, E. (1982) 'Persuasion as argument processing', in H. Brandstätter et al. (eds), *Group Decision-making*. London: Academic Press. pp. 103–24.

Burnstein, E., Miller, H., Vinokur, A., Katz, S. and Crowley, J. (1971) 'Risky shift is eminently rational', *Journal of Personality and Social Psychology*, 20: 462–71.

Burnstein, E. and Vinokur, A. (1973) 'Testing two classes of theories about group-induced shifts in individual choice', *Journal of Experimental Social Psychology*, 9: 123–37.

Burnstein, E. and Vinokur, A. (1975) 'What a person thinks upon learning he has chosen differently from others: nice evidence for the persuasive-arguments explanation of choice shifts', *Journal of Experimental Social Psychology*, 11: 412–26.

Burnstein, E. and Vinokur, A. (1977) 'Persuasive argumentation and social comparison as determinants of attitude polarization', *Journal of Experimental Social Psychology*, 13: 315–35.

Burnstein, E., Vinokur, A. and Trope, Y. (1973) 'Interpersonal comparison versus persuasive argumentation: a more direct test of alternative explanations for group-induced shifts in individual choice', *Journal of Experimental Social Psychology*, 9: 236–45.

Caldeira, C. (1988) 'Que "Educacâo Popular" par a Constituinte?' *Proposta*, 13: 42–8.

Campbell, D.T. (1956) 'Enhancement of contrast as a composite habit', *Journal of Abnormal and Social Psychology*, 53: 350–55.

Campbell, D.T. (1969) 'Reforms as experiments', *American Psychologist*, 24: 409–29.

Bibliography

Cantril, H. (1946) 'The intensity of an attitude', *Journal of Abnormal and Social Psychology*, 41: 129–35.

Cartwright, D. (1971) 'Risk-taking by individuals and groups: an assessment of research employing choice dilemmas', *Journal of Personality and Social Psychology*, 20: 361–78.

Castore, C.H. (1972) 'Group discussion and pre-discussion assessment of preferences in the risky shift', *Journal of Experimental Social Psychology*, 8: 161–7.

Castore, C.H. and Murningham, J.K. (1978) 'Determinants of support for group decision', *Organizational Behavior and Human Performance*, 22: 75–92.

Cattaneo, C. (1864) 'Dell'antitesi come metodo di psicologia sociale', *Il Politechnico*, 20: 262–70.

Cecil, E.A., Chertkoff, J.M. and Cummings, L.L. (1970) 'Risk-taking in groups as a function of group pressure', *Journal of Social Psychology*, 81: 273–4.

Charters, W.W. and Newcomb, T.M. (1952) 'Some attitudinal effects of experimentally increased salience of a membership group', in G.E. Swanson, T.M. Newcomb and E.L. Hartley (eds), *Readings in Social Psychology*. New York: Holt. pp. 415–20.

Chevigny, P. (1988) *More Speech: Dialogue Rights and Modern Liberty*. Philadelphia: Temple University Press.

Clark, R.D. (1971) 'Group-induced shift toward risk: a critical appraisal', *Psychological Bulletin*, 76: 251–70.

Clark, R.D. and Crockett, W.H. (1971) 'Subjects' initial positions, exposure to varying opinions, and the risky shift', *Psychonomic Science*, 23: 277–9.

Clark, R.D., Crockett, W.H. and Archer, R.L. (1971) 'Risk-as-value hypothesis: the relationship between perception of self, others and risky shift', *Journal of Personality and Social Psychology*, 20: 425–9.

Clark, R.D. and Willems, E.P. (1969) 'Where is the risky shift? Dependence on instructions', *Journal of Personality and Social Psychology*, 13: 215–21.

Coleman, J. (1973) *Community Conflict*. Glencoe, IL: Free Press.

Collins, B.E. and Guetzkow, H. (1964) *A Social Psychology of Group Processes in Decision-making*. New York: J. Wiley & Sons.

Coser, L.A. (1956) *The Function of Social Conflict*. New York: Free Press.

Crick, F. (1990) *What Mad Pursuit: a Personal View of Scientific Discovery*. Harmondsworth: Penguin Books.

Cvetkovich, G. and Baumgardner, S.R. (1973) 'Attitude polarization: the relative influence of discussion group structure and reference group norms', *Journal of Personality and Social Psychology*, 26: 159–65.

Davis, J.H. (1969) *Group Performance*. Reading, MA: Addison-Wesley.

Davis, J.H. (1982) 'Social interaction as a combinatorial process in group', in H. Brandstätter et al. (eds), *Group Decision-making*. London: Academic Press. pp. 27–58.

Davis, J.H. and Hinsz, V.B. (1982) 'Current research problems in group performance and group dynamics', in H. Brandstätter et al. (eds), *Group Decision-making*. London: Academic Press. pp. 1–20.

Davis, J.H., Kerr, N.L., Atwin, R.S., Holt, R. and Meek, D. (1975) 'The decision process of 6- and 12-person mock juries assigned unanimous and two-thirds majority rules', *Journal of Personality and Social Psychology*, 32: 1–14.

Davis, J.H. and Restle, F. (1963) 'The analysis of problems and a prediction of group problem-solving', *Journal of Abnormal and Social Psychology*, 66: 103–16.

Davis, J.H., Stasser, G., Spitzer, C.E. and Holt, R.W. (1976) 'Changes in group members' decision preferences during discussion: an illustration with mock juries', *Journal of Personality and Social Psychology*, 34: 1177–87.

Davis, J.H., Stasson, M., Ono, K. and Zimmerman, S. (1988) 'Effects of straw polls on group decision-making: sequential voting pattern, timing, and local majorities', *Journal of Personality and Social Psychology*, 55: 918–26.

Deconchy, J.P. (1980) *Orthodoxie religieuse et sciences humaines*, suivi de *(Religious) Orthodoxy, Rationality and Scientific Knowledge*. Paris: Mouton.

Deutsch, M. (1973) *The Resolution of Conflict*. New Haven, CT: Yale University Press.

Deutsch, M. (1985) *Distributive Justice*. New Haven, CT: Yale University Press.

Deutsch, M. and Gerard, H.B. (1955) 'A study of normative and informational social influences upon individual judgement', *Journal of Abnormal and Social Psychology*, 51: 629–36.

Dion, K.L., Baron, R.S. and Miller, N. (1970) 'Why do groups make riskier decisions than individuals?', in L. Berkowitz (ed.), *Advances in Experimental Social Psychology*, Vol. 5. New York: Academic Press. pp. 306–77.

Dion, K.L., Miller, N.H. and Magnan, M.A. (1971) 'Cohesiveness and social responsibility as determinants of group risk-taking', *Journal of Personality and Social Psychology*, 20: 400–6.

Doise, W. (1969a) 'Jugement collectif et prise de risque des petits groupes', *Psychologie Française*, 14: 87–96.

Doise, W. (1969b) 'Intergroup relations and polarization of individual and collective judgments', *Journal of Personality and Social Psychology*, 12: 136–43.

Doise, W. (1970) 'L'importance d'une dimension principale dans les jugements collectifs', *Année psychologique*, 70: 151–9.

Doise, W. (1971) 'An apparent exception to the extremization of collective judgments', *European Journal of Social Psychology*, 1: 511–18.

Doise, W. (1973) 'La structuration cognitive des décisions individuelles et collectives d'adultes et d'enfants', *Revue de psychologie et des sciences de l'éducation*, 8: 133–46.

Doise, W. (1978) *Groups and Individuals: Explanations in Social Psychology*. Cambridge: Cambridge University Press.

Doise, W. (1979) *Expériences entre groupes*. Paris: Mouton.

Doise, W. and Moscovici, S. (1984) 'Les décisions en groupe', in S. Moscovici (ed.), *Psychologie sociale*. Paris: Presses Universitaires de France. pp. 213–27.

Doise, W. and Mugny, G. (1981) *Le développement social de l'intelligence*. Paris: Interéditions.

Durkheim, E. (1978) *La Division du travail social*. Paris: Presses Universitaires de France.

Eagly, A.H. (1967) 'Involvement as a determinant of response to favorable and unfavorable information', *Journal of Personality and Social Psychology*, 7: 1–15.

Eagly, A.H. (1974) 'Comprehensibility of persuasive arguments as a determinant of opinion change', *Journal of Personality and Social Psychology*, 29: 758–73.

Eagly, A.H. and Himmelfarb, S. (1978) 'Attitudes and opinions', *Annual Review of Psychology*, 29: 517–54.

Eagly, A.H. and Manis, M. (1966) 'Evaluation of message and communication as a function of involvement', *Journal of Personality and Social Psychology*, 3: 483–5.

Ebbesen, E.B. and Bowers, R.J. (1974) 'Proportion of risky to conservative arguments in a group discussion and choice shift', *Journal of Personality and Social Psychology*, 29: 316–27.

Einhorn, H.J., Hogarth, R.M. and Klempner, E. (1977) 'Quality of group judgment', *Psychological Bulletin*, 84: 158–72.

Eiser, J.R. (1971) 'Comment on Ward's "Attitude and involvement in the absolute judgment of attitude statements"', *Journal of Personality and Social Psychology*, 17: 81–3.

Eiser, J.R. and Stroebe, W. (1972) *Categorization and Social Judgment*. London: Academic Press.

Ellis, H.D., Spencer, C.P. and Oldfield-Box, H. (1969) 'Matched group and the risky shift phenomenon: a defence of the extreme member hypothesis', *British Journal of Social and Clinical Psychology*, 8: 333–9.

Faucheux, C. and Moscovici, S. (1960) 'Études sur la créativité des groupes II: tâche, structure de communications et réussite', *Bulletin du Centre d'Etudes et de Recherches Psychotechniques*, 9: 11–22.

Festinger, L. (1950) 'Informal social communication', *Psychological Review*, 57: 271–82.

Festinger, L. (1954) 'A theory of social comparison processes', *Human Relations*, 7: 117–40.

Fiske, S.T. and Taylor, S.E. (1984) *Social Cognition*. Reading, MA: Addison-Wesley.

Flowers, M.L. (1977) 'A laboratory test of some implications of Janis's groupthink hypothesis', *Journal of Personality and Social Psychology*, 35: 888–96.

Forgas, J.P. (1977) 'Polarization and moderation of person perception judgements as a function of group interaction style', *European Journal of Social Psychology*, 7: 175–87.

Forgas, J.P. (1981) 'Responsibility attribution by groups and individuals: the effects of the interaction episode', *European Journal of Social Psychology*, 11: 87–99.

Fraser, C., Gouge, C. and Billig, M. (1971) 'Risky shifts, cautious shifts and group polarization', *European Journal of Social Psychology*, 1: 7–30.

Freedman, J.L. and Fraser, S.C. (1966) 'Compliance without pressure: the foot-in-the-door technique', *Journal of Personality and Social Psychology*, 4: 195–202.

French, J.R.P., Jr (1941) 'The disruption and cohesion of groups', *Journal of Abnormal and Social Psychology*, 36: 361–76.

Freud, S. (1981) *Essais de Psychanalyse*. Paris: Payot.

Gaskell, G.D., Thomas, E.A.C. and Farr, R.M. (1973) 'Effects of pretesting on measures of individual risk preferences', *Journal of Personality and Social Psychology*, 25: 192–8.

Gerard, H.B. (1961) 'Disagreement with others, their credibility, and experienced stress', *Journal of Abnormal and Social Psychology*, 62: 559–64.

Goethals, G.R. and Zanna, M.P. (1979) 'The role of social comparison in choice shifts', *Journal of Personality and Social Psychology*, 37: 1469–76.

Goffman, E. (1967) *Interaction Ritual*. New York: Anchor.

Goffman, E. (1983) 'The interaction order', *American Sociological Review*, 48: 1–17.

Gouge, C. and Fraser, C. (1972) 'A further demonstration of group polarization', *European Journal of Social Psychology*, 2: 95–7.

Gramsci, A. (1953) *Note sul Machiavelli*, Milan: Einaudi.

Grice, P.H. (1975) 'Logic and conversation', in P. Cole and J.L. Morgan (eds), *Speech Acts*, Vol. 3. New York: Academic Press. pp. 41–58.

Grice, P.H. (1982) 'Meaning revisited', in N.V. Smith (ed.), *Mutual Knowledge*. London: Academic Press. pp. 223–46.

Guetzkow, H. and Gyr, J. (1954) 'An analysis of conflict in decision-making groups', *Human Relations*, 4: 367–82.

Guyot, Y. (1970) 'Espace pédagogique et relations professeurs–étudiants', *Revue internationale de psychologie appliquée*, 19: 161–71.

Habermas, J. (1990) *Moral Consciousness and Communicative Action*, tr. C. Lenhardt and S.W. Nicolsen. Cambridge: Polity.

Hagstrom, W.O. (1965) *The Scientific Community*. New York: Basic Books.

Haley, H.J. and Rule, B.G. (1971) 'Group composition effects on risk-taking', *Journal of Personality*, 39: 150–61.

Hall, J. and Watson, W.H. (1970) 'The effects of a normative intervention on group decision-making performance', *Human Relations*, 23: 299–317.

Harkins, S.G., Latané, B. and Williams, K. (1980) 'Social loafing: allocating effort or taking it easy?', *Journal of Experimental Social Psychology*, 16: 457–65.

Hayek, F. von (1986) *Scientisme et science sociales*. Paris: Plon.

Hegel, G.W.F. (1965) *La Raison dans l'histoire*. Paris: Plon.

Heider, F. (1958) *The Psychology of Interpersonal Relations*. New York: J. Wiley & Sons.

Hermann, M.G. and Kogan, N. (1968) 'Negotiation in leader and delegate groups', *Journal of Conflict Resolution*, 12: 332–44.

Hewstone, M. and Jaspars, J. (1982) 'Explanations for racial discrimination: the effect of group discussion on intergroup attributions', *European Journal of Social Psychology*, 12: 1–16.

Hirschman, A.O. (1979) *Shifting Involvements*. Princeton: Princeton University Press.

Hoffman, R.L. and Maier, N.R.F. (1961) 'Quality and acceptance of problem solutions by members of homogeneous and heterogeneous groups', *Journal of Abnormal and Social Psychology*, 62: 401–7.

Horne, W.C. and Long, G. (1972) 'Effects of group discussion on universalistic-particularistic orientation', *Journal of Experimental Social Psychology*, 8: 236–46.

Hovland, C.I. and Sherif, M. (1952) 'Judgmental phenomena and scales of attitude measurement: item displacement in Thurstone scales', *Journal of Abnormal and Social Psychology*, 47: 822–32.

Hoyt, G.C. and Stoner, J.A.F. (1968) 'Leadership and group decisions involving risk', *Journal of Experimental Social Psychology*, 4: 275–84.

James, H. (1987) *Du roman considéré comme un des beaux-arts*. Paris: Bourgois.

Jamieson, B.D. (1968) 'The "risky shift" phenomenon with a heterogeneous sample', *Psychological Reports*, 23: 203–6.

Janis, I.L. (1972) *Victims of Groupthink*. Boston: Houghton Mifflin.

Jesuino, J.C. (1986) 'Influence of leadership processes on group polarization', *European Journal of Social Psychology*, 16: 413–23.

Johnson, D.L. and Andrews, I.R. (1971) 'Risky-shift phenomenon tested with consumer products as stimuli', *Journal of Personality and Social Psychology*, 20: 382–5.

Jones, E.E. and Gerard, H.B. (1967) *Foundations of Social Psychology*, New York: J. Wiley & Sons.

Jorgenson, D.O. and Papciak, A.S. (1981) 'The effects of communication, resource feedback, and identifiability on behavior in a simulated commons', *Journal of Experimental Social Psychology*, 17: 373–85.

Kalven, H. and Zeisel, H. (1966) *The American Jury*. Boston: Little, Brown & Co.

Kaplan, M.F. (1977) 'Discussion polarization effects in a modified jury decision paradigm: informational influences, *Sociometry*, 40: 262–71.

Kaplan, M.F. and Miller, C.E. (1977) 'Judgments and group discussion: effect of presentation and memory factors on polarization', *Sociometry*, 40: 337–43.

Kaplan, M.F., and Miller, C.E. (1985) 'Group discussion and judgment', in P.B. Paulus (ed.), *Basic Group Processes*. New York: Springer. pp. 65–94.

Kelley, H.H. and Thibaut, J.W. (1954) 'Experimental studies of group problem-solving and process', in G. Lindzey (ed.), *Handbook of Social Psychology*, Vol. 2. Cambridge, MA: Addison-Wesley. pp. 735–85.

Kelley, H.H. and Thibaut, J.W. (1969) 'Group problem-solving', in G. Lindzey and E. Aronson (eds), *Handbook of Social Psychology*, Vol. 4. Reading, MA: Addison-Wesley. pp. 1–101.

Kelly, J.R. and McGrath, J.E. (1985) 'Effects of time limits and task types on task performance and interaction of four-person groups', *Journal of Personality and Social Psychology*, 49: 395–407.

Kerr, N.L. and MacCoun, R.J. (1985) 'The effects of jury size and polling method on the process and product of jury deliberation', *Journal of Personality and Social Psychology*, 48: 349–63.

Keynes, J.M. (1964) *The General Theory of Employment, Interest and Money*. San Diego, CA: Harcourt Brace Jovanovich.

Kiesler, C.A. (1969) 'Group pressure and conformity', in J. Mills (ed.), *Experimental Social Psychology*. New York: Macmillan. pp. 235–306.

Kiesler, S. (1987) 'Flock by wire: group effects of new communication technology'. Heidelberg, conference on new media (mimeo).

Knorr-Cetina, K.D. (1981) *The Manufacture of Knowledge*. Oxford: Pergamon Press.

Kogan, N. and Wallach, M.A. (1967a) 'The risky-shift phenomenon in small decision-making groups: a test of the information-exchange hypothesis', *Journal of Experimental Social Psychology*, 3: 75–84.

Kogan, N. and Wallach, M.A. (1967b) 'Effects of physical separation of group members upon group risk-taking', *Human Relations*, 20: 41–8.

Kuhn, T.S. (1977) *The Essential Tension*. Chicago: University of Chicago Press.

Lamm, H., Trommsdorff, G., Burger, C. and Füchsle, T. (1980) 'Group influences on success expectancies regarding influence attempts', *Human Relations*, 33: 673–85.

Lamm, H., Trommsdorff, G. and Rost-Schaude, E. (1973) 'Group-induced extremization: a review of the evidence and a minority-induced change explanation', *Psychological Reports*, 33: 471–84.

Latané, B. and Darley, J.M. (1968) 'Group inhibition of bystander intervention in emergencies', *Journal of Personality and Social Psychology*, 10: 215–21.

Latané, B. and Darley, J.M. (1970) *The Unresponsive Bystander: Why Doesn't He Help?* New York: Appleton Century Crofts.

Laughlin, P.R. and Earley, P.C. (1982) 'Social combination models, persuasive arguments theory, social comparison theory, and choice shifts', *Journal of Personality and Social Psychology*, 42: 273–80.

Le Bon, G. (1963) *La Psychologie des foules*. Paris: Presses Universitaires de France.

Lécuyer, R. (1974) 'Rapports entre l'homme et l'espace'. PhD thesis, Paris, Laboratoire de Psychologie.

Lehrer, K. and Wagner, C. (1982) *Rational Consensus in Science and Society*. Dordrecht: Reidel.

Lemaine, G. (1975) 'Dissimilation and differential assimilation in social influence', *European Journal of Social Psychology*, 5: 93–120.

Lemon, N.F. (1968) 'A model of the extremity, confidence and salience of opinion', *British Journal of Social and Clinical Psychology*, 7: 106–14.

Lévy-Bruhl, L. (1952) *Carnets*. Paris: Vibert.

Lewin, K. (1936) 'Some social psychological differences between the United States and Germany', *Character and Personality*, 4: 265–93.

Lewin, K. (1943) 'Forces behind food habits and methods of change', *Bulletin of National Research Council*, 108: 35–65.

Lewin, K. (1947) 'Group decision and social change', in E. Swanson, T.M. Newcomb and E.L. Hartley (eds), *Readings in Social Psychology*. New York: Holt. pp. 197–211.

Lewin, K., Lippitt, R. and White, R. (1938) 'Patterns of aggressive behavior in experimentally created "social climates"', *Journal of Social Psychology*, 10: 271–99.

Lippitt, R. and White, R. (1960) 'Leader behavior and member reaction in three "social climates"', in D. Cartwright and A. Zander (eds), *Group Dynamics*. New York: Harper & Row.

Lord, C.G., Ross, L. and Lepper, M.R. (1979) 'Biased assimilation and attitude polarization: the effect of prior theories on subsequently considered evidence', *Journal of Personality and Social Psychology*, 37: 2098–109.

Lorge, I., Fox, D., Davitz, J. and Brenner, M. (1958) 'A survey of studies contrasting the quality of group performance and individual performance', *Psychological Bulletin*, 55: 337–72.

Lorge, I. and Solomon, H. (1955) 'Two models of group behavior in the solution of Eureka-type problems', *Psychometrika*, 20: 139–48.

McCauley, C.R. (1972) 'Extremity shifts, risk shifts and attitude shifts after group discussion', *European Journal of Social Psychology*, 2: 417–36.

McCurdy, H.G. and Lambert, W.E. (1952) 'The efficiency of small human groups in the solutions of problems requiring genuine cooperation', *Journal of Personality*, 20: 478–94.

McDougall, W. (1920) *The Group Mind*. Cambridge: Cambridge University Press.

Machiavelli, N. (1950) *The Discourses of Niccolò Machiavelli*, ed. and tr. L.J. Walker (2 vols). London: RKP.

Mackie, D. (1986) 'Social identification effects in group polarization', *Journal of Personality and Social Psychology*, 50: 720–8.

Mackie, D. and Cooper, J. (1984) 'Attitude polarization: effects of group membership', *Journal of Personality and Social Psychology*, 46: 575–85.

McLachlan, A. (1986) 'The effects of two forms of decision reappraisal on the perception of pertinent arguments', *British Journal of Social Psychology*, 25: 129–38.

Madaras, G.R. and Bem, D.J. (1968) 'Risk and conservatism in group decision-making', *Journal of Experimental Social Psychology*, 4: 350–66.

Mahoney, M.J. (1977) 'Publication prejudices: an experimental study of conformity bias in the peer review system', *Cognitive Therapy and Research*, 1: 161–75.

Mahoney, M.J., Kazdin, A.E. and Kenigsberg, M. (1978) 'Getting published', *Cognitive Therapy and Research*, 2: 69–70.

Maier, N.R.F. and Solem, A.R. (1952) 'The contribution of a discussion leader', *Human Relations*, 5: 277–88.

Main, E.C. and Walker, T.G. (1973) 'Choice shifts and extreme behavior: judicial review of the federal court', *Journal of Social Psychology*, 91: 215–21.

Manis, M., Gleason, T.C. and Dawes, R.M. (1966) 'The evaluation of complex social stimuli', *Journal of Personality and Social Psychology*, 3: 404–19.

Markova, I. (1987) 'On the interaction of opposites in psychological processes', *Journal for the Theory of Social Behaviour*, 17: 279–99.

Marquardt, D.I. (1955) 'Group problem solving', *Journal of Social Psychology*, 41: 103–13.

Marquis, D.G. (1962) 'Individual responsibility and group decisions involving risk', *Industrial Management Review*, 3: 8–23.

Maupassant, G. de (1979) *Sur l'eau*. Paris: ed. Encre.

Mead, G.H. (1964) *Selected Writings*. Chicago: University of Chicago Press.

Meindl, J.R. and Lerner, M.J. (1984) 'Exacerbation of extreme responses to an out-group', *Journal of Personality and Social Psychology*, 47: 71–84.

Miller, N.E. (1965) 'Involvement and dogmatism as inhibitors of attitude change', *Journal of Experimental Social Psychology*, 1: 121–32.

Moede, W. (1920) *Experimentelle Massenpsychologie*. Leipzig: Hirzel.

Morris, C.G. (1966) 'Task effects on group interaction', *Journal of Personality and Social Psychology*, 4: 545–54.

Moscovici, S. (1967) 'Communication processes and the properties of language', in L. Berkowitz (ed.), *Advances in Experimental Social Psychology*, Vol. 3. New York: Academic Press. pp. 225–70.

Moscovici, S. (1976) *Social Influence and Social Change*. London: Academic Press.

Moscovici, S. (1979) *Psychologie des minorités actives*. Paris: Presses Universitaires de France.

Moscovici, S. (1981) *L'Âge des foules*. Paris: Fayard.

Moscovici, S. (1985) *The Age of the Crowd*. Cambridge, Cambridge University Press.

Moscovici, S. (1986) 'The Dreyfus Affair, Proust and social psychology', *Social Research*, 53: 23–56.

Moscovici, S. (1987) 'The discovery of group polarization'. New York: New School for Social Research (mimeo).

Moscovici, S. (1988) *La Machine à faire des dieux*. Paris: Fayard.

Moscovici, S. and Doise, W. (1974) 'Decision-making in groups', in C. Nemeth (ed.), *Social Psychology: Classic and Contemporary Integrations*. Chicago: Rand McNally. pp. 250–87.

Moscovici, S., Doise, W. and Dulong, R. (1972) 'Studies in group decision II: differences of position, differences of opinion and group polarization', *European Journal of Social Psychology*, 2: 385–99.

Moscovici, S. and Faucheux, C. (1972) 'Social influence, conformity bias and the study of active minorities', in L. Berkowitz (ed.), *Advances in Experimental Social Psychology*, Vol. 6. New York: Academic Press. pp. 149–202.

Moscovici, S. and Lage, E. (1976) 'Studies in social influence III: majority versus minority influence in a group, *European Journal of Social Psychology*, 6: 149–74.

Moscovici, S. and Lage, E. (1978) 'Studies in social influence IV: minority influence in a context of original judgments', *European Journal of Social Psychology*, 8: 349–65.

Moscovici, S. and Lécuyer, R. (1972) 'Studies in group decision I: social space, patterns of communication and group consensus', *European Journal of Social Psychology*, 2: 221–44.

Moscovici, S. and Nève, P. (1973) 'Studies on polarization of judgments III: majorities, minorities and social judgments', *European Journal of Social Psychology*, 3: 479–84.

Moscovici, S. and Zavalloni, M. (1969) 'The group as a polarizer of attitudes', *Journal of Personality and Social Psychology*, 12: 125–35.

Moscovici, S., Zavalloni, M. and Louis-Guérin, C. (1972) 'Studies on polarization of judgments I: group effects on person perception', *European Journal of Social Psychology*, 2: 87–91.

Moscovici, S., Zavalloni, M. and Weinberger, M. (1972) 'Studies on polarization of judgments II: person perception, ego involvement and group interaction', *European Journal of Social Psychology*, 2: 92–4.

Murdoch, P., Myers, D.G. and Smith, C.F. (1970) 'Information effects on cautious and risky-shift items', *Psychonomic Science*, 20: 97–8.

Myers, D.G. (1975) 'Discussion-induced attitude polarization', *Human Relations*, 28: 699–714.

Myers, D.G. (1978) 'Polarizing effects of social comparison', *Journal of Experimental Social Psychology*, 14: 554–68.

Myers, D.G. (1982) 'Polarizing effects of social interaction', in H. Brandstätter et al. (eds), *Group Decision-making*. London: Academic Press. pp. 125–61.

Myers, D.G. and Arenson, S.J. (1972) 'Enhancement of dominant risk tendencies in group discussion', *Psychological Reports*, 30: 615–20.

Myers, D.G., Bach, P.J. and Schreiber, B.S. (1974) 'Normative and informational effects of group interaction', *Sociometry*, 37: 275–86.

Myers, D.G. and Bishop, G.D. (1970) 'Discussion effects on racial attitudes', *Science*, 169: 779–89.

Myers, D.G. and Bishop, G.D. (1971) 'Enhancement of dominant attitudes in group discussion', *Journal of Personality and Social Psychology*, 20: 386–91.

Myers, D.G. and Kaplan, M.F. (1976) 'Group-induced polarization in simulated juries', *Personality and Social Psychology Bulletin*, 2: 63–6.

Myers, D.G. and Lamm, H. (1976) 'The group polarization phenomenon', *Psychological Bulletin*, 83: 602–27.

Myers, D.G. and Murdoch, P. (1972) 'Is risky shift due to disproportionate influence by extreme group members?', *British Journal of Social and Clinical Psychology*, 11: 109–14.

Myers, D.G., Schreiber, B.J. and Viel, D.J. (1974) 'Effects of discussion on opinion concerning illegal behavior', *The Journal of Social Psychology*, 92: 77–84.

Myers, D.G., Wong, D.W. and Murdoch, P. (1971) 'Discussion arguments, information about others' responses, and risky shift', *Psychonomic Science*, 24: 81–3.

Nelkin, D. (1979) *Controversy: Politics of Technical Decisions*. Beverly Hills, CA: Sage.

Nemeth, C.J. (1977) 'Interactions between jurors as a function of majority vs unanimity decision rules', *Journal of Applied Social Psychology*, 7: 38–56.

Nemeth, C.J. (1984) 'Processus de groupe et jurys: les États-Unis et la France', in S. Moscovici (ed.), *Psychologie Sociale*. Paris: Presses Universitaires de France. pp. 229–51.

Nemeth, C.J. (1985) 'Dissent, group process and creativity: the contribution of minority influence', in E. Lawler (ed.), *Advances in Group Processes*, Vol. 2. Greenwich, CT: JAI Press. pp. 57–75.

Nemeth, C.J. (1986) 'Differential contributions of majority and minority influence', *Psychological Review*, 93: 23–32.

Nemeth, C.J. and Kwan, J.L. (1985) 'Originality of word associations as a function of majority vs minority influence', *Social Psychology Quarterly*, 48: 277–82.

Nève, P. and Gautier, J.M. (1978) 'Phénomènes de polarisation des décisions de groupe: étude expérimentale des effets de l'implication', *Bulletin de psychologie*, 31: 361–70.

Nève, P. and Moscovici, S. (1982) 'Implication et décision en groupe', *Bulletin de psychologie*, 35: 317–23.

Ng, S.H. (1984) 'Equity and social categorization effects on intergroup allocation of rewards', *British Journal of Social Psychology*, 23: 165–72.

Ng, S.H. and Cram, F. (1987) *Fairness and Biases in Intergroup Relations: a Study on Reward Allocation and Intergroup Differentiation*, Dunedin: University of Otago, Psychology Department.

Obershall, A. (1978) 'Theories of social conflict', *Annual Review of Sociology*, 4: 291–315.

O'Donovan, P. (1965) 'Rating extremity: pathology or meaningfulness?' *Psychological Review*, 72: 358–72.

Olson, M. (1965) *The Logic of Collective Action*. Cambridge, MA: Harvard University Press.

Paicheler, G. (1976) 'Norms and attitude change I: polarization and styles of behavior', *European Journal of Social Psychology*, 6: 405–27.

Paicheler, G. (1977) 'Norms and attitude change II: the phenomenon of bipolarization', *European Journal of Social Psychology*, 7: 5–14.

Paicheler, G. (1978) 'Argumentation, négociation et polarisation', *Bulletin de psychologie*, 31: 923–31.

Paicheler, G. (1979) 'Polarization of attitudes in homogeneous and heterogeneous groups', *European Journal of Social Psychology*, 9: 85–96.

Paicheler, G. and Bouchet, J. (1973) 'Attitude polarization, familiarization and group process', *European Journal of Social Psychology*, 3: 83–90.

Paicheler, G. and Flath, E. (1986) 'Changements d'attitude, influence minoritaire et courants sociaux'. Paris: EHESS, Laboratoire de Psychologie Sociale (mimeo).

Pallak, M.S., Cook, D.A. and Sullivan, J.J. (1980) 'Commitment and energy conservation', *Applied Social Psychology Annual*, 1: 235–53.

Pallak, M.S., Mueller, M., Dollar, K. and Pallak, J. (1972) 'Effect of commitment on responsiveness to an extreme consonant communication', *Journal of Personality and Social Psychology*, 23: 429–36.

Park, R.E. and Burgess, E.W. (1921) *Introduction to the Science of Society*. Chicago: University of Chicago Press.

Parsons, T. (1952) *The Social System*. Glencoe, IL: Free Press.

Pascal, B. (1985) *De l'esprit géometrique*. Paris: Flammarion.

Petrullo, L. and Bass, B.M. (1961) *Leadership and Interpersonal Behavior*. New York: Holt.

Polyani, M. (1964) *Personal Knowledge*. New York: Harper.

Preston, M. and Heinz, R. (1949) 'Effects of participatory vs supervisory leadership on group judgement', *Journal of Abnormal and Social Psychology*, 44: 345–55.

Pruitt, D.G. (1971) 'Choice shifts in group discussion: an introductory review', *Journal of Personality and Social Psychology*, 20: 339–60.

Pruitt, D.G. and Teger, A.I. (1967) 'Is there a shift toward risk in group conditions? If so, is it a group phenomenon? If so, what causes it? Paper presented at American Psychological Association Convention, Washington, DC (mimeo).

Putnam, H. (1979) *Mind, Language and Reality: Philosophical Papers*, Vol. 2. Cambridge: Cambridge University Press.

Putnam, H. (1981) *Reason, Truth and History*. Cambridge: Cambridge University Press.

Rabbie, J.M. (1982) 'The effects of intergroup competition and cooperation on intragroup and intergroup relationships, in V.J. Derlaga and J. Grzelak (eds), *Cooperation and Helping Behavior*. London: Academic Press. pp. 123–49.

Rabbie, J.M., Schot, J.C. and Visser, L. (1989) 'Social identity: a conceptual and empirical critique, from the perspective of a behavioural interaction model', *European Journal of Social Psychology*, 19: 171–202.

Rabbie, J.M. and Visser, L. (1972) 'Bargaining strength and group polarization in intergroup negotiations', *European Journal of Social Psychology*, 2: 401–16.

Rabow, J., Fowler, F., Bradford, L., Hofeller, M. and Shibuya, Y. (1966) 'The role of social norms and leadership in risk-taking, *Sociometry*, 29: 16–27.

Rawls, J. (1971) *A Theory of Justice*. Cambridge, MA: Harvard University Press.

Reid, F.J.M. and Sumiga, L. (1984) 'Attitudinal politics in intergroup behaviour: interpersonal vs intergroup determinants of attitude change', *British Journal of Social Psychology*, 23: 335–40.

Rettig, S. and Turoff, S.J. (1967) 'Exposure to group discussion and predicted ethical risk-taking', *Journal of Personality and Social Psychology*, 7: 177–8.

Roberts, J.C. and Castore, C.H. (1972) 'The effects of conformity, information and confidence upon subjects' willingness to take risk following a group discussion', *Organizational Behavior and Human Performance*, 8: 384–94.

Romilly, J. de (1986) *Problèmes de la démocratie grecque*. Paris: Hermann.

St Jean, R. and Percival, E. (1974) 'The role of argumentation and comparison processes in choice shifts: another assessment', *Canadian Journal of Behavioral Science*, 6: 297–308.

Sanders, G.S. and Baron, R.S. (1977) 'Is social comparison irrelevant for producing choice shifts?', *Journal of Experimental Social Psychology*, 13: 303–14.

Saussure, F. de (1972) *Cours de linguistique générale*. Paris: Payot.

Schachter, S. (1951) 'Deviation, rejection, and communication', *Journal of Abnormal and Social Psychology*, 46: 190–207.

Scheidel, T.M. (1986) 'Divergent and convergent thinking in group decision-making', in R.Y. Hirokawa and M.S. Poole (eds), *Communication and Group Decision-making*. Beverly Hills, CA: Sage. pp. 113–32.

Semin, G.R. (1975) 'Two studies on polarization', *European Journal of Social Psychology*, 5: 121–31.

Semin, G.R. and Glendon, J.A. (1973) 'Polarization and the established group', *British Journal of Social and Clinical Psychology*, 12: 113–21.

Shapiro, D. and Crider, A. (1969) 'Psychophysiological approaches in social psychology', in G. Lindzey and E. Aronson (eds), *Handbook of Social Psychology*, Vol. 3. Reading, MA: Addison-Wesley. pp. 1–49.

Shaw, M.E. (1932) 'A comparison of individuals and small groups in the rational solution of complex problems', *American Journal of Psychology*, 44: 491–504.

Sherif, C.W., Kelly, M., Rodgers, H.L., Sarup, G. and Tittler, B.I. (1973) 'Personal involvement, social judgment and action', *Journal of Personality and Social Psychology*, 27: 311–28.

Sherif, C.W. and Sherif, M. (1967) *Attitude, Ego-Involvement and Change*. New York: J. Wiley & Sons.

Sherif, C.W., Sherif, M. and Nebergall, R.E. (1965) *Attitude and Attitude Change: the Social Judgment-involvement Approach*. Philadelphia: Saunders.

Sherif, M. (1936) *The Psychology of Social Norms*. New York: Harper & Row.

Sherif, M. (1966) *In Common Predicament*. New York: Houghton Mifflin.

Sherif, M. and Hovland, C.I. (1961) *Social Judgment*. New Haven, CT: Yale University Press.

Sieber, J.E. and Lanzetta, J.T. (1964) 'Conflict and conceptual structure as determinants of decision-making behavior', *Journal of Personality*, 33: 622–41.

Siegel, S. and Zajonc, R.B. (1967) 'Group risk-taking in professional decisions', *Sociometry*, 30: 339–49.

Simmel, G. (1896) 'Comment les formes sociales se maintiennent?', *Année Sociologique*, 1: 71–109.

Simon, H. (1957) *Models of Man*. New York: J. Wiley & Sons.

Singleton, R. (1979) 'Another look at the conformity explanation of group-induced shifts in choice', *Human Relations*, 32: 37–56.

Skinner, M. and Stephenson, G.M. (1981) 'The effects of intergroup comparison on the polarization of opinions', *Current Psychological Research*, 1: 49–59.

Smith, C.E. (1936) 'A study of the automatic excitation resulting from the interaction of individual opinion and group opinion', *Journal of Abnormal and Social Psychology*, 31: 138–64.

Smith, K.A., Petersen, R.P., Johnson, D.W. and Johnson, R.T. (1986) 'The effect of controversy and concurrence seeking on effective decision-making', *Journal of Social Psychology*, 126: 237–48.

Soueif, M.I. (1958) 'Extreme response sets as a measure of intolerance of ambiguity', *British Journal of Psychology*, 49: 329–33.

Stasser, G. and Davis, J.H. (1977) 'Opinion change during group discussion', *Journal of Personality and Social Psychology*, 3: 252–6.

Stasser, G. and Davis, J.H. (1981) 'Group decision-making and social influence: a social interaction sequence model', *Psychological Review*, 88; 523–51.

Steiner, I.D. (1972) *Group Process and Productivity*. New York: Academic Press.

Steinzor, B. (1950) 'The spatial factor in face-to-face discussion groups', *Journal of Abnormal and Social Psychology*, 45: 552–5.

Stephenson, G.M. and Brotherton, C.J. (1975) 'Social progression and polarization: a study of discussion and negotiation in groups of mining supervisors', *British Journal of Social and Clinical Psychology*, 14: 241–52.

Stokes, J.P. (1971) 'Effects of familiarization and knowledge of others' odds choices on shifts to risk and caution', *Journal of Personality and Social Psychology*, 20: 407–12.

Stoner, J.A.F. (1961) 'A comparison of individual and group decisions involving risk'. Unpublished MSc thesis. Mass. Institute of Technology, School of Industrial Management.

Stoner, J.A.F. (1968) 'Risky and cautious shifts in group decisions: the influence of widely held values', *Journal of Experimental Social Psychology*, 4: 442–59.

Strodtbeck, F.L., James, R.M. and Hawkins, C. (1957) 'Social status in jury deliberations', *American Sociological Review*, 22: 713–19.

Stroebe, W. and Fraser, C. (1971) 'The relationship between riskiness and confidence in choice dilemma decisions', *European Journal of Social Psychology*, 1: 519–26.

Tajfel, H. (1981) *Human Groups and Social Categories*. Cambridge: Cambridge University Press.

Tajfel, H. (1982) *Social Identity and Intergroup Relations*. Cambridge: Cambridge University Press.

Tajfel, H. and Wilkes, A.L. (1964) 'Salience of attributes and commitment to extreme judgments in the perception of people', *British Journal of Social and Clinical Psychology*, 3: 40–9.

Tanford, S. and Penrod, S. (1983) 'Computer modeling of influence in the jury: the role of the consistent juror', *Social Psychology Quarterly*, 46: 200–12.

Tarde, G. (1895) *Les Transformations du pouvoir*. Paris: Alcan.

Tarde, G. (1910) *L'Opinion et la foule*. Paris: Alcan.

Taylor, D.W., Berry, P.C. and Block, C.H. (1958) 'Does group participation when using brainstorming facilitate or inhibit creative thinking?', *Administrative Science Quarterly*, 3: 23–47.

Teger, A.I. and Pruitt, D.G. (1967) 'Components of group risk-taking', *Journal of Experimental Social Psychology*, 3: 189–205.

Thibaut, J.W. and Kelley, H.H. (1967) *The Social Psychology of Groups*. New York: J. Wiley & Sons.

Thomas, E.J. and Fink, C.F. (1961) 'Models of group problem-solving', *Journal of Abnormal and Social Psychology*, 63: 53–63.

Thurstone, L.C. and Chave, E.J. (1929) *The Measurement of Attitude*. Chicago: University of Chicago Press.

Tocqueville, A. de (1961) *De la démocratie en Amérique*. Paris: Gallimard.

Torrance, E.P. (1954) 'The behavior of small groups under stress conditions of survival', *American Sociological Review*, 19: 751–5.

Touraine, A. (1978) *La Voix et le regard*. Paris: Seuil.

Trommsdorff, G. (1982) 'Group influences on judgments concerning the future', in M. Irle (ed.), *Studies in Decision-making*. Berlin: De Gruyter. pp. 145–65.

Tugendhat, E. (1981) 'Morality and communication'. Unpublished ms, Princeton University, Christian Gauss Lectures.

Turner, J.C. (1975) 'Social comparison and social identity: some prospects for intergroup behaviour', *European Journal of Social Psychology*, 5: 5–34.

Turner, J.C. (ed.) (1987) *Rediscovering the Social Group*. Oxford: Basil Blackwell.

Upmeyer, A. and Layer, H. (1974) 'Accentuation and attitude in social judgment', *European Journal of Social Psychology*, 4: 469–88.

Van Knippenberg, A. and Wilke, H. (1988) 'Social categorization and attitude change', *European Journal of Social Psychology*, 18: 395–406.

Vidmar, N. (1970) 'Group composition and the risky shift', *Journal of Experimental Social Psychology*, 6: 153–66.

Vidmar, N. (1974) 'Effects of group discussion on category width judgments', *Journal of Personality and Social Psychology*, 29: 187–95.

Vidmar, N. and Burdeny, T.C. (1971) 'Effects of group size and item type in the "Group Shift" effect', *Canadian Journal of Behavioral Science*, 3: 393–407.

Vinokur, A. (1969) 'Distribution of initial risk levels and group decisions involving risk', *Journal of Personality and Social Psychology*, 13: 207–14.

Vinokur, A. (1971) 'Review and theoretical analysis of group processes upon individual and group decisions involving risk', *Psychological Bulletin*, 76: 231–50.

Vinokur, A. and Burnstein, E. (1974) 'Effects of partially shared persuasive arguments on group-induced shifts', *Journal of Personality and Social Psychology*, 29: 305–15.

Vinokur, A. and Burnstein, E. (1978) 'Depolarization of attitudes in groups', *Journal of Personality and Social Psychology*, 36: 872–85.

Vinokur, A., Burnstein, E., Sechrest, L. and Wortman, P.M. (1985) 'Group decision-making by experts: field study of panels evaluating medical technologies', *Journal of Personality and Social Psychology*, 49: 70–84.

Visser, L. (1975) 'De invloed van de achterban op coöperatieve en competitieve intergroeps onderhandelingen'. Unpublished research report, Institute of Social Psychology, Utrecht.

Vroom, V.H. and Yetton, P.W. (1973) *Leadership and Decision-making*. Pittsburgh: University of Pittsburgh Press.

Walker, T.G. and Main, E.C. (1973) 'Choice shifts in political decision-making: federal judges and civil liberties cases', *Journal of Applied Social Psychology*, 3: 39–48.

Wallach, M.A. and Kogan, N. (1965) 'The roles of information, discussion and consensus in group risk-taking', *Journal of Experimental Social Psychology*, 1: 1–19.

Wallach, M.A., Kogan, N. and Bem, D.J. (1962) 'Group influence on individual risk-taking', *Journal of Abnormal and Social Psychology*, 65: 75–86.

Wallach, M.A., Kogan, N. and Bem, D.J. (1964) 'Diffusion of responsibility and level of risk-taking in groups', *Journal of Abnormal and Social Psychology*, 68: 263–74.

Wallach, M.A., Kogan, N. and Burt, R. (1965) 'Can group members recognize the effects of group discussion upon risk-taking?', *Journal of Experimental Social Psychology*, 1: 379–95.

Wallach, M.A. and Mabli, J. (1970) 'Information versus conformity in the effects of group discussion on risk-taking', *Journal of Personality and Social Psychology*, 14: 149–56.

Ward, C.D. (1966) 'Attitude and involvement in the absolute judgment of attitude statements', *Journal of Personality and Social Psychology*, 4: 465–76.

Weber, M. (1978) *Economy and Society*, ed. G. Roth and C. Wittich, tr. E. Fischoff et al. Berkeley: University of California Press.

Wehman, P., Goldstein, M.A. and Williams, J.R. (1977) 'Effects of different leadership styles on individual risk-taking in groups', *Human Relations*, 30: 249–59.

Wetherell, M. (1987) 'Social identity and group polarization', in J.C. Turner (ed.), *Rediscovering the Social Group*. Oxford: Basil Blackwell. pp. 142–70.

White, R. and Lippitt, R.' (1968) 'Leader behaviour and member reaction in three "social climates"', in D. Cartwright and A. Zander (eds), *Group Dynamics*. New York: Harper and Row. pp. 318–35.

Willems, E.P. and Clark, R.D., III (1969) 'Dependency of risky shift on instructions: a replication', *Psychological Reports*, 25: 811–14.

Willems, E.P. and Clark, R.D., III (1971) 'Shift toward risk and heterogeneity of groups', *Journal of Experimental Social Psychology*, 7: 304–12.

Windisch, U. (1987) *K.O. Verbal: La communication*. Geneva: L'Âge d'Homme.

Witte, E.H. (1979) *Das Verhalten in Gruppensituationen*. Göttingen: Hogrefe Verlag.

Zajonc, R.B. (1960) ' The process of cognitive tuning in communication', *Journal of Abnormal and Social Psychology*, 61: 159–67.

Zajonc, R.B., Wolosin, R.J., Wolosin, M.A. and Loh, W.D. (1970) 'Social facilitation and imitation in group risk-taking, *Journal of Experimental Social Psychology*, 6: 26–46.

Zaleska, M. (1972) 'Comparaison des décisions individuelles et collectives dans des situations de choix avec risque'. Doctoral thesis, Paris.

Zaleska, M. (1976) 'Polarization of group choices'. Paris, International Congress of Psychology (mimeo).

Zaleska, M. (1980) 'Climat de relations interpersonnelles et polarisation des attitudes', *Psychologie Française*, 25: 183–93.

Zaleska, M. (1982) 'The stability of extreme and moderate responses in different situations', in H. Brandstätter et al. (eds), *Group Decision-making*. London: Academic Press. pp. 163–84.

Zaleska, M. and Chalot, C. (1969) 'Réponses exprimées et inexprimées en fonction de l'extrémisme de l'attitude, du degré d'implication et de l'information', *Bulletin de Psychologie*, 23: 295–304.

Zander, A. and Medow, H. (1963) 'Individual and group levels of aspiration', *Human Relations*, 16: 89–105.

Zax, M., Gardiner, D.H. and Lowy, D.G. (1964) 'Extreme response tendency as a function of emotional adjustment', *Journal of Abnormal and Social Psychology*, 69: 654–7.

Ziller, R.C. (1957) 'Four techniques of group decision-making under uncertainty', *Journal of Applied Psychology*, 41: 384–8.

Zuber, J. (1988) *Extremisierungsphänomene in Gruppen*. Berne: Lang.

Index